Beyond Technique in Family Therapy

Finding Your Therapeutic Voice

George M. Simon

The Minuchin Center for the Family
and
Hofstra University

Boston   New York   San Francisco
Mexico City   Montreal   Toronto   London   Madrid   Munich   Paris
Hong Kong   Singapore   Tokyo   Cape Town   Sydney

To Gail and Gina,
whose loving voices echo in my own

———————————

Series Editor: *Patricia M. Quinlin*
Editorial Assistant: *Annemarie Kennedy*
Marketing Manager: *Taryn Wahlquist*
Composition and Prepress Buyer: *Linda Cox*
Manufacturing Buyer: *JoAnne Sweeney*
Cover Administrator: *Kristina Mose-Libon*
Editorial Production Service: *Chestnut Hill Enterprises, Inc.*
Electronic Composition: *Peggy Cabot, Cabot Computer Services*

For related titles and support materials, visit our online catalog at www.ablongman.com.

Library of Congress Cataloging-in-Publication Data
Simon, George M.
      Beyond technique in family therapy : finding your therapeutic voice / George M. Simon. — 1st ed.
      p.   cm.
   Includes bibliographical references and index.
   ISBN 0-205-34116-0
   1. Family psychotherapy.   I. Title.
RC488.5 .S542 2002
616.89'156—dc21   2002032676

Printed in the United States of America

10 9 8 7 6 5 4 3 2 1   08 07 06 05 04 03 02

CONTENTS

PREFACE

The field of family therapy has struggled mightily during the last decade or so to embrace diversity. It has labored to increase its awareness of and sensitivity to diversity associated with ethnicity, class, gender, religious affiliation, and sexual orientation.

At the same time that it has been working to celebrate diversity in the world at large, the field of family therapy has been showing a perplexing discomfort with a species of diversity within its own ranks. I am referring here to the theoretical diversity associated with the large number of therapeutic models that have currency within the field. While striving to honor diversity in its clients, family therapy has come to experience its own internal theoretical diversity as something akin to Babel (Miller, Duncan, & Hubble, 1997). Seeing only confusion in the large number of therapeutic models that are available to practitioners, teachers and scholars of family therapy have moved steadily toward an ethos of integration. It is the rare family therapy graduate program today that does not explicitly counsel its students to strive in their practice to construct some kind of systematic eclecticism.

This book sounds a dissenting note in the face of the growing chorus singing the praises of therapeutic eclecticism. To family therapists who experience the multitude of therapeutic models as a confusing chaos, this book offers a means of making sense of the field's theoretical diversity. It views the models of family therapy in the context of the broader Western philosophical tradition in which they arose. It sees the differences among the models as being rooted in differing "solutions" that Western philosophers have developed to some of the most perplexing quandaries about the human condition. While these "solutions" are discussed abstractly by philosophers, they are lived concretely by those who operate within the context of Western culture. Indeed, it is the multiplicity of these philosophical "solutions" that has given rise to the very diversity among its clients that family therapy has learned to embrace. For the same reasons that the field celebrates the latter kind of diversity, it should also celebrate the former. Rather than looking to integrate the various models of family therapy, the field should rejoice in and maintain their distinction.

The close connection that exists between the apparently abstract musings of philosophers and the concrete ways in which people live their lives provides a way for the individual family therapist to orient herself toward the numerous therapeutic models that are available to her. This book argues that each family therapist needs to search the major models of therapy to find the one that best expresses her personal worldview and values. Each therapist will find this privileged model is just about inevitable because the same cultural environment that gave rise to the models also provided the range of "solutions" from which the therapist has chosen in the process of constructing her own worldview. The therapist need only search for the model that is based on the same philosophical/cultural "solutions" on which she herself has built her own life.

This book endeavors to help family therapists, especially those who are just beginning their clinical careers, to make this search and to find this fit. Toward this end, it seeks to expose each major therapeutic model's underlying story about the human condition. It also attempts to guide the reader through a series of reflections that will help him to become explicitly aware of his own personal story about the nature of the human world. By helping to unearth both of these sets of stories, it hopes to bring the reader to a place where he can recognize the model of family therapy that tells the same story about what it means to be human that he tells.

The book follows a very straightforward organization. An introduction makes the case for a practice of family therapy that is model-pure rather than eclectic, and it details the means proposed for individual practitioners to find the model to which to commit themselves. The first five chapters then undertake to expose the major models' underlying worldviews and to help the reader discern her own worldview and values. Each of these chapters devotes itself in turn to one of the issues that have been fundamental in Western philosophical speculation about the human condition. Chapter 6 pulls together the discussions of the previous five and offers a summary statement of how each of the therapeutic models views the human condition. Chapter 7 describes a view of clinical supervision as a means whereby practitioners, having chosen the model that best expresses their worldview, refine their ability to use themselves as instruments of change in the way that the model prescribes. The final chapter invites the reader to bring the process of self-discovery and self-commitment in which she has been engaged to a close by telling the story of how she came to hold the worldview that has led her to her chosen model of therapy.

The style of this book has been determined by its desire to serve as a practical tool for readers who might easily be put off by discussions that remain overlong in the realm of abstraction. Thus, the book attempts to maintain a conversational tone, even when it presents philosophical material. Clinical vignettes, most of them of considerable length, introduce six of the eight chapters, and the characters and situations of the vignettes reappear repeatedly throughout these chapters. Scholarly apparatus has been kept to a minimum. References to the philosophical literature have been limited almost entirely to articles contained in two encyclopedias aimed at an educated, but lay, audience. If the reader chooses to consult any of these references, he will find both an excellent presentation of the philosophical issue in question, as well as suggestions for further reading that he can pursue should he choose to delve into the issue in greater depth.

Although this book welcomes, even seeks, novice family therapists as part of its readership, it has not attempted to serve as an introductory family therapy text. Had it made this attempt, its focus on its own distinctive argument and purpose would have been compromised. Thus, while I fully expect a novice therapist will leave this book with a deeper and more nuanced understanding of the major family therapy models than she had when she began, the book does presume in its reader at least a rudimentary knowledge of the therapeutic models. When the book is used in an academic setting for family therapy graduate students, it can well be assigned as a supplemental text in a theory course; however, it cannot serve as the primary text in such a course.

There is a very real sense in which this book has been almost fifty years in the making. Anything that has been that long in developing owes debts of gratitude to an exceedingly large number of people. Due to space constraints, I will be able to mention only a few of these people here.

To begin, I would like to acknowledge the contributions of the professors who taught me when I was studying for my master's degree in philosophy at Fordham University from 1976–1978. In a special way, I would like to single out Norris Clarke, S.J., Gerald McCool, S.J., Robert O'Connell, S.J., William Richardson, S.J., Joseph Donceel, S.J., Robert Johann, and Dominic Balestra. In addition to teaching me a lot about philosophy, these gifted teachers taught me the even more important lesson that philosophy matters mightily to the way that ordinary people live their lives.

I would also like to acknowledge two colleagues who were instrumental in helping me to crystallize some of the key ideas presented in this book. These ideas were spawned in numerous long and stimulating—to me, at least—conversations with Richard Holm, of The Minuchin Center for the Family, and Daniel Sciarra, of Hofstra University. While I do not wish to imply that either one of these men would necessarily like to be associated with any of the ideas presented in this book, I do want to attest to the role that their intelligent, thoughtful exchanges with me played in helping me to crystallize the outlook that I have presented here.

A book project is most vulnerable, I think, at its very beginning, when the inevitable vagueness of the plan for the project leaves it highly susceptible to being prematurely abandoned in the face of criticism or rejection. This particular project was fortunate to encounter Michael P. Nichols in this vulnerable early stage. With exquisite sensitivity, Mike offered just the right combination of cheerleading and constructive criticism to help bring the project to birth in the form that it has finally assumed.

The particular contours of my career as a family therapist have provided me with the opportunity of working with and/or watching several truly gifted clinicians plying their trade as therapists. All have had significant influence on the way in which I think about and conduct therapy. However, none has influenced me more than Salvador Minuchin, a man whom I have been privileged to have as a teacher, a mentor, and a colleague.

Christopher Lowney is not a family therapist. He is, however, a good friend who has done for me what all good friends do: He has helped me to respect and to believe in myself. The self-respect that he helped engender was crucial in the conception and execution of this book.

I also extend my appreciation to the reviewers of the manuscript: Ralph Cohen, Central Connecticut State University; David Kleist, Idaho State University; Ameda Manetta, Winthrop University; Volker Thomas, Purdue University; and Joseph Walsh, Virginia Commonwealth University.

Finally, there is my wife, Gail, and my stepdaughter, Gina. The presence of these two intelligent and profoundly humane women so permeates every nook and cranny of my world that to acknowledge them as having contributed to this book seems to me nothing less than trite. I dedicate this book to them with a gratitude that goes beyond words.

INTRODUCTION

"What do I do now?"

Maria was sitting opposite the eighth family she had seen in her very brief career as a family therapist. Six months into her internship, she thought that by now she would no longer be experiencing the kind of utter confusion that was gripping her at this moment. Yet, here it was, happening all over again.

It was not anxiety that Maria was experiencing. To be sure, she had been a nervous wreck during her initial sessions with her first two or three client families. But by this point, Maria had become fairly comfortable acting in the role of therapist. She felt relatively relaxed doing an interview with a family, and her last few client families had responded well to her. When she was assigned the Tanner family, she could not wait to have her first session with them. "This first session," she thought, "will go differently from the previous ones."

The intake packet had informed Maria that the Tanner family consisted of Tanisha, a woman in her early forties, and her sixteen-year-old son, Douglas. There had been no unsettling surprises when Maria had greeted the Tanners in the clinic's waiting room. Tanisha had smiled affably when Maria introduced herself. Douglas, on the other hand, had barely mumbled a greeting. Instead, he had stared fixedly at the magazine that he was reading, clearly intending Maria to understand that the magazine was far more interesting than anything she possibly could say to him now or at any point in the future. Douglas's sullenness, however, had not thrown Maria. As she had prepared mentally for this first session, she had considered the very real possibility that a sixteen-year-old boy would not be turning somersaults at the prospect of being dragged by his mother into the presence of a therapist. And so, when Douglas had refused the handshake that Maria had proffered, she had not felt hurt or dismayed. Wearing a smile as affable as Tanisha's, she had guided the mother and son to the room where the camcorder was already running, ready to record what Maria was confident would be a smooth, focused initial session.

The session had begun well, in Maria's estimation. After a few minutes of light social banter, she had asked Tanisha to describe what it was that had led her to call the clinic for an appointment.

"Douglas hates his father," Tanisha had responded. "He's doing very poorly in school, and I just think that he needs some help."

Tanisha had gone on to explain that Douglas's father had physically abused both him and his younger brother David throughout their childhood. Feeling powerless to get the man to stop beating her children, she had developed the strategy of provoking him when he began beating one of the boys so as to divert his anger away from the boy and toward herself. Most times, the strategy succeeded. "I have the scars to prove it," she told Maria, still flashing that affable smile that Maria had first seen in the waiting room.

About a year ago, Tanisha had had enough. She had served her husband with divorce papers. To her surprise, he had accepted the prospect of divorce

1

without a struggle. Within days after she had served him with the papers, he had moved out and gotten an apartment across town. David visited with his father every weekend; but Douglas refused to have any contact at all.

"Six months ago," Tanisha continued, "David and I had a fight. You know, the kind of argument mothers and fourteen-year-olds have. That weekend, when David was at his father's, he called me and told me that he had decided to stay with him. So, I let him. I mean, what could I do? Go over there and kidnap him?" *It was from that point on that Tanisha began to notice the deterioration in Douglas's school performance.*

Tanisha had told this story with few prompts from Maria. Listening intently to the story, Maria began to ponder how she should proceed when Tanisha was finished. Not yet having heard Douglas's voice, she decided that the thing to do would be to ask him his view as to why he was sitting in a family therapist's office.

"So, Douglas, what's your opinion? Why do you think you guys need to be here?"

Douglas shrugged.

"Your mom thinks that you're having trouble at school. Do you think so?"

"Nope."

Seeing that Douglas's mood had not changed significantly since their first encounter in the waiting room, Maria quickly turned her thoughts to how she would begin intervening with the Tanners. She had been struck by the connection that Tanisha had made at the beginning of her narrative between Douglas's anger at his father and his deteriorated school performance. Tanisha had not elaborated on what she thought the connection was; to her, it was clearly obvious. It was not so obvious to Maria. And so Maria decided to begin there. "By asking her to spell out a connection that she considers obvious," *Maria thought,* "perhaps I can introduce some uncertainty into her story, and so open up the possibility for re-storying."

Maria asked Tanisha to give her view of the connection. Tanisha shifted in her chair. The smile that she had worn throughout the session to that point faded ever so slightly. When she began to respond to Maria's question, her answer was a bit halting, nowhere near as seamless and fluid as her initial description of the presenting problem had been.

Maria tried to listen carefully to Tanisha's response, but she was almost immediately distracted. A remarkable thing had occurred. Douglas, who up to that point in the session had mutely stared out the window as intently as he had stared at the magazine in the waiting room, had turned to look at his mother. Something in her changed posture had clearly caught his attention. As Tanisha continued to try to answer Maria's question, Douglas had begun to help her, supplying a word when she fumbled for one, gently correcting a detail that she got wrong, elaborating an idea that he apparently felt she had not adequately explained.

As Maria watched this interaction, a new interventive tack occurred to her. "Perhaps Douglas's problems at school," *she thought,* "are related to enmeshment between him and Tanisha." *The circumstances in which they had lived would certainly have invited enmeshment. Tanisha had already described* to Maria how she had felt the need to protect both Douglas and his brother from their father's abuse. Perhaps Douglas, too, had developed a protective stance toward his mother. Each might now be hypervigilant of the other, always on the alert for possible signs of distress. Perhaps with David's departure from the household, Douglas had felt the need to devote even more energy toward being watchful of his mother, with his school performance suffering as a result.

Maria decided to test this hypothesis of disabling enmeshment between Tanisha and Douglas. Thus, when Tanisha finished responding to Maria's request that she describe the connection she saw between Douglas's anger at his father and his poor school performance, Maria elicited an enactment between the mother and son, asking them to talk together about the theory that Tanisha had just propounded.

Maria intended to watch the enactment closely, to discern whether Douglas and Tanisha were, in fact, overinvolved with each other. However, she was once again distracted. Early in the enactment, Tanisha and Douglas made passing reference to a two- or three-week period a couple of months before when Douglas's grades had briefly improved. "Aha," Maria thought, "an exception to the presenting problem! Maybe I should underline it and ask them to think about what each of them did at the time to produce the improvement. Then they'll be able to construct a solution to the problem based on the behaviors that they identify." Excited by this latest strategy, Maria looked for the first opportunity to interrupt the enactment that she herself had elicited.

"I heard the two of you refer to a period a couple of months ago when Douglas got mostly Bs and Cs instead of Ds and Fs. I think that may be significant. Could you think about anything either of you might have been doing differently at that time that might have helped bring about the improvement?"

Maria waited expectantly for their responses, but Tanisha and Douglas did not appear to share her excitement. In fact, they looked confused and distinctly put off. They had been able to discern no pattern to Maria's interventions up to that point in the session. Maria's request to Tanisha that she explain the connection that she saw between Douglas's feelings toward his father and his school performance had unsettled Tanisha, asking her to reflect on something that she simply took for granted. Yet, she had accommodated and put some effort into responding to Maria's request. After all, she assumed that Maria knew what she was doing. Moreover, she had a strong feeling that she could grow to like this therapist. But then, Maria's next intervention appeared to disregard the effort that Tanisha had put into responding to the previous one. Neither Tanisha nor Douglas could see why Maria now wanted them to talk together. Nonetheless, they accommodated her. And, as they talked together, their conversation had developed a real momentum as it drifted into an area of deep importance to both of them, namely, their relationship with each other. However, just as the conversation was developing some intensity, Maria had cut it short. Worse, her next intervention had focused on a small piece of the conversation that felt to Douglas and Tanisha insignificant compared to the turn that the conversation had taken.

As for Maria, she was unsettled by her clients' obvious consternation. She glanced at her watch; there were only five minutes remaining in the

session. It was happening again: she was approaching the end of an initial session feeling that she and her clients were not even close to being on the same wavelength. Tanisha and Douglas simply sat there, staring at her.
   "What do I do now?"

Therapeutic Models

Despite her best intentions and her newfound comfort in interviewing families, Maria had once again conducted an initial session that had turned out to be unfocused and meandering. The same thing had happened in every one of her previous cases. To be sure, she had been successful in developing a therapeutic focus in each of these previous cases, but only after her supervisor had supplied her with one. Why was it that, left to her own devices, Maria interviewed in such a rambling, unfocused way, one that invariably left her feeling confused and disconnected from her clients?

   The answer to this question is quite simple: Maria's interviews are unfocused because she has not committed herself to a particular model of family therapy. A therapeutic model can be thought of as a filter, such as one might affix to a camera. Such filters let only certain colors of light into the camera and reflect or absorb all the others. In the same way, a model of therapy focuses the therapist to look for certain kinds of events during a session and to disregard all others. The model then gives the therapist guidance as to how she should respond to these events that get through the filter that the model provides.

   Because Maria did not have the filter that a therapeutic model would have provided, she paradoxically saw both too much and too little during her session with the Tanners. She saw too much: once she started down the postmodern path opened by her request that Tanisha describe the connection she saw between Douglas's anger toward his father and his school functioning, it was not useful for her to make the structural observation of possible enmeshment between the mother and son. In the same way, when Maria began exploring that possible enmeshment, it was not useful for her to hear, as a solution-focused therapist would, Douglas and Tanisha's passing reference to an exception to their presenting problem.

   Maria saw too much. But because she was not guided by a model, she also saw too little. Distracted as she was by her thoughts of possible enmeshment, Maria did not hear Tanisha's answer to her question. She did not hear Tanisha explain that, in her experience, young African American men like her son already feel so marginalized in the school setting that the added burden of emotional agitation, such as Douglas's intense anger toward his father, is enough to propel them into failure, and, before very long, into dropping out. Had she heard this explanation, Maria could have focused the session on exploring with Tanisha and

Douglas the ways in which their lives, both past and present, have been shaped by cultural images about black men and black women.

Similarly, Maria's excitement at having identified a possible exception to the Tanners' presenting problem kept her from seeing and hearing the emotional intensity that developed during the enactment between Tanisha and Douglas, as their conversation drifted onto the topic of how constrained each feels by the other's behavior. Had Maria observed this intensity, she could have prolonged the conversation past its natural cutoff point in order to observe how the mother and son handle, or possibly avoid, conflict. She might have found herself faced with the opportunity to shape a conflictual exchange between Tanisha and Douglas in the interest of promoting a less reactive kind of emotional involvement between the two of them.

Without the filter that a commitment to a model of therapy would have provided her, Maria lacked a compass to guide her through her session with the Tanners. She was blown now in this direction, now in that, by her chance encounters with in-session events that triggered for her recollections of techniques or ideas that she had studied in her coursework. Having taken so many detours over the course of the session, she found near its end that, despite having competently delivered several technically correct interventions, she had actually wound up covering little ground. The upshot: Tanisha and Douglas were disoriented, and Maria was confused.

This book is based on the premise that family therapy is best practiced, by seasoned clinicians and even more so by novices like Maria, when it is informed by an established therapeutic model. Having stated this premise, let me immediately make clear that I am not disqualifying all eclecticism in the practice of family therapy. My own practice is informed by the model of structural family therapy. Nonetheless, I find myself with some regularity utilizing techniques that belong to other models. However, whenever I do so, it is always for good structural reasons. The *thinking* underlying my occasional use of a Bowenian or a postmodern or a solution-focused *technique* is always structural. This kind of occasional technical eclecticism is in no way at odds with a model-driven therapy, and is compatible with my premise that the practice of family therapy should be informed by an established therapeutic model.

If the practice of family therapy should be based on one of the established models, then why is it that, as many sources suggest, so many family therapists have chosen not to commit themselves to a model, preferring instead to identify themselves as eclectic (Prochaska & Norcross, 1994; Raitt, 1988)? The path to the current widespread popularity of eclectic practice most likely begins with the robust finding of outcome research, that across the broad spectrum of presenting problems and client populations, none of the established family therapy models has demonstrated superiority over the others (Shadish et al., 1993; Shadish, Ragsdale, Glaser, & Montgomery, 1995).

By and large, family therapy educators have responded to this research result by institutionalizing an encyclopedic approach to the presentation of therapeutic models to students like Maria. Theory courses tend to be organized along the lines of, "Here's Bowen family systems theory, and now here's structural family therapy, and now here's collaborative language systems therapy, and now here's. . . ." These year-long or semester-long expositions usually end with one of two punch lines: either, "In each case, pick the model that best fits the client system," or, "Now pick the model that best fits your style." Both of these punch lines are grossly inadequate, in my estimation.

The first punch line is inadequate because it glosses over the fact that nothing even approaching a consensus has emerged among proponents of eclecticism as to how clinicians should go about the task of matching client system to therapeutic model (Held, 1995). In order to achieve such a match, therapists need a set of ideas that will allow them to scan the range of family therapy models in order to compare and contrast them. Necessarily, these ideas have to be more abstract and general than the ideas that make up the models themselves. Breunlin, Schwartz, and Mac Kune-Karrer (1992) have called such ideas "metaframeworks." Miller, Duncan, and Hubble (1997) refer to them as "common factors." Whatever they are called, these ideas are intended to help therapists "float above" the various models of family therapy. From this elevated position, it is hoped, therapists will be able to see that which is common to all of the models of family therapy and then to use these common, presumably therapeutic, practices in their work with all client systems. More to the point, a therapist can use the perspective that her elevated position gives her to find a noncommon practice, idiosyncratic to a particular model, that shows promise of being particularly suited to use with the particular client system that she is working with at that time. In this way, therapists can match clients to the model of therapy that best fits them.

This approach to constructing a systematically eclectic practice of family therapy has what researchers call "face validity." It looks as if it should work. However, difficulty has arisen when theorists have actually attempted to distill the "meta" ideas that will allow therapists to match model to clients. Different theorists, it turns out, have distilled different ideas. As a result, they have offered different, and sometimes conflicting, schemes as to how a therapist should go about the process of matching client system to therapeutic model. In their metaframeworks approach, for example, Breunlin and his colleagues counsel therapists to use feedback provided by clients in response to the therapists' hypothesizing to decide where to begin focusing therapy. Peter Fraenkel's integrative approach, which he calls The Therapeutic Palette (Fraenkel & Pinsof, 2001), also advises therapists to make use of client feedback, though in a strikingly different way than Breunlin and his colleagues do. Fraenkel's approach values brevity in treatment in a way that the metaframeworks approach does not. Thus, while the latter approach uses client feedback simply to refine the hypothesis that will guide the therapy, the former uses feedback for the much more specific purpose of determining which model of therapy will likely produce the briefest, most economical treatment with this particular client system. A third integrative approach, called Integrative Problem Centered Therapy (IPCT), devised by William Pinsof, also values brevity and cost-effectiveness (Fraenkel & Pinsof, 2001). However, it seeks to achieve economy very differently than does Fraenkel's approach. Where

The Therapeutic Palette relies on client feedback to determine which model will produce the briefest treatment with a particular client system, IPCT prescribes a fixed sequence in which techniques and ideas from various therapeutic models should be applied to a given client system. Behavioral and structural family therapy techniques should be applied first. If these fail, biologically based interventions should be delivered. If these are inappropriate or fail, experiential techniques should be used, and so on.

Thus, the family therapist who is interested in practicing a systematic eclecticism is faced with the ironic situation of having to choose among several credible, competing approaches to integrative practice. Advocates of eclecticism could, perhaps, try to address this situation by subjecting the competing approaches to research designed to compare their relative effectiveness. I have a sneaking suspicion that such research would reach the same conclusion that was reached when the various primary models of family therapy were compared. Just as the primary models have been shown to be equally effective, I would not be in the least surprised if the competing integrative approaches also proved to be about equally effective. If that were to turn out to be the case, would we then be poised to launch an effort to integrate the various integrative approaches? Parenthetically, it should be noted at this point that the outcome research that has been conducted to date has not established that any of the available integrative approaches are more effective than "purist" practice based on a single model.

The second punch line that family therapy educators typically use to draw the theory courses that they teach to a close is, "Now pick the model that best fits your style." This punch line is as inadequate as the first. The inadequacy of this second punch line flows out of its use of the word *style*. In my practice and my teaching, I have met several superb structural family therapists whose "styles" were as dramatically different as can be imagined (Minuchin, Lee, & Simon, 1996). Whatever it is that makes one a good structural family therapist, or a good narrative therapist, or a good practitioner of any one of the established models, it is not what is commonly conveyed by the word *style*.

Maria was taught family therapy theory in the encyclopedic manner described above. Like most of her fellow students, she came out of her theory courses with an adequate grasp of the various therapeutic models, but with little idea either of how to construct a systematically eclectic practice or of how to go about the task of finding the therapeutic model that best fits her. The immediate negative impact of this state of affairs was obvious in the clinical vignette that opened this discussion. Maria found herself repeatedly conducting first sessions whose meandering character hindered the development of a therapeutic alliance with her clients. Because it was her supervisor who wound up providing her with a focus in each of her cases, Maria was on the verge of becoming overly dependent on her supervisor, something to which beginners are prone anyhow.

Not immediately obvious in the vignette above is a possible long-term negative consequence of Maria's muddled relationship with the established therapeutic models. Not only do models orient therapists as they conduct sessions, they also provide criteria by which therapists can judge their performance. Without a model to guide her, it is difficult for Maria to assess for herself what she does well in therapy and where she needs improvement. As a result, it is difficult for her to set herself an agenda for growth and development. A therapist not actively engaged in a project of self-growth is a therapist well on the way to stultification. Maria runs the risk of becoming such a therapist. Again, let me state my contention that it is in the best interest of both Maria and her clients for her to commit herself to one of the established models of family therapy.

Still, the problem remains: if neither outcome nor style provides adequate means for choosing a model of therapy, then how are novices such as Maria to be guided in making this choice? There is, in fact, another means available, and it is the purpose of this book to describe that means.

The Underlying Story

We tend to think of therapeutic models as pragmatic affairs, designed to tell clinicians a relatively simple story about human behavior that provides them with an answer on a moment-to-moment basis to the all-important question, "What do I do now?" However, therapeutic models also tell another story, one that is much deeper and broader. Each tells a story about the fundamental nature of human beings and their place in the broader nature of things (Rediger, 1996). This story addresses perennial philosophical themes. It tells whether it is the individual or the group that is the fundamental unit of the human. It asserts whether self-actualization or self-sacrifice constitutes the ultimate human value. It proclaims whether human beings are intrinsically motivated toward good or are capable of evil. It describes the relationship between mind and body. It tells whether primacy in the human domain belongs to being or becoming.

This deeper story told by each model of family therapy is not told explicitly. It lies between the lines, implicit in the main story that the model tells about human behavior and about therapy. Yet this deeper story is the foundation of that main story. Though apparently abstract, this deeper story dictates what the model asserts about the very pragmatic business of doing therapy. This deeper story is whispering in the background every time that the model answers the therapist's question, "What do I do now?"

Though she may not be explicitly aware of it, Maria has her own personal story about the fundamental nature of human beings and their place in the world. Though she may never have studied philosophy and would shudder at the thought of being made to do so, she has her own answers to the questions of whether it is the individual or the group, self-actualization or self-sacrifice, being or becoming, that has primacy in the human world. Her story about these matters may lie latent in the contours of her day-to-day living, but it is there and it is central to who Maria is.

It stands to reason that that story should also be central to how Maria approaches therapy. In order for it to be so, Maria would have to become aware of her personal story about the human condition. She would also need to become aware of the story about the human condition that underlies each of the models of family therapy. That done, Maria would be in a position to commit herself to the therapeutic model whose underlying story about the human condition, whose worldview and values, best fits with her own.

Here, then, is the means proposed by this book for choosing a model of therapy to guide one's practice. There is, indeed, a "fit" to be looked for between yourself and the model to which you choose to commit. But the fit is not in the superficial domain of "style." Rather, it is between your own deeply held values and worldview and the values and worldview that inform your chosen model.

Looking for this fit is not any easy matter. Most of us are only dimly aware, if at all, of our personal stories about the fundamental nature of the human condition. To make matters worse, rarely, if ever, do family therapy educators expose us to the deeper stories about the human condition that underlie the various models of family therapy. Finally, there is little guidance provided us to help us see the intimate connection between these deeper stories and those moments in session when we hear within us that inexorable question, "What do I do now?"

This book will attempt to remedy these difficulties. It will endeavor to sensitize you to how common clinical situations, ones that you face almost every day in your practice, inevitably bring into play deeper philosophical issues. It will try to help you increase your awareness of your own deeply held and cherished values and view of the world. And it will lay bare the values and worldview that inform the major models of family therapy.

Table I.1 provides you with a list of the family therapy models that we will be discussing in this book. It also lists for you the five major issues on which Western philosophers have tended to focus over the centuries as they have tried to make sense of the human condition. In each of the first five chapters, we will examine one of these issues and determine where each of the therapeutic models stands on the issue. In Chapter 6, which will synthesize the discussions in the previous five, Table I.1 will reappear. However, this time the cells that are currently empty will be filled with adjectives that, taken together, will describe each of the models' underlying story about what it means to be human.

Finding Your Therapeutic Voice

If this book does its job well, by its end you will have a working knowledge of the story about the human condition that underlies each of the major models of family therapy. As significantly, you will also have cultivated an awareness of your own personal story about this matter. Thus, ideally, as the book closes, you will be in a position to commit yourself to the therapeutic model whose underlying worldview best fits your own.

Once you make this commitment, your chosen model will begin to guide your practice. It will filter the events that you notice and to which you respond during your sessions. It will provide you with a range of intervention options and help you to decide which option is most likely to be helpful in a given clinical

TABLE I.1 Therapeutic Models and Philosophical Issues to Be Discussed in This Book

	Individual/Group	Freedom from/ Freedom for	Good/Evil	Mind/Body	Being/Becoming
Structural Family Therapy					
Strategic Therapies					
Collaborative Language Systems Therapy					
Solution-Focused Therapy					
Narrative Therapy					
Bowen Family Systems Therapy					
Symbolic Experiential Family Therapy					
Psychoanalytic Family Therapy					

situation. It will help you to assess how well you are doing your job as a family therapist.

The last paragraph makes it sound like, when you commit yourself to a therapeutic model, you will be submerging your individuality to the dictates of the model. Indeed, it is, I think, the fear of such submersion that helps to keep many beginners from committing themselves to a model. However, if you choose your guiding model in the way that this book suggests, the fear is unfounded. For if you are led to a therapeutic model by the congruence between its values and your values, between its worldview and your worldview, then the model becomes, not a mechanism for submerging your individuality, but a vehicle for expressing those core beliefs that make you who you are.

The result of choosing a model in this way is that therapy becomes highly personalized, both for the therapist and for her clients. When they participate in a therapy that is guided by a model which their therapist chose because of its fit with her worldview, clients encounter not an abstract theoretical edifice, but the personhood of their therapist. Even when the therapist employs the model's techniques, her clients ultimately encounter, not a depersonalized technique, but the core values of the therapist. And the therapist herself, when she uses the model, ultimately uses herself. Therapy thus becomes what it always is at its best—an encounter between persons.

This book will lead you on a journey that should end with your committing yourself to a therapeutic model. When you make that commitment, your therapy will begin to be transformed. If it is now a therapy of isolated techniques, it will cease being so. It will become instead a therapy marked with a consistent, characteristic voice. And that voice will not be the voice of your chosen model's founders. It will be yours. For in committing yourself to the model, you will have begun to find your therapeutic voice.

1

The Individual and the Group

Whose Life Is It, Anyway?

"It feels like I'm walking around with an anvil on each shoulder and one on my chest." Carrie was describing her depression to her therapist, Collette.

This was the beginning of Collette's third session with Carrie and her husband, Steve. It had become clear to Collette within five minutes of meeting the couple that it was Carrie who had been the one to instigate their entrance into therapy. It was Carrie who did most of the talking, Carrie who articulated the agenda for the therapy. Steve looked on with an expression that was difficult for Collette to read, making no attempt to break into his wife's monologues.

"We're here because we've grown distant from each other," Carrie had told Collette during the first session. Although Carrie had defined the presenting problem for the therapy in relational terms, in both of the first two sessions it was not long before she had led the talk in the direction of her depression. Once the focus moved onto this topic, it remained there. Now, at the beginning of the third session, Carrie was once again talking about the depression.

Collette was aware that she had not been a passive bystander to the way in which the first two sessions—and now, by all appearances, the third, as well—developed. She had allowed and even colluded in stabilizing the focus on Carrie's depression. She had done so because she was, quite frankly, confused. She was not sure how she should think about Carrie's quite evident depression. Was the depression something inside of Carrie, rooted in her psyche or her biology? The psychiatrist who was treating Carrie apparently thought so, because he was prescribing medication for the depression.

At several points during the first two sessions, Collette had had thoughts of a very different kind about the depression. Noting Steve's utter lack of response to his wife's pain during the sessions, she found herself wondering whether Carrie's depression was an expression of her extreme loneliness in the face of her husband's uninvolvement. She wondered whether that impassive expression on Steve's face was the end product of years of listening to Carrie drone on about her sadness and her pain. She wondered whether Steve's lack of presence, in the sessions and probably at home, was his way of insulating himself from Carrie's pain. She wondered whether Steve's strategy for coping with his wife's depression accomplished nothing more than the deepening of the depression. Collette wondered, in short, whether Carrie's depression did not belong primarily to Carrie but to the marital relationship, to the patterned way in which Steve and Carrie related to each other.

Collette was called back from these thoughts by Carrie's narration of the fact that she had suffered bouts of depression long before she had met Steve. She had grown up in a family rife with alcoholism. The drinking was never talked about, nor were the episodes of depression that she experienced with regularity. When she was twenty, she had finally taken herself to a psychiatrist. He had prescribed a medication different from the one that she was currently taking. The medication had worked, leaving her symptom-free for years. As Collette listened to this story, she began to wonder whether Carrie's depression did indeed reside inside of her.

Then Carrie added that the depressive symptoms had returned when she and Steve married. Collette glanced over toward Steve, saw that blank expression on his face, and her confusion about how to think about the depression returned. Not a little depressed herself, Collette postponed for the moment thinking about how to intervene with the couple and just went with the flow. Steve continued to stare into space; Carrie droned on about her depression.

The Individual and the Group

This was the first time in her clinical career that Collette was faced with the decision about where to locate a client's dysfunction, whether inside the client in some way, or in some social group to which the client belongs. This might have been the first time, but it will by no means be the last. Collette will be faced with this decision regularly in her practice. When she hears a wife complain about her husband's excessive drinking, when she hears parents describe their eight-year-old son's "out-of-control" behavior, when she hears a husband describe his wife's compulsive housecleaning rituals, she will be faced with the same decision.

It might strike you as strange that I am casting this matter as something that requires a *decision* on Collette's part. Aren't matters like this questions of objective fact, answerable by scientific research? Won't the growing body of research on depression and alcoholism and attention deficit disorder ultimately provide answers to the question of where the dysfunction in each of these conditions is located?

If Collette believes that she can pass the buck to researchers on this matter, then she has a flawed understanding of the nature of research. Before the researcher ever begins to gather data, she makes decisions that will vitally influence the outcome of her research (Boss, Dahl, & Kaplan, 1996). She decides where she will look for data. She decides what kind of data she will collect. She decides how she will interpret the data. All of these decisions inevitably color the so-called "results" of the research. And these decisions are not themselves data-driven. They flow out of the researcher's biases, her values and view of the world. No less than Collette, then, the researcher who investigates conditions like Carrie's needs to make an a priori decision about whether she is going to view the conditions as lying inside of people or outside of them, in some larger social system. If Collette is genuinely of a mind to consult research in her attempt to think about Carrie's depression, then that is extremely commendable. However, the intent to consult research does not let Collette off the hook about making a decision. For if she is going to be an informed consumer of the research that she consults, Collette will need to take note of the assumptions that have driven the research, and she will need to decide how well those assumptions fit with her own.

Moreover, Collette's decision about where to locate the dysfunction in the case of major disorders like depression or alcoholism or attention deficit disorder is simply a corollary of a more encompassing decision that will dictate how she responds to therapeutic situations of a far less dramatic character. Every time that Collette in her role as therapist focuses on a piece of human behavior and tries to understand it and change it—whether it be a husband's withdrawal from his wife's overtures for closeness, or a mother's refusal to discipline her son, or a twelve-year-old boy's aggressive behavior toward his younger siblings—she will inevitably have to identify the behavior as belonging either to an individual or to some larger social group. The decision that Collette makes on this clinical question will itself be rooted in a decision that she has made on a more fundamental, more personal question: whether in her world it is the individual or the group that constitutes the fundamental unit of the human.

Historical Backdrop

The reason that Collette has been called on to make a decision in her personal life on this fundamental question is that the question itself has been a pivotal one in the evolution of Western culture. Over the course of the centuries, Western philosophers have revisited time and again the issue of whether the individual or the group represents the fundamental human unit. While the average person knows little about these philosophical speculations, they have both reflected and shaped the broader culture's story about what it means to be human. Thus, despite the fact that Collette neither knows nor cares to know about philosophy, the question about what is the fundamental unit of the human is one that she has absorbed, as if by osmosis, simply as a result of having been raised in the West.

Political Philosophy

The first Western philosophers to focus specifically on the human condition were a group of Greek thinkers who in their own time were called (especially by their critics) Sophists. The most prominent members of this group were Protagoras, Gorgias, Thrasymachus, Callicles, and Critias.

In studying the human condition, Protagoras reached the conclusion that knowing is the same as perceiving. However, you know from your own experience that what a person perceives depends on that person's moment-to-moment state and situation. Thus, for Protagoras, and for all the Sophists after him, "[t]he consequence is that knowledge is not only relative but is relative to each perceiver at the moment of [perception]. . ." (Nahm, 1964, p. 221). The ground was thus laid for the radical individualism and relativism that came to characterize Sophist reflections on the human condition. For the Sophists, the fundamental human unit was unambiguously the individual. Each individual's perceptions provided the sole measure of what would constitute "reality" for that person. Law and tradition, the elements that provide cohesiveness to groups of people, were seen by the Sophists as lacking any "objective" foundation. They were merely "custom," to be overcome by the individual in pursuit of personal integrity.

The Sophists' designation of the individual as the fundamental unit of the human provoked a predictable reaction. No less a philosophical figure than Socrates undertook to challenge the individualism and relativism of the Sophists. And when Socrates' philosophizing resulted in his execution by the city-state of Athens, Plato, his student and admirer, devoted his entire philosophical career to constructing a rebuttal of the Sophists' position. For Plato, the group, the collectivity of humans, is not a matter of mere convention or convenience, secondary to the desires and projects of the individuals that it encompasses. The group—in Plato's thought, the city-state—has ontological status in its own right, which is to say that not only its existence but the form that it should ideally take is rooted in the very nature of reality. Plato describes his vision of the ideal human group in his *Republic* and in his *Laws*.

As the philosophical tradition of the West evolved over the course of the ensuing centuries, philosophical reflections on the human condition, and political philosophy in particular, continued to oscillate between seeing the individual and the group as the fundamental human unit. When the eighteenth century spawned the political philosophy known as liberalism, the political philosophy that has most influenced the rise and development of democracies in the West, that oscillation did not cease. Instead, it was not long before two distinct traditions developed within liberalism.

The cornerstone of liberalism is the concept of human liberty. For liberals like Locke, Voltaire, and Montesquieu, liberty meant freedom of the individual from the constraints of the state (Cranston, 1967). Here, in rationalist eighteenth-century garb, was a reprise of the Sophists' designation of the individual as the fundamental human unit.

It was not long, however, before some liberals, building on the thought of Rousseau, began to identify liberalism with the *extension* of liberty, especially to those deprived of it, such as the poor. The intervention of the state in this project of extending liberty came to be seen as both necessary and salutary. The focus of Lockean liberalism on protecting the individual from the activity of the state came to be replaced in this brand of liberalism by a focus on how the state may best act to extend liberty. With its interest in the state and its activity, this brand of liberalism reprised, again in eighteenth-century garb, Plato's designation of the group as the fundamental unit of the human.

And the debate continues. To this day, "one might divide liberals into those who see freedom as something which belongs to the individual, to be defended against the encroachments of the state, and those who see freedom as something which belongs to society and which the state, as the central instrument of social betterment, can be made to enlarge and improve" (Cranston, 1967, p. 461).

Philosophy of the Social Sciences

The debate as to whether the fundamental unit of the human is the individual or the group has dominated not only political philosophy but also that branch of philosophy that examines the assumptions and premises of the social sciences, which include family therapy. Here, the debate is formulated as

> whether we should treat large scale social events and conditions as mere aggregates or configurations of the individual men and women who participated in, enjoyed, or suffered them. Methodological individualists say we should. Methodological holists (or collectivists, as some prefer to be called) claim, rather, that social phenomena may be studied at their own autonomous, macroscopic level of analysis. Social 'wholes,' they say, not their human elements, are the true historical individuals (Dray, 1967, p. 461).

Put more simply, methodological individualists see the individual as the fundamental human unit. So-called group phenomena (such as the interactional patterns in a family) are seen by these philosophers to be nothing more than the sum of the thoughts, feelings, intentions, and behavior of the individuals comprising the group. Methodological collectivists, on the other hand, see the group as the fundamental human unit. Group phenomena are for them not mere sums; they are, in fact, what really exist in the human domain, and it is they that explain the behavior of individuals, not the other way around, as the individualists claim.

Therapeutic Ramifications

Having been raised in the context of Western culture, Collette has been exposed, perhaps explicitly, but more likely implicitly, to the question of whether it is the individual or the group that constitutes the fundamental unit of the human. As part of the process of crystallizing an adult identity, she has answered this question for herself, again perhaps explicitly, but more likely implicitly.

The way in which Collette has chosen to answer this question should have an impact on the way in which she operates as a family therapist. If she has defined herself to be an individualist, someone who sees the individual as the fundamental unit of the human, she needs to choose a model of therapy that is based on the same premise. If, on the other hand, she is a collectivist, seeing the group as the fundamental human unit, she needs to commit herself to a collectivist model of therapy, one that makes the same assumption about the fundamental unit of the human.

A question immediately comes to mind. Because it is specifically models of *family* therapy that we are concerned with in this book, is it not safe to assume that all of them take the group rather than the individual to be the fundamental human unit? There was indeed a time, early in the development of the field, when this assumption was not far from being correct (although, as we will soon see, it was not, even then, entirely correct). As the field has evolved, however, and especially in recent years, it has become decreasingly so.

So, if we are interested in seeing what positions the various models of family therapy take on this question of the fundamental unit of the human, we will actually have to examine them for indications regarding their position. But these models are fairly complex conceptual systems; where within them can we look so as to discern as quickly as possible the stance that they take on this fundamental question?

This task is not as daunting as it might first appear. We need only look at what each of the models asserts about the cause of the problems that bring families into therapy in order to discern where the model stands on the issue of the individual versus the group as the fundamental human unit. Some of the models, we will find, ascribe problem causation to group-level processes. These are collectivist therapies, which take the group as the fundamental human unit. We will discover that other models see problems as rooted in processes that occur within individuals. These are the individualist therapies.

The Collectivist Therapies

Structural Family Therapy.   In structural family therapy, the problems that bring a family into therapy are seen as being caused by a family structure, a family organizational map, if you will, that is preventing the family from responding adequately to the developmental needs of its members and/or to the demands being exerted on the family by its sociocultural surround. As structural family therapists understand it, family organization may be thought of as a collection of informal and largely unarticulated rules or routines that regulate how the individual members of the family will behave toward each other. Put simply, it is faulty family organization that is the culprit that lands families in therapy. Because family organization is manifestly a group-level rather than an individual-level construct, when structural therapy ascribes problem-causation to flawed family organization, it positions itself squarely as a collectivist therapy.

Not so fast, you might find yourself thinking at this point. Even if we grant that family organization is the cause of the problems that bring families into therapy, who is responsible for having created the organization in the first place? Was it not the family members themselves? And if so, is it not the individual family members who are ultimately the "culprits" who have brought themselves into therapy, making structural therapy in the final analysis an individualist therapy?

Well, no, the structural family therapist would answer, it is not quite that simple. To be sure, the individual members of a family are involved in the creation of the family's organization. However, the family organization cannot be considered to be their creation in the same way that this book can be considered my creation. In the case of this book, I have exercised something close to unilateral control over the final product. No member of a family ever exerts anything like that degree of control over the form that her family's organization takes. Instead, the organization is the product of countless daily interpersonal encounters, in which I accommodate to your behavior at the very moment that you are accommodating to me accommodating to you, and so on. When our mutual accommodation becomes routinized, that transaction will become part of our family's organization. You and I were both involved in the creation of the transaction. However, the form that it has assumed is not something that I in isolation or you in isolation could ever have produced. Nor is it simply the sum or aggregate of what you and I could have produced in isolation. Rather, it is the product of our relationship. It is, in fact, very similar to a child. If you and I produce a child, that child will have something from me and something from you, but he will be none-theless an independent entity in his own right. In an entirely analogous way, the individual members of a family cannot be seen as creating the family's organization; the family itself, as an organism in its own right, creates the organization.

As was noted above, once an organizational map has stabilized within a family, it regulates the behavior of individual family members. However, it never exhausts the capabilities of the individual family members. Precisely because family structure is the product of mutual accommodation, it always leaves untapped a reserve of behavioral possibilities in each and every family member. If the current organization is disrupted, and you and I are prevented from returning to our old pattern of mutual accommodation, then the next time we find ourselves in a situation where I am accommodating to you as you are accommodating to me accommodating to you, and so on, we will each find ourselves using aspects of our behavioral repertoire that were not activated by the old organization (Minuchin & Fishman, 1981; Minuchin & Nichols, 1993).

This is precisely what intervention in structural family therapy is all about. The therapist challenges and disrupts the family's organizational map. At the same time, utilizing enactments, he creates contexts in which new patterns of mutual accommodation between family members can emerge (Simon, 1995).

A structural family therapist meeting with Carrie and Steve would experience no quandary about where to locate Carrie's depression. He would see both the depression and Steve's impassive stance toward it as being the product of the organization that currently regulates day-to-day life in Carrie and Steve's family. Though Steve and Carrie helped to conceive this organization, it is bigger than both of them and now has a life of its own. Disrupting this organization would be the first major task that the structural family therapist would set for himself. The second major task would be to help Carrie and Steve produce a new organizational map that elicits more vital and satisfying parts of both of them.

The Strategic Therapies. The term *strategic therapy* is admittedly somewhat nebulous. Following common usage, I include among the strategic therapies the MRI Brief Therapy approach, the strategic therapy developed and taught by Jay Haley and Cloe Madanes, and the systemic therapy of the first Milan team (the late Mara Selvini Palazzoli, Luigi Boscolo, Gianfranco Cecchin, and Giuliana Prata) (Nichols & Schwartz, 1995).

Among the strategic therapies, the MRI approach has the simplest—and, some would add, the most elegant—theory of problem causation. To begin, the MRI approach anticipated later developments in the field of family therapy by asserting that there are no objectively defined problems that require treatment. Problems are only problems when a family defines them to be so. Once a family defines a certain behavior to be a problem, family members invariably take steps to solve it. If the steps taken are successful, a therapist will not be called on for help. However, suppose the steps taken by family members fail to solve the problem. The family then faces a decision. It can respond to the failure by taking new steps to solve the problem. The MRI therapist is confident that if the family responds in this way, it will eventually be able to resolve the problem on its own without help from a therapist. However, the family can respond to the failure of its first attempted solution by repeating the steps originally taken, perhaps with more gusto this time around. It can easily happen in such a situation that the sheer repetition of the attempted solution steps unwittingly begins to elicit intensification of the problem. If the family responds to this development with yet another repetition of the attempted solution steps, a vicious cycle is born. The problem behavior, which may have been circumscribed and fairly innocuous at its first appearance, becomes part of a circular sequence of behaviors involving several, if not all, the members of the family.

The MRI therapist sees her task in therapy as bringing about the interruption of this interactional sequence in the family in which the presenting problem has become embedded. She will accomplish this task mainly through the use of directives delivered to the family. To increase the chance that family members will comply with her directives, the MRI therapist reframes the presenting problem, redefining it in such a way as to make her directives appear reasonable.

Some of the thoughts that Collette had about Carrie's depression were actually MRI thoughts. When she saw Steve's impassivity as an attempt on his part to "solve" his wife's depression (at least insofar as it impacted him), when she hypothesized that this attempted solution on Steve's part only intensified Carrie's depression, when she saw Steve responding to this development by simply repeating his attempted solution of withdrawal, Collette was thinking as an MRI therapist would. Had she followed through in this MRI mode, her next task would have been to devise and "sell" to Carrie and Steve directives that, when implemented, would have interrupted the problem-maintaining interactional sequence being played out between the two of them.

The strategic therapy of Jay Haley and Cloe Madanes also sees families' presenting problems as being embedded in circular interactional sequences in the families that serve to maintain the problems. However, Haley and Madanes have a more involved theory than does the MRI Brief Therapy group regarding why such problem-maintaining sequences come about within a family. Madanes and Haley share with structural family therapy the notion that the behavior of family members is regulated by an organizational map that holds sway in the family. An organization that allows a family to respond adequately to the developmental needs of its members and to the demands exerted on the family by the broader society is seen as functional. Such an organization will not spawn symptoms and the interactional sequences that maintain them. However, in some families, the organizational map does hinder them from performing these tasks; moreover, despite this fact, the families display a reluctance to change the organization. In such families, symptoms are likely to be generated. As described by the MRI group, the symptoms become embedded in circular interactional sequences that serve to maintain them. If you examine these sequences closely, Haley and Madanes assert, you will see that they have the effect of buttressing the family's organization, especially those aspects of it that are being most threatened by the developmental and/or environmental pressures to which the family is being subject. Thus, the famous dictum that "the system maintains the symptom, and the symptom maintains the system."

Like their MRI counterparts, Madanes and Haley deliver directives to families designed to interrupt problem-maintaining sequences. In doing so, they see themselves as also intervening to change the families' organization, especially in the area of hierarchy, which is that aspect of family organization that they see as most crucial to adaptive family functioning. Thus, while their means are quite different, the end toward which Madanes and Haley aim in their strategic therapy is quite similar to that sought by the structural family therapist.

A strategic therapist of the Haley-Madanes variety would see Carrie's depression as being part of the same interactional loop that Collette observed between Steve and Carrie when she was having her MRI thoughts about the case. However, whereas an MRI therapist would have no thoughts about why the loop between Carrie and Steve came to be, the Madanes-Haley strategic therapist would likely develop a fairly involved hypothesis about the origins of the loop. Tuned in as he is to hierarchy issues, he would likely see the loop as originating in a power struggle between the spouses, in which each has tried to maneuver him- or herself into a position to control the rules of the relationship. In the struggle, each has turned to a weapon: Carrie has used her depression as a means to gain the one-up position; Steve has countered by emotionally withdrawing. Each may have sought allies in the struggle. Perhaps Carrie has confided with her mother; perhaps Steve is having an affair.

The strategic therapy of the first Milan team can be thought of as lying somewhere between the theoretical minimalism of the MRI Brief Therapy group and the structuralism of Haley and Madanes' strategic therapy. Like Madanes and Haley, the Milan team believed that symptoms and the interactional sequences in which they are embedded function to allow families to hold on to a flawed organizational map. However, whereas Madanes and Haley's theory of family functioning is so fully articulated as to practically predetermine what organizational flaws the therapist would find in the client family—no doubt a disturbance in the family hierarchy—the Milan group approached each family as a new puzzle to be figured out. The interviewing technology invented by the first Milan team—circular questioning, the observing team, the guidelines of hypothesizing, circularity, and neutrality—was devised to allow the idiosyncratic interactional game being played out in each family to be ferreted out as quickly as possible.

Once the Milan therapists felt that they had a pretty good read on a family's organization and the way in which the presenting problem fit into it, they would tell the family, via a message from the observing team, how they saw the system maintaining the symptom and the symptom maintaining the system. The message would tell the family how necessary it was for family stability for everyone in the family to continue doing what they were doing, and they would advise all family members to continue doing so. Of course, the intent of this positively connoting message was paradoxical: the message was intended to provoke the family into changing its organization so that the symptom was no longer required.

A strategic therapist trained in the practice of the first Milan team would be as convinced as a Haley-Madanes strategist that Carrie's depression was both produced by and helped to maintain the organizational map of Steve and Carrie's family. Like the Madanes-Haley therapist, the Milan therapist would engage in fairly elaborate hypothesizing about the family organization and the way in which Carrie's depression was embedded within it. However, whereas the Haley-Madanes strategic therapist would base his hypotheses on some preconceived ideas about where the flaw in the family organization probably lies, the Milan practitioner would try her best to base her hypotheses primarily on the idiosyncratic details of the case. Thus, the Milan therapist might wonder what it means for the family organization that, despite the fact that he has been passive during the sessions, it was Steve who called Collette's clinic to arrange the couple's entrance into treatment. She might also wonder about the relationship between Carrie and her psychiatrist, and how that relationship fits into the family's organization. These and any other details of the case could serve as the starting point for hypothesizing by the Milan therapist. Any of these details, positively connoted, might figure in the paradoxical message by which Milan therapy attempts to provoke change in the family organization.

Whatever their differences, all three kinds of strategic therapies share the viewpoint that human behavior does not belong to individuals, but rather to larger social entities (problem-maintaining interactional sequences, family organizational maps). The unit of clinical analysis is not the individual, but a social group. It is this perspective that makes the strategic therapies collectivist.

Collaborative Language Systems Therapy.   As in the MRI approach, problems are not seen as having any kind of objective status in the collaborative language systems approach pioneered by Harlene Anderson and the late Harold Goolishian.

Problems do not exist on their own; they are defined into existence by people who, in conversation together, decide to label something as problematic. In the collaborative language systems approach this group of people is called the problem-organizing system.

The language systems approach departs radically from earlier family therapy approaches in refusing to identify problem-organizing systems with family systems. As a matter of fact, true to their social constructionist underpinnings, collaborative language systems therapists are wary of any ready-made, predefined systems (e.g., "the" family, "the" couple). Of clinical relevance to them is the group of people who are in ongoing conversation together about something that they have decided to call a problem. These people may happen to be members of the same family, but they may not. They may include part of one family and part of another. They may also include people who have entered the conversation in their capacity as professionals.

It is the conversation among these people that maintains the problem in existence. Note that I said that it is the *conversation* in the problem-organizing system that keeps the problem in existence. It is not the structure, the organization, of the system that elicits and maintains the problem. True postmodernists, collaborative language systems therapists see all properly human phenomena, including the problems that people bring into therapy, as existing solely in the domain of meaning. Thus, attempts to deal therapeutically with human problems should not rely on concepts like organization and hierarchy and problem-maintaining sequences; they should instead attend to the meanings put forth as part of the ongoing conversations that define problems into existence.

Thus, the language systems therapist endeavors to join the problem-organizing system. She does so with the intention of managing her participation in the conversation in such a way as to keep the conversation fluid. This is her goal because she is convinced that if the conversation flows and evolves, it will eventually define the problem out of existence, or as Anderson and Goolishian (1988) put it, the conversation will dis-solve the problem.

The language systems therapist attempts to keep the problem-organizing conversation fluid by adopting the attitude that no meaning expressed as part of the conversation is simple, clear, and easily understandable. This posture Anderson and Goolishian refer to as an attitude of not-knowing. "It is this attitude that leads the therapist to accord plausibility to any idea and, at the same time, to consider any idea as needing to be questioned to elicit further elaboration" (Minuchin, Lee, & Simon, 1996, p. 53). Participating in the problem-organizing conversation in this way, the language systems therapist helps keep the conversation tending in the direction of the not-yet-said. As the conversation moves in this direction, it is inevitable, given the evanescence of meaning, that the problem will eventually be defined out of existence.

If a collaborative language systems therapist were to meet with Carrie and Steve, she would try very hard to enter into that meeting without any preconceived ideas about depression, or about marriage, or about anything else, for that matter. Nor would she construct any hypotheses about Carrie's depression or about Steve and Carrie's marriage. Instead, she would try to elicit the conversation that was currently being held about Carrie's depression. Toward that end, she might ask Carrie how she understood her depression. She would likely ask Steve the same question. She might ask Carrie how she understood Steve's reticence on the matter of her depression. She might ask who else had an opinion or was concerned about Carrie's depression, this with an eye toward inviting these other participants in the problem-organizing system to join a later session. The therapist would listen carefully to the answers given to her questions, not so that she could understand the answers, but so that she could be slow to understand, asking for further elucidation that would keep the problem-organizing conversation fluid and developing, tending toward the inevitable dissolution of the presenting problem.

It is clear that, in considering collaborative language systems therapy, we have entered into a world of conceptualization and practice that differs dramatically from that inhabited by structural family therapy and the strategic therapies. Yet, collaborative language systems therapy shares one very important characteristic with these earlier models of family therapy: for it, as for them, the phenomena that are the focus of the therapeutic enterprise are collective, or group, phenomena. To be sure, the language systems therapist conceives of and intervenes in these phenomena very differently than does the structural or strategic therapist. Where the latter sees and attempts to modify organizational realities, such as hierarchy and interactional sequences, the former hears and attempts to facilitate conversation. However, whether one sees organizational maps or hears meaning-generating conversations, one is operating out of the position that it is group-level processes that are most relevant to the therapeutic enterprise. For all of these therapies, it is the group that is the fundamental unit of the human.

The Individualist Therapies

Psychoanalytic Family Therapy.   To begin, the title of this section is a misnomer. There is not a single psychoanalytic approach to family therapy, but several such approaches, each differing significantly from the others in conceptualization, technique, and length of treatment. Whatever the differences, however, all these approaches have a crucial element in common: dysfunctional behavior in a person is seen to be rooted in that person's childhood experiences of being parented. These experiences produce in the person intrapsychic structures that determine how that person will interact with significant others across the life span. When inadequate parenting leaves an individual beset by unresolved conflicts, that individual will almost certainly couple with someone who provides him with an opportunity continuously to revisit and reenact those conflicts. Additionally, it is almost invariably the case that the individual provides his partner with the same opportunity. Thus, the relationship between these two adults becomes little more than an arena within which each, with the help of the other, makes continual unsuccessful efforts to gratify unmet childhood needs. If the couple produces or adopts children, the way in which they parent the children will also be determined by their intrapsychic difficulties. By thus parenting their children inadequately, the couple assures that yet another generation of impaired individuals is produced.

Differently from their classical psychoanalytic forebears, psychoanalytic family therapists are interested in interactional phenomena. They attend to the manner in which each member of a couple "cooperates" with the other by behaving in ways that allow the other's intrapsychic conflicts to be played out. They note, too, how each member induces such "cooperation" through the process that analytic therapists refer to as "projective identification." Nonetheless, it remains the case for analytic family therapists that such interactional phenomena are mere by-products of the intrapsychic structures of the individuals involved. Psychoanalytic family therapy aims at helping each family member gain insight into and work through her own individual conflictual issues. The result of such work is that the family members become freer to experience themselves and each other more realistically (Sander, 1998). Interactional processes in the family become healthier, but as a result of the intrapsychic restructuring of the individual family members that preceded it.

As would a structural family therapist, an analytic therapist working with Carrie and Steve would note the complementarity between Carrie's depressed monologues and Steve's impassivity. However, the analytic therapist would interpret this observation very differently than the structural therapist. The latter would see the pattern as something into which Steve and Carrie had drifted in the course of their mutual accommodation to each other. The pattern currently governs their behavior, but it is not hardwired and it does not exhaust their interpersonal resources. The structural therapist would assume that if the pattern is interrupted Carrie and Steve can crystallize a new, more adaptive pattern in fairly short order.

For the psychoanalytic family therapist, on the other hand, the pattern is hardwired. While the details are not yet apparent, an analytic therapist working with Steve and Carrie would assume that the complementary behavior of each toward the other is rooted in his and her respective developmental histories. In watching their interaction, the analytic therapist would not see two fundamentally sound people being victimized by a maladaptive relational organization, but two disturbed people playing out core conflicts whose roots extend deeply into their psyches and into their pasts. In viewing a group-level process (Carrie and Steve's interactional pattern) as being the result and mere sum of individual-level processes (Carrie and Steve's respective intrapsychic dynamics), the psychoanalytic family therapist gives expression to his assumption that it is the individual, not the group, that is the fundamental unit of the human.

Bowen Family Systems Therapy.   What is it, from the perspective of the Bowenian therapist, that gives rise to the kinds of problems that lead people into therapy? No less than in psychoanalytic family therapy, Bowen family systems therapy attributes symptoms to flawed intrapsychic structure. What differs between the two approaches is the way in which intrapsychic structure is described.

No matter how much it has evolved and developed over time, analytic thinking still has its roots in drive theory. Intrapsychic structure is still thought of as arising from the interplay between instinctive impulses and needs of the individual—sexual and aggressive impulses, needs for attachment and appreciation—and the parental environment. When analytic therapists describe intrapsychic structure, the individual is the star and the environment is supporting cast.

Murray Bowen, on the other hand, was among the first to develop an interest in family-level phenomena in their own right. His description of processes within the nuclear and intergenerational family was seminal. When Bowen sought to describe intrapsychic structure, he did so as a family theorist. Thus, he did not ascribe primacy to individual drives and needs. He took the language that he had used to describe family relational processes and used it to describe intrapsychic processes as well. Thus, just as Bowen described family relationships in terms of how much emotional fusion characterized them, he described individuals in terms of how differentiated they are. Fused relationships are characterized by emotional reactivity between the participants, who respond to each other in times of stress in a stereotyped knee-jerk fashion rather than from a base of calm deliberation. Similarly, undifferentiated individuals are described as people whose cognitive functioning is especially vulnerable to being flooded in times of stress by overwhelming feelings, resulting either in impulsive behavior or reactive distancing. By describing intrapsychic functioning in language drawn from a systemic analysis of family processes, Bowen avoided the psychoanalytic bias of describing the family (and the world, for that matter) as if its sole reason for existing was to serve as a foil for the needs and drives of the developing individual.

So why, then, have I included Bowen therapy within the ranks of the individualist therapies? Despite the fact that Bowen describes intrapsychic structure in what we might term "family-friendly" language, it is no less true for him than it is for psychoanalytic therapists that human behavior is ultimately driven by individual intrapsychic structure. A child triangulated into the relationship between undifferentiated parents will herself wind up even less differentiated than her parents. In Bowen's view, this intrapsychic state of affairs all but determines her destiny. When she couples, this individual will almost assuredly do so with someone whose level of differentiation approximates hers. Their respective intrapsychic deficits make it just about inevitable that they will construct a fused relationship, marked by such a high degree of free-floating anxiety that triangulation will almost certainly be required to stabilize the relationship.

A Bowenian therapist meeting with Carrie and Steve would assume that they were such a couple. The therapist would certainly observe the complementarity between Carrie's emotion-ridden monologues and Steve's reactive, withholding distancing. However, similarly to the psychoanalytic therapist, the Bowenian would see these role-behaviors as hardwired, issuing from Steve and Carrie's respective intrapsychic deficits. Like the analytic therapist, the Bowenian would see the therapeutic task as involving the restructuring of Carrie and Steve's psyches so that they can relate to each other in a healthier fashion. Because the Bowenian and the analyst conceive of intrapsychic structure differently, each will go about this task of intrapsychic restructuring differently. However, the one as much as the other will construct a therapy that sees group processes as being the product of individual processes. Each will construct a therapy based on the assumption that it is the individual that is the fundamental unit of the human.

Symbolic Experiential Family Therapy.   Carl Whitaker and the symbolic experiential therapists who have come after him have liked to proclaim that theirs is an atheoretical approach to therapy. In doing so, they have given expression to what is perhaps the fundamental tenet of their approach: optimal human functioning involves first of all the ability to experience deeply, without the filters of "rationality" by which we try to tame and domesticate life, and secondly the ability to give expression to our experience by whatever combination of verbal and nonverbal means best gets the job done.

"Experience" is an individualist concept. It is individuals who experience, not groups. In exalting deepened experiencing as the goal of therapy, symbolic experiential therapists have placed their therapy squarely within the ranks of the individualist therapies. David Keith, a colleague of Whitaker, is succinct on this matter: "The goal of psychotherapy, the definition of growth, is for the patient to have as much access to the self as possible" (1998, p. 180).

If they are interested in the self, then why do experientialists see families? Keith provides us with the answer: "Access to the self is greatest in the context of a deeply intimate relationship (e.g., marriage). Marriage is one of the best ways of getting a PhD in being a person" (1998, p. 180). Symbolic experientialists are interested in seeing families because the emotional intensity of family life provides a crucible wherein access to deep experiences of self is available. The well-functioning family, in the experientialists' view, is one that nurtures and supports the growth and experiencing of the individual members. By contrast, the malfunctioning family, the one that gives rise to symptoms, is one that requires its members to repress feelings and drives, to hide from each other, and, ultimately, from themselves.

When the symbolic experientialist meets with such a family, he will not focus his attention on group-level phenomena, such as organizational maps or problem-bearing interactional sequences. Instead, he will key on in-session moments when the behavior of individual family members appears to be arising out of an experiencing of self that is stunted, repressed, or somehow truncated. In such moments, the therapist will use his own (hopefully unrepressed) experiencing to craft interventions whose spontaneity, creativity, and unconscious wisdom work to unblock family members, to deepen their self-awareness, and to enhance their ability to communicate their experiencing to each other.

Because the very essence of symbolic experiential therapy is that it flows out of the idiosyncratic way in which a particular therapist experiences particular clients, it is impossible for me to say what a "generic" experiential therapist would focus her interventions on while working with Carrie and Steve. If she experiences Steve's impassivity as repressed rage at his wife, the therapist might focus on that. If she experiences Carrie's depressed and depressing monologues as a mechanism used by her to keep Steve (and the therapist) at arm's length, she might tell her so. If sitting with Steve and Carrie causes the therapist to remember a cousin of hers who committed suicide, she might share that. This much can be said with certainty: the "stuff" used by the symbolic experiential therapist to construct her therapy will be her experiencing of the way in which her clients appear to be experiencing. "Good" therapy, like good family life, will be characterized by deep, intense experiencing on the part of all the participants, and the free-flowing, uncensored communication of that experiencing.

Narrative Therapy. The term *narrative therapy* has come to be used widely and somewhat loosely over the past few years. In this book, I will use the term narrowly to refer to the postmodern therapeutic approach developed by Michael White.

In our quest to discern which therapies are collectivist and which are individualist, we have been examining what the various models assert about how the problems that lead families into therapy arise. Another way of saying this is that we have been exploring what the models have to say about where these problems "really" reside. The collectivist therapies assert that problems reside in group-level phenomena, like family organization or problem-organizing systems. The individualist therapies that we have discussed thus far assert that problems reside in individual people, who are conceived, depending on the model, as being intrapsychically conflicted, undifferentiated, or repressed.

For Michael White, the problem with the people who enter therapy is that they believe that they are the problem. White does not. He believes that the problems that bring people into therapy have their ultimate source in cultural practices and social institutions. These "hide" their culpability by presenting themselves to people as essential, necessary, objectively valid, grounded in truth that transcends time and place. When social institutions and cultural practices give rise to problems in living and yet obscure the fact that alternative practices and institutions are possible, the people who experience the problems have no choice but to see themselves as the source of the problems.

The first task for therapy, as White sees it, is to help people see that, far from being the source of their problems, they are in fact being oppressed by problems whose source lies at the level of sociocultural practices. White thus externalizes presenting problems, using the language of his therapeutic questions to help clients see the problems as "out there" rather than "in here." He then endeavors to empower his clients to overcome their victimization by their problems. He does this in a couple of ways. First of all, he leads his clients into an exploration of what he calls unique outcomes, episodes in the past when the clients have succeeded in rendering themselves less oppressed by the problems. In recounting such episodes, clients are sensitized to a resilience and a resourcefulness that was likely obscured by their previous acceptance of the story that they themselves were the problem. Next, White begins to call into question the "obviousness" and the "essentialness" of the cultural practices and the social institutions that are the ultimate source of the clients' problems. By doing so, he empowers clients to resist social pressures to conform to dominant cultural practices, and to choose instead practices that they would prefer.

A narrative therapist meeting with Steve and Carrie would likely be struck by the degree to which Carrie identifies herself with her depression. To attenuate this debilitating story, the therapist would externalize the depression. He might begin the process of externalization by giving the depression a clever name. Seizing on Carrie's own metaphor, he might call the depression "The Anvil Lifestyle." He might then proceed to ask Carrie what the effects are on her life when The Anvil Lifestyle succeeds in getting her into its clutches. Similarly, he might ask Steve how his life is affected when The Anvil Lifestyle has its way with Carrie. The narrative therapist might go on to ask Carrie the particular devices The Anvil Lifestyle uses to seduce her. Steve might be asked how The Anvil Lifestyle enlists his aid in seducing Carrie. The therapist might now begin to ask Steve and Carrie about times that they have succeeded, separately or together, in resisting The Anvil Lifestyle's overtures. Empowered by this conversation, Carrie and Steve might then be led by the narrative therapist into a consideration of what sociocultural practices give The Anvil Lifestyle its power and make its seductions difficult to resist. This dialogue might expose that our society's prescriptions for gender role behavior sustain The Anvil Lifestyle by telling the couple that it is primarily Carrie's responsibility to nurture and maintain the quality of their relationship. The therapist might then go on to ask Carrie and Steve to think about alternative stories about gender, stories that they like better and that might help them keep The Anvil Lifestyle in its place.

Narrative therapy sees the problems that lead people into therapy as being rooted ultimately in sociocultural practices, such as gender role prescriptions. These are undeniably group-level phenomena. Why, then, have I included narrative therapy among the individualist therapies? The reason is that narrative therapy sees group-level phenomena as being inevitably dehumanizing. For narrative therapy, that which is authentically human is always found at the level of the local and the particular. The further one moves from the level of the individual, the more one moves into the domain of the impersonal, the coercive, and the dehumanizing. Griffith and Griffith, narrative therapists who acknowledge their indebtedness to Michael White, state this view plainly: "Authentic expression of personal experience is always fluid, idiosyncratic, and unpredictable. It does not know the bounds imposed by cultural practices. It inevitably takes a stand against some type of cultural practice. . ." (1994, p. 58).

Like the symbolic experiential therapist, the narrative therapist assigns primacy to individual experiencing and sees therapy as a quest to free individuals from the forces that inhibit their idiosyncratic experiencing. For the experientialist, these forces lie within the individual herself and within the family; for the narrative therapist, these forces are to be found in cultural practices and social institutions that inevitably work to rob individuals of their humanity. Symbolic experiential therapy and narrative therapy see different "enemies" opposing the integrity of the individual. They are, however, of one mind in proclaiming the individual the fundamental unit of the human.

Solution-Focused Therapy

What about solution-focused therapy? Is this currently popular approach a collectivist or an individualist model of treatment?

The solution-focused model evolved out of the MRI model, which, as we have seen, is collectivist. Thus, we might be inclined to assume that solution-focused therapy, too, is collectivist. However, the "mutation" that produced the evolution from the MRI model to the solution-focused model was a radical one that should make us cautious about attributing to solution-focused therapy things that can be accurately said about MRI therapy.

The mutation that gave birth to solution-focused therapy entailed a reversal of the perspective of the MRI approach. MRI therapy, you will recall, focuses on identifying and interrupting interactional sequences that maintain problems in existence. It is this focus on a group-level process that makes the model a collectivist one. Steve de Shazer (1985) accepted the MRI conceptualization of what it is that keeps problems in existence. However, he noted that no problem presented by clients, no matter how severe and chronic, is happening all the time, twenty-four hours a day, seven days a week. Thus, even in systems in which a problem-maintaining sequence is operative, there must also be interactional sequences at work that have nothing to do with the presenting problem. Now, therapy can focus on interrupting the problem-maintaining sequence; this is the MRI way of thinking about therapy. But, de Shazer wondered, why can't therapy focus instead on amplifying the problem-free sequences that are already operating in the system? The goal in such a therapy would be to amplify the problem-free sequences to the point that they "crowd out" the problem-maintaining sequence. The presenting problem would thus be resolved, not because it was addressed in therapy, but because it was neglected to the point where it died from lack of attention (de Shazer, 1985; de Shazer et al., 1986).

This early theoretical formulation of the solution-focused perspective marked a reversal of the MRI perspective and a radical departure from the problem-focused ethos that had characterized all approaches to family therapy up to that point. Nonetheless, de Shazer's early conceptualization of the approach, as I have just outlined it, can still be characterized as collectivist. Human behavior is still seen as belonging to larger social entities (interactional sequences) rather than to individuals.

In more recent publications about the solution-focused model, the tenor has shifted in a decidedly more individualist direction. The factor that appears most to account for this development is the fact that de Shazer in recent years has joined the growing number of those in the field who make the postmodern assumption that language creates reality rather than reflects it (Berg & de Shazer, 1993; Miller & de Shazer, 1998). Once this turn is made, it is inevitable that interest in group-level phenomena, like interactional sequences, wanes, because neither the client's nor the therapist's "observation" and "description" of these phenomena can any longer be seen as telling us something "real" about the client system. Instead, reflection on the activity of doing therapy tends to focus simply on language. The goal of solution-focused therapy is no longer seen as the amplification of problem-free interactional sequences, but rather as the amplification of problem-free talk (Berg & de Shazer, 1993).

A therapeutic focus on language does not necessarily produce an individualist therapy. The collaborative language systems approach certainly focuses on language; however, its conceptualization of "the problem-organizing system" renders this model collectivist. In his relentless quest for therapeutic brevity and simplicity, de Shazer has avoided theorizing about any conversations that might be occurring "out there," outside of the therapy room. The only talk that interests him is that which occurs between the client and the therapist. It is this narrow focus that has imparted to de Shazer's version of linguistically focused therapy its individualist feel. When de Shazer operates as therapist, the only thing that is "really real" for him is what this particular client is saying to him. Even if the current client system happens to contain more than one person, de Shazer has no intrinsic interest in the way that these people talk with each other. He is interested in the way that each talks with him, and in how he can respond so as to amplify problem-free talk from them. This is a therapy that treats the individual as the ultimate human unit. It is an individualist therapy.

If you conceptualize it as de Shazer did in his earlier works, solution-focused therapy can be practiced as a collectivist model. If you conceptualize it as de Shazer has done more recently, the model can be practiced as an individualist approach. Thus, whether you are an individualist or a collectivist, some variant of the solution-focused model is available to you.

Personal Reflection

As it is for Collette, it is crucial for you that you choose a model of therapy whose stance on the question of the fundamental unit of the human matches your own. Thus, you need to decide now whether you are in fact an individualist or a collectivist.

Some of you might object at this point to being maneuvered by me into an either/or position on this matter. Aren't either/or positions universally condemned in the family therapy literature? Isn't reality more complex than can be captured in an either/or proposition? Wouldn't it be better to give a both/and response to the question as to whether it is the individual or the group that constitutes the fundamental human unit?

As a matter of fact, this is the first of several times in this book that I will be prompting you to take a position on a matter that I have defined in either/or terms. Why have I made such a politically incorrect blunder? I have defined these questions in either/or terms to highlight the fact that they are not about some reality "out there." When we answer these questions, it is ourselves that we are defining. These questions are not like scientific questions, answerable by data-gathering and hypothesis-testing. Both sides of the either/or polarity in these matters are plausible and philosophically tenable. Neither side, however, is provable. Thus, when we give an answer to these questions, we are talking in the first place about ourselves. We are defining ourselves, announcing to ourselves and to the world who we are and how we intend to conduct ourselves in the business of living. A both/and response to these questions is a dodge, an attempt to avoid self-definition and the commitment that it entails. Moreover, on many of these matters, a refusal explicitly to commit to one or the other of the either/or poles is nothing less than a camouflaged endorsement of one of the poles. (While it would be interesting to discuss in detail how this is so, such a discussion would take us too far afield from the purpose of this book.) One goal of this book is to help you in the process of self-definition, so that you can choose the model of family therapy that best fits your values and view of the world. It is in the interest of promoting your self-definition that I have cast these matters in either/or terms.

Some of you may have been aware throughout your reading of this chapter exactly where you stand on the question of the fundamental unit of the human. If you have, it may be because you have studied some academic philosophy and in doing so have crystallized an explicitly defined philosophical worldview. Others of you may have reached a decision on this question as a result of an interest in politics. Indeed, one of the issues that distinguishes different political viewpoints is precisely this matter of the fundamental human unit. With exceptions, left-tending political philosophies tend to be collectivist, while right-tending political philosophies tend to be individualist.

It is probably safe to say, however, that many, if not most, of you have until this moment never given explicit thought to whether it is the individual or the group that constitutes the fundamental human unit. That does not mean, however, that you have not taken a position on this crucial matter. All it means is that you have taken your position implicitly, at the level of behavior rather than at the level of articulated ideology. Discerning what your position is will be a bit like solving a murder mystery; you will need to look for clues to your position in your behavior, in decisions that you have made, in the way that you have constructed your life.

An important place to begin to look for clues is your family life. As you examine the rituals and routines of your family, does it appear that these have been constructed to foster a sense of togetherness, a sense of group identity, or does it appear instead that these rituals and routines serve the primary purpose of helping individual family members preserve a sense of privacy and autonomy? Is care taken to plan a family activity in such a way as to accommodate members' individual schedules, or is such an activity planned with the unspoken expectation that everyone will adjust his or her individual schedule to accommodate the activity?

As you examine your family life to answer these questions, it is of some relevance whether you are still living with your family of origin. If you are, it is important to note how you feel about your family's ethos of collectivity or individuality. If your family's manner of proceeding in this domain feels comfortable to you, then you have a significant indication that you have internalized and endorsed your family's position on this matter. If, on the other hand, you experience considerable discontent with the way that your family handles the issue of individuality versus collectivity, if you find yourself accommodating to family routines simply out of deference to your parents and/or grandparents, it may indicate that you have crystallized a position on this matter that is different from that of your family of origin. If so, it can be expected that, when you are in a position to exercise greater latitude in constructing family life, the life that you help to construct will differ significantly from that lived in your family of origin.

Another area to examine in your quest to discern whether you are a collectivist or an individualist is your work history. What kinds of jobs have you gravitated toward and thrived in? Are they jobs where you have functioned as a member of a closely knit team, where your activity depended in a palpable way on that of your colleagues? Or have they instead been jobs where you have been able to function more or less as a free agent, responding primarily to your own rhythms, impulses, and inspirations? If you find a pattern here, it may provide a significant clue as to whether, in the world that you have constructed, the fundamental unit of the human is the individual or the group.

The nature of your spirituality may also provide you with an important clue. (Throughout this book, the terms *spirituality* and *spiritual life* will be taken to denote the means by which you endeavor to relate to God, or to whatever it is that you consider the ground of the universe.) A spiritual life, like a family life and a work life, can be either individualist or collectivist in tenor. For some of you, the exercises that constitute your spiritual life may be activities that are intrinsically communal. Liturgy, prayer meetings, communal scripture reading and the like lie at the very heart of your spirituality. Even when you pray or meditate alone, you are at least peripherally aware that you are part of a larger praying community. If such is the case, you are practicing a collectivist spirituality. For others of you, the very essence of spirituality is that it is a private affair, wholly incommunicable to another person. Yours are the sentiments of the philosopher Plotinus, who described the spiritual ascent as "the flight of the alone to the Alone." If this description captures the flavor of your spiritual life, then it is an individualist spirituality that you are practicing.

Yet another dimension of your life worth exploring for clues is your recreational life. When you feel acutely in need of rejuvenation, to what kind of activities do you turn for sustenance? Do you take long, solitary bike rides or call your friends to arrange a volleyball game? Do you take a trip by yourself to a museum or attend a meeting of a book discussion group? Do you spend a few hours by yourself gardening or call a few friends to suggest a movie outing? Chances are, your recreational life includes a mixture of both solitary and group activities. But in all likelihood, one type of activity predominates over the other, and there is one type of activity to which you turn instinctively when things get bad and you are in need of a quick boost. It is this predominant, preferred type of recreational activity that can provide you with a clue as to whether you are a collectivist or an individualist.

As you examine the various dimensions of your life in the way just suggested, you are liable to find an interweaving of individualist and collectivist elements. Few of us are entirely consistent and unconflicted. Yet almost all of you will recognize that you tend to privilege one element over the other. One of these approaches to life will feel as if it lies more closely to who you take yourself to be than the other. Most of you will come out of the exploration with a good sense of whether in your world it is the individual or the group that constitutes the fundamental unit of the human.

Reprise: Collette, Carrie, and Steve

In order for her to be therapeutic for Carrie and Steve, Collette needs to know whether in her world it is the individual or the group that is the fundamental human unit. Without such knowledge, it will be impossible for Collette to position herself vis-à-vis Carrie's depression. Instead, she will drift, as she has done through the first three sessions of the therapy, and in the process, she will unwittingly become a party to whatever is amiss with Steve and Carrie.

However, armed with an awareness of what she considers to be the fundamental human unit, Collette can begin to tell herself a story about Carrie's depression. If Collette is a collectivist, she can tell a story drawn from one of the collectivist therapeutic models, a story that locates the depression in a family organizational map, or in a problem-maintaining sequence, or in a problem-organizing system. If she is an individualist, she can tell a story taken from one of the individualist models, locating Carrie's depression in her internal conflicts, or in her lack of differentiation, or in her repression of her anger, or in her oppression by cultural gender narratives. The story that Collette tells herself about Carrie's depression will be one that fits with her broader worldview. As a result, it is a story that she can own. And owning it, she will find it easier to act on, delivering interventions that are focused, consistent, and suffused with the very same passion that binds Collette to her view of the world.

But a problem remains. If Collette is an individualist, which of the several individualist stories about Carrie's depression should she tell herself? If a collectivist, which of the possible collectivist stories? Having decided what she considers to be the fundamental human unit has landed Collette in one of two camps, but it has not provided her with any means to begin choosing among the numerous models that populate each camp. In order to begin distinguishing among these various models, Collette, and you with her, will now have to reflect on another issue whose roots extend far back into the history of Western culture.

2

Freedom

"From" or "For"

"Why do you think you're having trouble with this case?"

Manny was talking with his supervisor about his work with Gwen and Raoul. He sensed no judgment or impatience in the supervisor's question. Yet, he was reluctant to answer it. He was indeed having trouble in his work with Raoul and Gwen, and the trouble he was having was the result of the discomfort that he was feeling with the direction that he was receiving from the supervisor.

Gwen and Raoul were a couple, sort of. . . . And therein lay the rub. Gwen had contacted the clinic and requested individual therapy. Manny met with her and discovered that her presenting problem was Raoul. More precisely, Gwen was extremely agitated over what she saw as the precarious nature of their relationship. They had been dating now for several years, and while Raoul was not giving any clear indication that he was on the verge of breaking up with her, Gwen was certain of the fact that she was now and had always been much more committed to the relationship than he was. "I'll do anything to hold on to him," Gwen told Manny tearfully. Manny asked Gwen if she thought Raoul would consent to attend the next session with her. Gwen agreed to ask him.

Raoul did indeed attend the next session, arriving, in fact, almost twenty minutes before Gwen did. (Gwen and Raoul lived in different counties, almost an hour's drive distant from each other.) Manny took an immediate liking to Raoul. They were about the same age and, Manny sensed, had fairly similar life experiences. As the session progressed, it became clear to Manny that Raoul genuinely cared for Gwen. However, Gwen was absolutely correct: she was much more committed to the relationship than was Raoul. She was unequivocal in asserting her desire that the two of them have a future together. Raoul, on the other hand, was vague and evasive in addressing this topic.

"I just don't know what kind of a future I envision with Gwen. I like being with her, I want to be with her now, but the future. . . ?" Raoul gave a slight shrug.

"You see, that's what I always get." Gwen began to cry. Manny's heart went out to her. Raoul, too, seemed moved. The air of light jocularity that he had affected throughout the session to that point disappeared. He pulled his chair close to Gwen's and began to stroke her arm. As he did so, Gwen's tears began to subside. She composed herself. Within a couple of minutes, she was

speaking normally, even managing a smile. Precisely at that moment, Raoul stopped stroking her arm and withdrew his chair to its previous position. Gwen visibly deflated.

It occurred to Manny that he might have just observed a cycle that repeats itself in the life of this couple. He inquired about it. Sure enough, there was a pattern operative here, one that Gwen and Raoul were at least vaguely aware of themselves.

"She's a very emotional person," Raoul explained. "She's easily hurt, and when she gets hurt, you know it. Even when I'm not the one who's upset her, she'll call me crying, telling me all about it. And I just can't stand to see her cry. So I'll drop everything and come running to make her feel better. I like being able to make her feel better."

"And I like when he comforts me," Gwen added. "But it always gets my hopes up, and there I am thinking, 'Maybe he's finally realizing just how much he loves me.' And all of a sudden, I look up and he's gone."

"And then the crying starts all over again," Raoul said, with more than a hint of frustration in his voice.

Manny and his supervisor agreed that the pattern that he had unearthed during the session was one that could keep Gwen and Raoul connected indefinitely. "But clearly at great cost to Gwen, and quite possibly to Raoul, as well," the supervisor observed. The pattern needed to be interrupted, the supervisor asserted, and what would interrupt it is the defining of the relationship.

"Gwen has already explicitly offered what she would like to see as the definition of the relationship," the supervisor said. "She would like the relationship to be defined as a committed one with a future. Raoul, however, is offering an ambiguous response to her offer. He's there for her and yet he's not there. He won't say that they have a future together, and yet he won't say that they don't. You need to press him for a definition. She's liable to panic when you do, because at least in the current arrangement she has him part-time, so to speak. But you need to press him anyhow."

The strategy seemed to make sense to Manny, and so he tried to implement it in his next session with the couple. He labeled the disparity in the partners' apparent commitment to the relationship. Gently, but firmly, he challenged Raoul to offer a clearer definition of the relationship.

"Don't you think that I would like to be able to tell her where I stand?" Raoul asked, frustration written all over his face. "That would make things so much easier for both of us. The reason that I can't tell her what I want is that I just don't know, I genuinely don't know."

Raoul himself now seemed to be on the verge of tears. As Manny watched, his confidence in the therapeutic strategy that he was employing began to evaporate. There was no doubt that Raoul's indecision, which was being played out right there in front of him, was part of a larger transactional pattern that was clearly stuck. And there was no doubt that that pattern was causing both Raoul and Gwen considerable pain. "But what right do I have to tell Raoul that he needs to make a decision about the relationship now?" Manny thought.

"So why do you think that you are having trouble with this case?" Manny's supervisor asked. Manny hesitated, then finally worked up the

*courage to express his misgivings to his supervisor. "What gives me the right,"
he asked, "to tell Raoul that he needs to decide now? Isn't a decision like the one
he is facing intensely personal? Shouldn't he be free to make it when he sees
fit?"*

Freedom

Manny's question was not a speculative one. On the contrary, it was intensely
pragmatic, emerging as it did out of his concern about how he should proceed in
his work with Gwen and Raoul. Manny will need to find an answer to his question. He is likely unaware of it at this point, but how he answers this question will
be crucial in determining not only how he works with this couple, but how he
works with innumerable other couples and families over the course of his clinical
career. For Manny's question about Raoul is part of a much larger question concerning how human beings should go about the process of decision making.

Let us begin to reflect on the bigger issue raised by Manny's question. What
was it that made Manny uncomfortable with his supervisor's therapeutic strategy? That strategy appears to be based on the notion that because Raoul's decisions
(or lack thereof) are part of a larger relational system, he is obligated to act in the
best interests of that relational system. Because his indecision is part of a stuck,
pain-producing pattern, he is obligated to take a more defined stand toward the
relationship.

Manny was ready to accept this logic until he experienced firsthand the consternation that it caused Raoul. When he saw that consternation, Manny began to
experience the situation differently. Isn't the preeminent factor here Raoul's freedom? What is more precious than a human being's freedom to choose how she or
he will conduct her or his life? As the couple's therapist, shouldn't Manny's first
concern be to protect and expand both Gwen's and Raoul's essential autonomy
and freedom?

It is unlikely that Manny's supervisor is an opponent of human freedom, so
the bigger question operative in this case is not the simplistic one of freedom versus coercion. Rather, it is a matter of emphasis. Is freedom an end in itself, to be
preserved at all cost? Or is freedom an instrument that finds its ultimate meaning
when it is used in the service of a higher good? Freedom from, or freedom for?
That is the bigger question operative in this case. Like the question of the individual or the group as the fundamental human unit, it is a question whose roots
extend far back into the history of Western culture.

Historical Backdrop

Reflection on how human beings should go about the process of decision making
in their day-to-day lives has been a perennial concern among Western philosophers.

Such reflection constitutes the philosophical specialization known as ethics. In the course of Western history, two distinct ethical traditions have emerged. Briefly examining these two traditions will help us understand better the dilemma that Manny is facing.

Eudaimonistic Ethics

As is true with practically every major theme in Western culture, it was the ancient Greeks who were the first to have something to say on the question of human decision making. Differently from the matter of the individual versus the group, Greek philosophers spoke with one voice on the matter of ethics. For the Greeks, it was self-evident that the point of human existence was to pursue *eudaimonia,* which, with due acknowledgment to Abraham Maslow, we may loosely translate as "self-actualization." According to Aristotle, a thing is good when it performs its characteristic function well (Korsgaard, 1998). A good person, then, is someone fully actualized, someone who has, to a high degree, activated and expressed her potentialities.

This eudaimonistic ethic is a self-focused ethic. "[T]he possibility that morality might require the sacrifice of the agent's *eudaimonia* for the good of others, or of society, is hardly canvassed" (Taylor, 1998, p. 451). Yet, we have seen in the previous chapter that some Greek philosophers, like Plato, proclaimed the group to be the fundamental unit of the human. How can these two positions be reconciled? Plato manages the reconciliation by asserting that there is an isomorphism, a similarity of structure, between the individual human being and the community of which he is a part. Therefore, what is good for one is good for the other. In pursuing their individual self-actualization, human beings automatically pursue the good of their community (Taylor, 1998).

For the ancient Greeks who were collectivists like Plato, relationships were central to the human condition. However, their eudaimonism led them to a particular understanding of what the ideal relationship should look like. Such a relationship should be structured in such a way as to elicit the *eudaimonia,* the self-actualization, of the parties involved. This kind of relationship, termed *philia* by the ancient Greeks, was thus instrumental. It was a means used by individuals to further their own self-interests. A contemporary rendition of this view of human relationships is contained in Thibaut and Kelley's (1959) social exchange theory that was so influential in the early development of behavioral family therapy. This theory assumes that people enter into and remain in relationships in order to get something out of them. The ideal relationship is thus one in which "partners work to maximize mutual rewards, while minimizing costs" (Nichols & Schwartz, 1995, p. 327).

When ethical decision making is pursued within a eudaimonistic framework, the focus moves almost immediately onto the issue of preserving the freedom of individuals to seek their self-actualization. Anything that curtails such freedom is seen to be bad and to be avoided. Self-sacrifice by an individual makes sense in this perspective only if it somehow ultimately redounds to her benefit, and thus is not really self-sacrifice at all. In the eudaimonistic tradition, freedom is an ultimate human value, an end in itself to be preserved at all costs. Freedom is freedom from.

Eudaimonistic ethics survived through the Middle Ages and became a dominant influence in modern political philosophy. There, it helped to shape that branch of liberalism that trumpets the preservation of individual freedom against the encroachments of the state.

Deontological Ethics

The individualism of the Sophists was quick to generate the collectivist response of Socrates and Plato. We might expect that eudaimonism would also generate a dissenting response. Indeed, it did. However, this response was rather slow in coming. It began to emerge in the Middle Ages and, in the estimation of some, found its ultimate expression in the work of the eighteenth-century German philosopher, Immanuel Kant.

In eudaimonistic ethics, the good (i.e., optimal human functioning) has priority over and determines what is right. In the Middle Ages, Duns Scotus and William of Ockham, two philosophers who were Franciscan friars, attempted to address some perennial philosophical issues in a way that they felt was compatible with their Christian faith. When they turned to the matter of ethics, they were profoundly dissatisfied with the eudaimonistic tradition, even as it had been Christianized by the Dominican friar, Thomas Aquinas. A morality based on the pursuit of self-actualization did not appear to them to do justice to the Christian concept of love. *Philia* did not appear to jive with *agapé*, the Christian ideal of relationship founded upon selfless concern for the other (Nussbaum, 1998). Therefore, Scotus and Ockham constructed ethical systems based on the idea that moral behavior was behavior in which the individual freely sacrifices his self-interest for the sake of something that lies outside himself, namely, the good of other people, and, ultimately, conformity with the will of God. These are ethical systems in which right (i.e., obligation to something larger than oneself) has precedence over and determines what is good (Larmore, 1998). Ethical systems constructed in this way have come to be known as *deontological*.

Immanuel Kant is usually considered to be the consummate exponent of deontological ethics. In developing the ethical tradition begun by Scotus and Ockham, Kant gave it a decidedly modernist twist. For Scotus and Ockham, the ultimate source of the obligation to which human beings should freely submit themselves is God. While Kant was a theist, he thought that both God and human beings were subject to a higher authority, namely reason. Human beings act morally, Kant maintained, when they freely deny their own whim and self-interest and act according to principles that reason reveals to be necessary and universal.

As those of you who are familiar with postmodernism know, reason no longer is considered to have the almost divine status that Kant accorded it. Nonetheless, deontology remains alive and well in contemporary ethical discussions, where it has given rise to the related concepts of solidarity and communitarianism.

Solidarity is generally seen in two ways. First, as a commitment to other members of a group to abide by the outcome of their collective decision-making. Second, as a concern for other members of a group, which may require an unwillingness to receive a benefit unless the others do, or an unwillingness to receive a benefit when this will harm them (Mason, 1998, p. 23).

Solidarity leads one so to identify with a community that the goals and values of the community come to be seen as one's own goals and values (Buchanan, 1998).

In any of its various forms, deontological ethics views human freedom as a means rather than an end. Freedom is seen as an instrument that human beings use to transcend their narrow concerns and interests and to identify with something larger than themselves. In the deontological tradition, freedom is freedom for.

Therapeutic Ramifications

As is the case with the question of the individual versus the group, the issue of freedom from versus freedom for is deeply embedded within Western culture. Manny, who has never heard the issue formally stated, was caught up in the midst of it as he met with Gwen and Raoul and as he talked with his supervisor. It would indeed be surprising if this issue has not left its traces within the various models of family therapy. It would be reasonable for us to expect that the models have polarized around this issue as they have around the question of the individual versus the group.

Such is, in fact, the case. There are models of family therapy that can aptly be called eudaimonistic models, and there are models that are deontological. As a first guess, we might assume that it is the individualist models that are eudaimonistic and the collectivist ones that are deontological. While this assumption makes some prima facie sense, we need to be wary. The example of the ancient Greeks reminds us that, while some consider it to be inconsistent (e.g., Taylor, 1998), it is possible to be a collectivist and a eudaimonist at the same time.

Thus, if we wish to discover which therapeutic models belong to which ethical tradition—and Manny's dilemma tells us that it is crucial that we do so—we are going to have to do some work. We are going to have to examine the various models for indications as to their ethical leanings. Specifically, we need to see whether any of the models ask clients to sacrifice their self-interests for the sake of the well-being of the relational systems to which they belong. These will be the deontological therapies. Similarly, we need to discover which of the models aim their interventions at protecting individuals from the constraints and restrictions that relationships can impose on them. These are the eudaimonistic therapies.

The Deontological Therapies

Structural family therapy and the strategic therapies see the behavior of the individual as being regulated by dynamics occurring within larger social entities of which the individual is a part. For the structural family therapist, both Raoul's and Gwen's behavior, for example, is dictated by the organizational map of their relationship, which is itself merely part of the organizational maps of their respective families of origin. The MRI therapist would see Raoul's chronically unsuccessful attempts to cheer Gwen up as part of an interactional loop involving at least both him and Gwen, a loop that produces the very pain in Gwen that Raoul tries endlessly and futilely to ameliorate. A Haley-Madanes strategist would observe the same interactional loop and would assume that it has arisen out of Raoul's and Gwen's attempts each to assume the one-up position in their relationship. A strategic therapist practicing in the mode of the first Milan team would also observe the same interactional loop. Like Haley or Madanes, he might see the loop as being the product of some kind of power-focused game being played out between Gwen and Raoul, but he would be interested in ferreting out in considerable detail the idiosyncratic particulars of that game.

Seeing the behavior of individuals as being regulated by larger social systems makes structural family therapy and the strategic therapies collectivist. In and of itself, it does not make them deontological. The fact that these models share a deontological outlook begins to become evident when we examine what these models have to say about what individuals perceive—or, more accurately, fail to perceive—about the larger social systems of which they are a part.

All of these models agree in asserting that clinical families, the kind that need and seek treatment, are families whose individual members do not see the big picture. Individual members of these families do not see that their behavior is part of a larger dynamic pattern involving all the other family members. Various explanations for this myopia are given. Jay Haley (1976) reports the hypothesis of Braulio Montalvo, who was influential in the development both of Haley's strategic model and of structural therapy, that the attention span that we bring to bear on our day-to-day lives is insufficient to observe the interactional sequences of which our behavior constitutes a part. The developers of the MRI model hypothesize that family members persist in failed attempts to solve a problem because of their rigid adherence to a cognitive set that demands that they attempt to solve the problem in this way. Their allegiance to this cognitive set blinds them to the fact that their attempted solutions have become part of an interactional sequence that is maintaining the problem. For the Milan group, individual family members' blindness to the big picture is caused by the members' single-minded attention to their own goals and intentions. So riveted is each family member on her own interests and plans that she is unaware that her behavior has simply become a predictable move in a larger, highly patterned family game.

Whatever the details, individual family members do what they do and keep on doing it because it makes sense to them. The structural or strategic therapist brings a wide-angle lens to bear on the situation and sees that the individual member's behavior is part of a larger malfunctioning pattern. The therapist can view the situation through this lens because he is not a player in the family's life. His vision is not narrowed by the cognitive and emotional demands entailed by actually living the client–family's life or playing the client–family's game. Looking through his lens, the structural or strategic therapist sees that the larger pattern must change: the family map must be redrawn, the problem-maintaining sequence must be interrupted, the family game must develop new rules.

Caught up in living her family's life, the therapist's client does not see this. She is dedicated to doing what, in her constricted view of things, makes sense. Thus, as he meets with Manny, Raoul remains committed to doing what feels right to him, that is, helping Gwen in a way that she appears to value, while giving voice to his lack of clarity about where he would like to see the relationship go. Gwen remains committed to what feels right to her, that is, letting Raoul know how much she needs him and how very much she wants their relationship to have a future. Manny's supervisor, a structural family therapist, sees Raoul's and Gwen's behaviors as eliciting and reinforcing each other. He wants Manny to intervene in a way that will change the complementary organization of the relationship. The intervention makes sense to the supervisor. Before he began to deliver it, the intervention made sense to Manny. However, it will not any time soon make any kind of visceral sense to Gwen and Raoul. The supervisor predicted to Manny Gwen's possible negative reaction to the intervention; Manny experienced first-hand Raoul's negative reaction.

Manny was thrown by the adverse reaction triggered by his intervention and he backed down. It is not likely that his supervisor will back down. In the view of the structural and strategic models, therapy requires that individual family members make changes that make sense only when they are viewed from the metaperspective provided by the therapist's collectivist theoretical lens. There may come a time when Gwen and Raoul are able to see and to endorse the systemic wisdom of the supervisor's intervention. For the moment, however, the intervention is asking them to abandon what makes sense to them. It is pushing them to sacrifice their self-interest.

Structural family therapy and the strategic therapies routinely ask individual family members to sacrifice their self-interest for the sake of changing the larger social systems of which they are a part. Thus, while they do not explicitly say so, these models treat the freedom of individual family members not as an end in itself, but as a means to be used in the service of a larger, more encompassing good, that is, improved family functioning. Freedom in these models is thus viewed as freedom *for* rather than freedom *from*. It is this outlook that makes these therapies deontological.

The Eudaimonistic Therapies

Collaborative Language Systems Therapy. The alert reader will have noticed that collaborative language systems therapy is a collectivist model that was not discussed above as a deontological therapy. Why is this so? What is it about this model's collectivism that makes it eudaimonistic rather than deontological?

It is the language systems therapist's postmodern emphasis on meaning that ultimately propels him into the eudaimonistic ethical tradition. True to its postmodernist roots, the collaborative language systems model views the self-authoring of meaning by individuals as the ultimate human value (Anderson, 1997). Meaning is always created in conversation, including the definition of something as a "problem." It is in their conversation with each other that Gwen and Raoul have decided to call their different outlooks about the future of their relationship a "problem." There may be others who are involved in this problem-defining conversation. Together with Gwen and Raoul, they constitute what the language systems therapist calls the "problem-organizing system."

The language systems therapist conceives of therapy as his entrance into the problem-organizing system. It is this conceptualization that renders his therapy collectivist. However, the language systems therapist enters into this system with goals that are very different from those that guide the structural or strategic therapist's work with family systems. The latter use their theoretical lenses to discern malfunctioning interactional patterns that they then intervene to modify. We have just seen how their interventions routinely require individuals to abandon their own perspectives and to sacrifice their self-interests in behalf of improved systemic functioning.

When the collaborative language systems therapist joins the problem-organizing system, he does not do so with the intention of asking anybody to abandon his or her perspective or to sacrifice his or her self-interest. Quite the contrary, in fact. The language systems therapist joins the problem-organizing system with the goal of influencing the conversation among the system's members in such a way as to protect and preserve the perspective and interests of each member. The language systems therapist's ideal of a "good" conversation is one that enhances the freedom of each participant to self-author preferred meanings. Such a conversation does not aim at consensus among the participants (Anderson, 1997; Anderson & Goolishian, 1988). It aims instead at diversity and fluidity, the ongoing creation and exploration of differing and even divergent perspectives among the participants. A collaborative language systems therapist working with Gwen and Raoul would not try to move the two of them toward some kind agreement about the future course of their relationship. Instead, the therapist would attempt to create a climate in which Raoul and Gwen could each explore aspects of their perspective on the relationship that, to this point, have gone unarticulated due to the monologic nature of the conversation that has been occurring between the two of them (Anderson, 1997).

A language systems therapist sees a conversation that is informed by this kind of climate as therapeutically useful because, as Gwen and Raoul each develop and embellish their perspective, it is inevitable that they will reach the point where they define their "problem" out of existence. In the ethical domain, the language systems therapist sees this kind of conversation as "good" because of the way in which it protects and promotes Raoul's and Gwen's uniqueness, freedom, and self-agency.

As collectivists, language systems therapists see relationships as central to the human condition. "Conversation is more than simply talking. In its fullest sense it can be thought of as the very essence of our existence" (Anderson, 1997, p. 111). However, their therapy aims at producing relationships of a certain kind, relationships that are carefully structured to protect the individual participants from constraint and to nourish the individual participants' self-determination. A relationship so constructed is nothing else than *philia,* the ancient Greek ideal of instrumental relating that promotes the participants' self-interest. Aiming as it does to produce *philia,* the collaborative language systems model is thoroughly eudaimonistic.

The Individualist Therapies.   We were correct in supposing above that the therapies that we identified in the last chapter as individualist are also eudaimonistic. With their focus on the individual as the fundamental unit of the human, eudaimonism comes naturally to the individualist therapies. Though they conceive of it differently, all of these therapies direct their efforts toward the enhancement of the functioning of individuals—their self-actualization.

For narrative therapy, the goal of the therapeutic encounter is to encourage in individuals a sense of authorship, a sense of ownership, of the story of their lives. A narrative therapist working with Gwen and Raoul would seek to free them from stories about themselves that have been written by large, impersonal forces "out there" somewhere, stories scripted by the dominant culture and by the societal institutions that support it. Her goal would be to help each of them author a story about himself or herself that is authentically self-generated, an idiosyncratic story that represents his or her lived experience far better than any premade, culturally sanctioned story ever possibly could.

Symbolic experiential therapy also prizes individual lived experience. Not sharing with narrative therapy, however, its postmodern concern with meaning and story, symbolic experiential therapy focuses its efforts on eliciting and amplifying experience itself, rather than a story about experience. A symbolic experientialist working with Gwen and Raoul would be interested in pushing each of them beyond her or his habitual, repressed experiencing of self, and in unearthing deeper, less predictable, and, for that reason, more authentic self-experiencing.

For psychoanalytic family therapy, the "holy grail" of therapy is the uncovering and working through by individuals of intrapsychic conflict. An analytic therapist would endeavor to lead Raoul and Gwen on a journey into themselves to discover the intrapsychic issues that they are playing out in their relationship with each other. Resolution of these issues will allow Gwen and Raoul, separately or together, to resume a trajectory of intrapsychic development that, for each of them, has become stalled.

A Bowen family systems therapist would also aim at restructuring Raoul's and Gwen's individual psyches. She, too, would lead them on a journey, though not into themselves, as would an analytic therapist, but back into their respective families of origin. By coaching new behavior between them and key members of their families of origin, the Bowenian would seek to increase their intrapsychic differentiation.

Each of these therapies aims ultimately at producing some kind of change at the level of the individual. Each defines the optimal human functioning toward which it leads its clients in individual terms. Thus, inevitably, each of these models treats relationships as a means rather than as an end. A relationship is defined as "good" if it promotes optimal functioning, as that particular model conceives it. For the narrative therapist, a good relationship is one that provides an "audience" to the individual's self-authoring of his story about himself (White & Epston, 1990). For the symbolic experientialist, a relationship is good if it provides the individual with opportunities for deep, nonrational, creative self-experiencing. In the world of psychoanalytic therapy, a good relationship is one that provides "holding," an envelope of safety and empathy that promotes the intrapsychic development of the individual. "Within this space, the family members provide the material and experience for each others' internal objects" (Scharff & Scharff, 1987, p. 71). The Bowenian sees a good relationship as one in which the individual retains the freedom to act on self-generated, cognitively evaluated choices.

Freedom is, in fact, the underlying motif in all of these versions of the good relationship. In these therapies, a relationship is good if it does not place the individual under constraint, if it provides her with space to pursue self-actualization. For these therapeutic models, freedom is freedom from. It is this outlook that makes the individualist therapies eudaimonistic.

Solution-Focused Therapy.   We saw in the last chapter that solution-focused therapy can be practiced either in a collectivist or in an individualist mode. However, both variants of the model are united in being eudaimonistic.

The eudaimonism of solution-focused therapy is more a matter of pragmatism than of ideology. Neither its early, collectivist version nor its more recent, individualist rendition have a notion of what optimal human functioning is or of what a "good" relationship looks like. Solution-focused therapy has no particular target toward which it aims. Its simple goal is to take problem-free interactional sequences (or problem-free talk) that are already occurring in the client system and amplify them.

Solution-focused therapy does not ask clients to stop doing things. A practitioner of the collectivist version of the approach would not ask Raoul or Gwen to change his or her part in the problem-maintaining interactional dance that Manny identified during his first session with the couple. Asking clients to stop doing things that seem to be in their best self-interest is what makes structural family therapy and the strategic therapies deontological. But the solution-focused therapist would not ask for this change. Instead, she would work with Gwen and Raoul to identify what each of them is doing when their problem is not occurring. Whatever it is, she would ask them simply to do more of it.

So, too, the solution-focused therapist of the postmodern/individualist variety would not try to challenge or interrupt any kind of talk produced by Raoul and Gwen. Instead, he would intervene with the simple goal of trying to amplify any kind of problem-free talk that either one of them produces. Thus, in either one of its versions, solution-focused therapy asks clients to do nothing more than what they are already doing that they themselves define as problem-free. Solution-focused therapy does not ask clients to change for the sake of some larger good. It asks them to do more of what they have self-defined to be good. Though not heavily theorized, this is clearly a eudaimonistic stance.

Personal Reflection

As I mentioned above, the dilemma about the nature of freedom that Manny is encountering in his work with Raoul and Gwen is one that he will encounter repeatedly over the course of his professional career. You, too, in your clinical work will constantly bump up against the question of whether to promote self-actualization or self-sacrifice on the part of your clients. The discussion that we have just completed has exposed where each of the major models of family therapy stands on the issue of freedom from versus freedom for. However, the discussion will have no value to you unless you are aware of which ethical tradition you personally endorse. Armed with this awareness, you can use the discussion above to discern which models of family therapy fit with your personal view about the nature of human freedom.

As was the case with the matter of the individual versus the group, some of you may already have reflected on and reached a decision about this issue of freedom from versus freedom for. Some of you may already know whether you are eudaimonists or deontologists. Once again, it may have been an interest in politics that motivated your reflection. The question of the nature of freedom is one that is central in politics and political philosophy.

For the vast majority of you, however, this is the first time that you are giving explicit thought to this matter. As you did when discerning your position on the individual versus the group, those of you who are in this situation will need to examine your life to look for clues regarding where you stand on this issue.

Before you begin your search for clues, however, it may be worthwhile to spend a moment on a concern that may be troubling some of you. Once again, as I promised I would in the last chapter, I have in this chapter defined an issue in either/or terms. It may seem to some of you that this kind of dichotomous thinking is particularly inappropriate when it comes to the question of human freedom. Why does one need to see freedom either as freedom from or freedom for? Why can't one have it both ways? Isn't it possible to conceive of a kind of human existence in which ethical decision making based on self-sacrifice leads ultimately to self-fulfillment? Can't one be a eudaimonistic deontologist or a deontological eudaimonist?

To be sure, it is possible at an abstract level to tell a story about human existence that reconciles the eudaimonistic and deontological ethical traditions. However, our lives are not lived at the level of abstract theorizing. Our lives are constructed out of day-to-day decisions made in the rough-and-tumble world of human relationships. And in that world, fortunately or unfortunately, decisions usually take on the dichotomous form described in this chapter: in this concrete situation, shall I act in the best interest of something larger than myself or in what

I perceive to be my own best interest? Down the road somewhere, or at some level of conceptualization, it may turn out that the two interests coincide somehow. But right now, in the heat of the moment, it does not look or feel that way. So I must decide, and in my deciding, I must endorse either a eudaimonistic or a deontological approach to decision making. There is no escaping the either/or situation. Because that is so, let us turn to the business of helping you to discern how you have gone about the matter of decision making in your own life.

The quest to discover whether you are a deontologist or a eudaimonist is going to be a little more difficult than was your effort to discern whether you are an individualist or a collectivist. The difficulty arises from the fact that our society strongly endorses both positions. In some societal contexts, we receive strong messages telling us that it is desirable to sacrifice self for the sake of a higher good. In other contexts, we receive equally strong messages inviting us—even seducing us—into constructing lives based on the pursuit of self-fulfillment. Not infrequently, both messages are sent within the same context. (Take a good look at the next television commercial that you see during the Christmas season.) Because we are subjected to such pressure, it can feel somehow wrong or inappropriate to identify with one of the ethical traditions, thereby implicitly rejecting the other. If we proclaim ourselves eudaimonist, we may feel guilty that we are "selfish." If we endorse a deontological ethical approach, we may be wary of being called "co-dependent" or "self-righteous." So, as you search your life for clues regarding your ethical position, try very hard to read the clues that you find dispassionately and without deference to our society's confused and confusing messages about appropriate decision making.

A good place to start your search for clues would be in the gut reactions that you experienced while reading the clinical vignette about Gwen and Raoul that opened this chapter. How did you feel about the intervention strategy proposed to Manny by his supervisor? Did it feel correct to you that Raoul be pushed to take a position regarding the future of the relationship? Or did you feel, as Manny himself came to, that, despite the relational difficulties that Raoul and Gwen were experiencing, Raoul's freedom to choose how he wanted to position himself in the relationship is sacrosanct, to be preserved at all costs? The former is a deontological reaction, the latter a eudaimonistic one.

The reason that you had a reaction as you read the vignette is that it likely echoes relational situations that you have encountered, indeed might now be encountering, in your own life. To be sure, it is not often that we are faced with the need to declare whether or not we will commit ourselves to a relationship. However, we do frequently find ourselves having to decide between something that appears good for us and something that would be judged good in a larger context.

As you examine how you respond in such situations, keep in mind the following proviso. In the matter of relational decision making, there is sometimes—and, for some of us, frequently—a difference between intention and performance. We may intend to act in one way, and find ourselves acting in another. (We will have much more to say about this in the next chapter.) In your search to determine your ethical leanings, it is to your intentions that you should look for clues rather than to your performance. The only exception would be if you consistently find a disparity between what you intend to do and what you actually do. In this latter case, your actual behavior may be telling you more about your ethical position than your conscious intentions do.

So, when you are faced with a relational decision, what kind of criteria do you use to evaluate the situation? Do you find yourself giving primary weight to criteria that lie outside yourself, for example, loyalty, a sense of duty, a perception of the needs of your relational partners? Or do you instead advert mostly to variables that lie inside of you, for example, how much you can be yourself in the relationship, or how well the relationship is meeting your needs? If you tend to evaluate relational situations in the first way, you have a significant clue that you are a deontologist; if the latter way comes naturally to you, you may be a eudaimonist.

As it was in the matter of the individual versus the group, your work history can also be a source of clues as to your ethical position. To unearth those clues, you need to examine the way in which you approach career decisions. Do you evaluate a job primarily in terms of the service that your work provides for others? Or is the most important criterion the degree to which the job is meeting your needs, however you may define them (e.g., the need for personal growth, the need for security, the need for expanding income, etc.). Because all of us are therapists or studying to be therapists, it would be safe to presume that all of us are interested in being of service to others. However, what if you were to find yourself in a job situation in which being of service to others compromised the satisfaction of your own career-related needs? In such a situation, to which set of criteria would you give ultimate weight? Once again, if you find yourself in such a situation responding primarily to interests external to you, you have a significant clue that your ethical leanings are deontological. If, instead, you would find yourself responding primarily to an internal frame of reference, it may be that you are ethically eudaimonistic.

Your spiritual life provides you with another, perhaps crucial, set of clues regarding your ethical position. Spirituality can take two very distinct forms. Some people experience spiritual growth as a process of increasing ex-centration. For such people, the spiritual journey is primarily one of self-denial and self-emptying, a transfer of one's center of mass, if you will, out of oneself into something or someone larger than oneself. If you recognize your own spirituality in this description, then yours is a spirituality that has a strong deontological flavor. Other people, on the other hand, experience the spiritual life as a process of self-discovery and individuation. It is a journey not out of oneself but deeply into one oneself, with the intention of uncovering the unique gem that lies there. If this description fits your own spiritual experience, then your spirituality has a distinctly eudaimonistic feel to it.

As you examine your spiritual, relational, and work lives for clues regarding your ethical leanings, remember that it is trends that you are looking to discover. No one decision looked at in isolation is sufficient to reveal to you your instinctive way of going about decision making. However, as you explore the various dimensions of your life, you are likely to discover that, more often than not, you tend to focus on certain criteria rather than others when faced with a significant decision. It is this overall tendency that will reveal to you whether, in your world, freedom is freedom from or freedom for.

Reprise: Manny, Gwen, and Raoul

How Manny works with Gwen and Raoul will vary greatly depending on whether he is a eudaimonist or a deontologist. If he is the former, Manny can work with the couple in a psychoanalytic or a symbolic experiential manner. He can follow the Bowen family systems or the solution-focused models. He can do narrative work with them, or he can conduct himself as would a collaborative language systems therapist. If Manny discerns himself to be a deontologist, he can apply the structural model or any one of the strategic models in his work with Raoul and Gwen.

However, our discussion in the last chapter alerts us to the fact that Manny's decision about how to work with Gwen and Raoul does not depend only on his ethical position. How Manny conceptualizes and intervenes in the couple's situation will also depend on whether he is an individualist or a collectivist. If, for example, Manny is a eudaimonist but also a collectivist, conceptualizing the case from the individualist perspective of the analytic, symbolic experiential, Bowenian, or narrative models would conflict with who Manny is as a person, with his values and experience of the world. These models would not fit Manny well. Trying to work within them would be akin to wearing an ill-fitting suit of clothes. Only the collaborative language systems model would fit Manny well if he is both a eudaimonist and a collectivist.

The individual or the group as the fundamental human unit. Freedom from or freedom for. Our discussion in these first two chapters has revealed that the position one takes on these perennial issues is crucial in determining how one goes about the business of doing family therapy. Are there any other issues of this kind that distinguish the models of family therapy from each other, and that constitute part of our own underlying, perhaps unspoken, stories about human existence? Indeed, there are. Let us go on to examine the next one.

CHAPTER

3

Good and Evil

Tasneem was demoralized. And the Aherns, of course, were fighting.

This was the sixth time that Tasneem was meeting with the Aherns. As a result, she had a pretty good idea of what would happen in the next few minutes. Right now, Peggy was berating her nineteen-year-old son Joe for the way in which his drinking and irresponsibility were wreaking havoc in the family. Joe was responding in his usual way, matching each escalation in Peggy's volume and rhetoric with a corresponding escalation of his own.

This will go on, Tasneem thought, for a few more minutes. Then Mike, Joe's stepfather, will launch a tirade of his own against Joe. And that will be when all hell breaks loose. Without missing a beat, Peggy will divert her fury from Joe and aim it squarely at her husband. Tasneem felt that she could predict almost exactly what Peggy would say.

"Sure, you're vocal enough when it comes to my son's behavior, but God forbid that you should raise your voice to your little princess. Melissa says 'Jump,' and you say, 'How high?' The little princess over there has your undivided attention and I get shit from you."

Tasneem knew that that would be the cue for Peggy's fourteen-year-old stepdaughter Melissa to jump to her father's defense.

"You have no idea how much my father does for you. You're just an ungrateful bitch." As Peggy and Melissa now engaged in an exchange of increasing ferocity, Mike would look on with an expression that blatantly signaled approval of his daughter's action.

Tasneem was also pretty certain about the way in which this enactment of the family drama would end. There would come a point when Joe would decide that Melissa's attacks on his mother had gone too far. Once that point was reached, he would suddenly lash out at Mike, recalling some affront that he had experienced at Mike's hands several days ago. His stepfather would readily accept Joe's invitation to fight, and the two would be off and running, their vocabulary growing ever more abusive, until one or the other of them would stand up and leave the room, probably slamming the door as a final flourish.

Tasneem did not consider it a sign of great clinical acumen on her part that she was able to predict in such detail how the fight in the Ahern family would develop. The only reason that she could make her prediction was that she had seen the same process unfold in front of her in each of her five previous sessions with the family. And the reason that the process had occurred so many times is that not a single one of Tasneem's interventions had achieved the slightest bit of success in interrupting or modifying the process that was once again being enacted in the session.

It was the utter failure of her interventions that now had Tasneem demoralized. She could not make any sense out of why she was failing. The stuckness of the therapy might be understandable if she had simply repeated the same intervention strategy over and over again. But Tasneem had not fallen into this blunder. When her first attempts to teach the Aherns communication skills had failed, she had switched gears. She abandoned the cognitive–behavioral track that she was on and tried instead to engage the family members in an exploration of the obviously intense emotions that all of them experienced in their dealings with each other. When this strategy had failed, Tasneem had moved into a structural mode, attempting to elicit new outcomes to the episodes of familial conflict by marking and maintaining boundaries around subsystems. And when these interventions produced no movement, she had even given some tasks to the family culled from the strategic therapy tradition with which her supervisor was familiar. Not one of the interventions that she had tried had appreciably modified what was happening among the Aherns.

In her desperation to make sense out of the situation, Tasneem had even considered whether cultural differences between herself and the family had anything to do with the impasse. Tasneem had been born in India and had spent part of her childhood there. She had now lived in the United States for twenty years and felt that she had a good visceral appreciation for the nuances of American culture. However, her failure with the Aherns led her to wonder whether some lack of fit between this family's Irish American rendition of the dominant culture and her own Indo-American rendition was getting in the way of therapeutic progress.

From time to time over the course of her work with the Aherns, Tasneem had found herself mulling over another possible explanation for the stuck situation that the therapy was in. Maybe, she thought to herself, these people just don't want to change. Maybe for some reason they prefer the predictability of their verbal assaults on each other to the unpredictability of what might replace them. Maybe this is just a highly resistant family.

It was precisely to thoughts such as these that Tasneem's mind drifted in this, her sixth session with the Aherns. She was called back into a focal awareness of what was going on around her by the slam of her office door. Her predictions had played out to the letter. It was Joe who had put the punctuation mark at the end of this go-round of the family drama by getting up and leaving the session. As she made arrangements with Peggy and Mike regarding the timing of the next session, it occurred to Tasneem in a flash that she had done next to nothing during this session. And the family, it seems, had not noticed. If they did notice, they didn't seem to care. For here they were, readily setting an appointment for another opportunity to reenact in her presence what they do on an almost daily basis at home. As the parents left her office, Tasneem felt the unmistakable first dull throbs of a headache creep into her consciousness.

Good and Evil

It may or may not console Tasneem to know that the phenomenon that she was encountering in her work with the Aherns has also caused quite a headache to the whole field of family therapy over the course of its development. Several different words have been used to label the phenomenon. *Resistance, homeostasis, negative feedback*—these and other terms have been employed by theoreticians in the field to name the baffling and seemingly paradoxical phenomenon of families asking for change by entering into therapy, and then failing to respond to therapeutic intervention, insisting instead on retaining the very processes that have proven problematic for them.

We will be examining shortly the twists and turns that the concept of resistance and related concepts have undergone as the field of family therapy has developed. Some models of family therapy, we will find, have understood resistance and its conquest to be crucial to the therapeutic enterprise. Others have denied that there is any such thing as resistance. Clearly, these two disparate positions on the question of resistance produce very different ways of going about the task of doing therapy. Thus, in order to proceed with the Aherns, and with other families that she experiences similarly, Tasneem will need to decide where she stands on this controversial issue.

It will be easier for Tasneem to decide where she stands on the question of resistance if she realizes that the debate in the field of family therapy around this issue is but a recent rendition of a debate that has been going in Western culture for the past 2,500 years. During these two and a half millennia, philosophers repeatedly have struggled to understand why human beings do things that are harmful to themselves and to others. In trying to make sense out of this fact of human existence, philosophers have utilized the concepts of good and evil. These are concepts that family therapists do not often use, at least in their professional lives. The unabashedly moral provenance of these terms is likely to make family therapists uncomfortable. Family therapy, after all, emerged out of the matrix of the social sciences, and so has inherited the social sciences' pretensions of being value-free. Most family therapists think of themselves, when engaged in the practice of their profession, as operating in a domain that has little to do with questions of morality, with the matter of good and evil.

In recent years, the postmodern critique of the mental health field has alerted many practitioners to the fact that a whole host of value-laden assumptions do, in fact, underlie the practice of psychotherapy. While models of family therapy may not employ terms like *good* and *evil,* we saw in the last chapter that each clearly has a notion of what well-functioning human beings "should" do and what they "should not" do. This realization hopefully will allay whatever misgivings you might have about exploring the matter of good and evil.

The usefulness of exploring this issue will quickly become evident to you in the next section. There you will see that Western philosophy has evolved two distinct approaches to the question of human evil, approaches that anticipate the two positions that have developed within the family therapy field on the question of resistance. The discussion will make you aware that where you stand on the clinical matter of resistance is a corollary of where you stand on the broader philosophical issue of good and evil.

Historical Backdrop

The Intellectualist Approach

For Socrates, and for Plato after him, the essence of what it means to be human is to be a knower. It is human beings' cognitive abilities that distinguish them from all other animals. This perspective is expressed in the term *homo sapiens*, which translated from the Latin means "man, the wise."

In the Socratic view of the human condition, knowledge is the pilot that guides people through their daily lives. If Socrates saw someone doing something that did not make sense to him, his invariable response was to ask that person what he was *thinking*. For Socrates, and for the intellectualist tradition that he helped to found, doing always follows thinking. Understand how a person thinks, and her behavior will then make perfect sense to you.

This vision of how human beings function leads to some interesting results when it is applied to the matter of human evil. If Socrates observed someone doing something evil, something that was somehow harmful, he would assume that, in performing that action, the person was merely acting on what he was thinking. If the action was evil, Socrates was certain that it must have arisen out of thinking that was faulty. People always act on the basis of what their knowledge informs them it is good for them to do. If they act poorly, it must be because they are in possession of incorrect or partial knowledge. In the intellectualist view, no human being ever knowingly wills an evil act (Scanlan, 1967).

The intellectualist approach to evil absolves human beings from any culpability for their evil actions. The approach, in a sense, defines human evil out of existence. What appears to be evil is, in this view, really ignorance. "The remedy for evil, consequently, is moral education that imparts genuine knowledge of the good and strengthens the intention to act on it" (Kekes, 1998, p. 464). Because human beings are attracted to knowledge as a moth is to light, intellectualists assume that people who unwittingly do evil as a result of their faulty knowledge will welcome interventions designed to correct their ignorance.

This intellectualist understanding of human evil has been the most influential one in the course of the development of Western philosophy (Kekes, 1998). It has played a crucial role in the rise of the liberal democracies in the modern period, and it accounts for the priority placed on widespread education in these democracies.

Given postmodernism's thoroughgoing rejection of the concept of "objective knowledge," it might be thought that the recent rise of this philosophical movement has signaled a decrease in the influence of the intellectualist approach to human evil. In point of fact, however, postmodernism has merely revised the intellectualist tradition. Postmodernism continues the premise that how a person thinks—in postmodern terminology, the "stories" that she tells herself—determines how she acts. What has been abandoned is the idea that it is possible to think correctly, that is, to possess knowledge that is valid for all times and in all places. As a result, it is also impossible to think incorrectly. A story is a story is a story, without any external criteria available to evaluate or pass judgment on it. Thus, postmodernism has taken the intellectualist approach to evil one step further. Whereas the earlier tradition redefined human evil as simply a cognitive mistake, postmodernism has denied that it is even possible to make cognitive mistakes. All stories have equal validity, and, thus, the actions to which they give rise cannot be subjected to any kind of critical judgment. The moral relativism of postmodernism can be viewed as the ultimate expression of the redefinition of human evil produced by the intellectualist tradition.

The Voluntarist Approach

In the last chapter, we met William of Ockham as one of the first dissenters to the eudaimonistic ethical tradition that had held sway in Western thought up to his time. In this chapter, we encounter him again, this time as an early critic of the intellectualist approach to human evil.

Ockham did not see the human person as the thinking machine depicted in the intellectualist tradition. For him, human dignity did not lie in people's capacity to know, but in their capacity for moral goodness and responsibility. Ockham wished to describe human beings in such a way that their moral behavior, good or evil, would not be redefined as something essentially amoral, that is, derived from correct or incorrect knowledge. Thus, Ockham asserted that free will, and not the power of thinking, is what makes human beings human (Moody, 1967). In making this assertion, he helped give rise to the voluntarist tradition. (*Voluntas* is the Latin word for *will*.)

In Ockham's view, our will is not shackled by what we know. "Ockham thinks we can knowingly reject happiness or whatever else seems in all ways best, and will evil because it is evil rather than because we think it in some way good" (Leftow, 1998, p. 663). There is no explaining away of human evil for Ockham. As he sees it, we can clearly perceive something to be evil and choose to do it anyway. What he achieves by taking this point of view is the ability to hold people responsible for their actions. Doing good is now commendable in a way that it is not for intellectualists, who see the doing of good as the inevitable by-product of having correct knowledge. Evildoing is now imputable in a way that it is not for intellectualists, who see evildoing as the excusable result of having incorrect or partial knowledge.

It was the nineteenth-century philosopher Arthur Schopenhauer who, in the estimation of many, gave the ultimate expression to the voluntarist tradition. Schopenhauer saw will not only as the central faculty of human beings, but as the underlying and ultimate source of the entire universe. "The will was described by

Schopenhauer as a blind and all powerful force that is literally the inexhaustible creator of every visible thing" (Scanlan, 1967, p. 272).

In living things, including human beings, will's fundamental manifestation is the sexual appetite, which Schopenhauer described "as a blind urge to live and to perpetuate existence without any goal beyond that. . ." (Scanlan, 1967, p. 272). Will in human beings not only has nothing to do with reason or intelligence, more often than not it is opposed them. "Our mental processes are always at a deeper level subservient to the 'blind' will to life. . . . [Schopenhauer's] idea that the intellect is often forced to follow the 'secret purposes' of an underlying will which it cannot control has been seen as a precursor of Freud's view of the unconscious" (Janaway, 1998, p. 550).

In Schopenhauer's voluntaristic world, each person is driven by an instinct for self-preservation that takes no note of the interests of any other people who might be in the vicinity. This instinct easily gives rise to actions that may be harmful to others, and ultimately to ourselves, as well, actions that may aptly be termed "evil." This instinct is not easily overcome. Knowledge is practically useless in reining it in, because knowledge is seen in Schopenhauer's voluntarism as little more than an appendage of the human condition. The most common road to the overcoming of will passes through the terrain of crisis and suffering. Only crisis and suffering have sufficient power to overcome the will's blind march toward self-preservation.

Therapeutic Ramifications

The intellectualist and voluntarist traditions tell two diametrically opposed stories about human beings. The intellectualist story is an optimistic one. In this story, human beings are intrinsically motivated toward good. Moreover, change among human beings is easy to effect. If a person is acting in a manner that is harmful or self-defeating, one need only point out to the person the underlying cognitive error, or, in the postmodern version of the tradition, invite the person to revise his story. The person will readily accept the intervention, and change will occur.

The voluntarist tradition tells a darker story. Human beings, the tradition says, are ruled not by intellect, but by will. Even in the face of evidence that they are doing something that is harmful, people can stubbornly insist on doing more of the same. As a result, change in the human domain can be difficult to bring about. Interventions aimed at producing change will need to focus on breaking or defeating the will. These interventions will need to operate in the will's domain of affect and impulse, rather than in the intellect's domain of language.

Early in its development, family therapy began to reflect on the clinical phenomenon that was causing Tasneem headaches in her work with the Aherns. In its attempts to make sense out of the phenomenon of clients apparently clinging tenaciously to behaviors that are causing them harm, it was inevitable that the family therapy field would turn to the solutions to the problem of human evil that were already available in the broader culture. Thus, it should come as no surprise to us that the field developed two distinct approaches to the problem of resistance.

One approach applied to the business of doing therapy is the voluntarist understanding of the problem of evil. This approach saw it as natural, even expected, that therapy clients would willfully hold on to behaviors that were causing them harm. Thus, it viewed resistance to change as an expected part of the therapeutic endeavor. Therapy, in this understanding, will inevitably take the form of a struggle, in which the therapist, as an advocate for change, engages and seeks to defeat the forces at work in the family that oppose change. Steve de Shazer (1982) aptly calls the models of therapy that subscribe to this voluntarist point of view "contest models."

The second approach to the problem of resistance laid claim to the intellectualist understanding of the problem of evil. This approach took the position that families in therapy are intrinsically motivated to change in ways that are in their best interest. The therapist, therefore, need not expect to find herself engaged in struggle with her client families. If the therapist intervenes correctly, the families will respond readily to her interventions, with the result that therapy will be a collaborative rather than an adversarial affair.

The Voluntarist Therapies

Psychoanalytic Family Therapy.   In the discussion of Schopenhauer above, it was noted how his voluntarist ideas anticipated some of Sigmund Freud's conceptualizations. Thus, we should not be surprised to find psychoanalytic family therapy included prominently among the voluntarist therapies.

The concept of resistance lies at the heart of all versions of psychoanalytic family therapy. However, each of the variants of the analytic approach offers somewhat differing accounts of the origin of resistance. Analytic family therapists who have remained close to Freud's description of intrapsychic functioning see resistance to change as arising from three sources (Marshall, 1982). The first source of resistance is the sexual and aggressive drives that are rooted in our biology, and that, in the classic analytic view, are the engines that drive much of our psychic life. These drives are primitive, blind, and not easily denied. One way or the other, they insist on making their presence felt in our behavior. The second source of resistance is the ego's need to protect itself from perceived threat. The final source of resistance is secondary gain, the interpersonal "payoffs" that frequently accrue to someone who exhibits symptomatic behavior.

Object relations family therapists de-emphasize the role of biological drives in human psychology. For them, resistance arises in clients as a misguided effort to protect themselves. Having been inadequately parented, clients have internalized the criticism or neglect that they have experienced at the hands of their caregivers. When a family meets a therapist, family members project onto her their expectation that they will be mistreated by those with whom they relate. Not unexpectedly, family members then protect and hide themselves from the therapist, utilizing in this effort the very same maladaptive interpersonal strategies that they use with each other (Scharff & Scharff, 1987).

Whatever their explanation of the source of resistance, psychoanalytic family therapists agree that experiencing the client-family's resistance can be useful to the therapist. The family members' resistance to her interventions invariably induces feelings and fantasies in the therapist. This, of course, is the phenomenon known as countertransference. Provided that she does not simply act on these feelings, countertransference provides the therapist with a privileged means of acquiring an experiential, "in-the-gut" grasp of the dysfunctional processes at work in the family.

If therapy is to succeed, resistance must be overcome. Analytic therapists of all persuasions use interpretation as their main weapon in their struggle against resistance. Interpretation unmasks resistance by naming it for what it is, an attempt to avoid change. Not sharing the intellectualist's optimism about human nature, analytic family therapists do not expect that the simple act of labeling resistance is going to induce clients to surrender the resistance. In fact, interpretation, even if it is well timed, is likely to elicit escalation in the family's resistance as family members scurry to protect themselves from the exposure produced by the interpretation. With heightened resistance will come more countertransference and greater danger that the therapist will blunder into an action that will cause a therapeutic impasse. In the face of this assault, the therapist must endeavor to stay the course and not be seduced by the family's resistance. Ultimately, just surviving the family's resistance and projections is the most therapeutic thing that the therapist does. In the object relations formulation of analytic family therapy, this survival by the therapist provides the holding environment that will allow the family eventually to work through its difficulties and to crystallize more mature ways of relating (Scharff & Scharff, 1987, 1991).

If Tasneem's supervisor were a psychoanalytic family therapist, he would likely be very interested in having her describe to him in some detail the feelings of demoralization that she was experiencing while sitting with the Aherns. He would want her to observe which particular piece of family interaction seemed to trigger the feelings in her. He would ask her to describe the in-session thoughts and fantasies that she was using as an escape hatch from the hurtful interpersonal drama that was being repeatedly enacted in front of her. The supervisor would use this material to construct with Tasneem an understanding of the intrapsychic terrain of each of the Aherns, and of the way in which the terrain fits together to produce the repeating sequences of behavior that Tasneem had observed. Armed with this understanding, Tasneem could begin to provide the Aherns with interpretations of their behavior. This understanding could also help Tasneem avoid behaving with the Aherns in a way that colluded with their attempts to resist change.

Symbolic Experiential Family Therapy. In the view of the symbolic experiential family therapist, repression of feelings and drives by family members is the very thing that lands a family in therapy in the first place. The experiential therapist does not think that such repression is going to cease simply because the family is sitting with a therapist. Indeed, the family's interest in making a socially appropriate presentation to the therapist may increase the repression of feelings that are experienced by the family as "bad" or "primitive." Thus, the symbolic experientialist expects that the families he sees will resist doing the very thing that is required in his view in order for them to be delivered from their difficulties. They will resist allowing their members to experience themselves in depth and to give expression to their experience. As much as the analytic family therapist, the experiential therapist sees struggling with this resistance as his primary therapeutic task.

The way in which the experientialist struggles against resistance is determined by his view of what gives rise to repression and resistance. Quite simply, repression and resistance are produced by fear, a lack of courage on the part of family members to face and to deal with their impulses. In order to overcome their resistance, the experiential therapist needs to convince his client families that there is nothing to fear in the world of feelings, drives, and impulses (Whitaker & Bumberry, 1988). This he does by providing families with an intense experience of the very thing that they fear. The experiential therapist resolutely goes where his clients are afraid to go. He shares his own in-session feelings, fantasies, and impulses. He confronts family members who appear to be avoiding their own in-session experiencing. In the process, he inevitably escalates the amount of anxiety in the consulting room. "I do not want to relieve their anxiety. I want their anxiety to be the power that makes things move" (Whitaker & Bumberry, 1988, p. 11).

Carl Whitaker, the father of symbolic experiential family therapy, was convinced that client families would not summon the courage to venture into territory that felt dangerous to them unless the therapist could do the same thing. Whitaker believed that, in order to be effective, therapy must feel as risky to the therapist as it does to the family. As a result, the therapist stands to get as much out of a good therapy as does his clients. "The real question becomes one of courage, both theirs and mine. Are we willing to take the risk of sailing into uncharted waters" (Whitaker & Bumberry, 1988, p. 20)?

The fact that the Aherns were resisting change in therapy would come as no surprise to the symbolic experiential therapist. What would likely disconcert the symbolic experientialist is the way in which Tasneem is responding to the resistance. He would note her reliance on techniques and would likely criticize her failure to enter into a personal struggle with the Aherns' resistance. An experiential supervisor might confront Tasneem's intellectual ruminations about the Aherns' resistance and challenge her to get in touch with the feelings and fantasies that she was experiencing while sitting with the family. He would counsel Tasneem to take these fantasies seriously, perhaps sharing them with the Aherns or using them in the formulation of provocative questions. He might suggest that Tasneem tell the Aherns that they are giving her headaches.

Structural Family Therapy.   As we saw in Chapter 1, structural family therapy does not share the individualist worldview of symbolic experiential therapy and psychoanalytic therapy. As a result, it does not privilege the drives, impulses, and feelings of individual family members as these therapies do. However, the concept of resistance plays as important a role for the structural family therapist as it does for the analytic therapist and the experientialist.

For the structural therapist, resistance has its origin in the natural (and adaptive) tendency of family structure to preserve itself. If a family's organizational map were not relatively stable, there would be no day-to-day predictability in family members' dealings with each other. Thus, the tendency for family structure to maintain itself over time is a good thing, freeing up family members to devote their focal attention to emergent situations that require creativity and problem solving. From time to time over the course of a family's life, however, an emergent situation being faced by the family is of such a kind that it can only be adequately dealt with if the family's organization changes. At times like these, the family's tendency to maintain itself, while not disappearing, must couple with a capacity to adapt and to modify itself. With both system-maintaining and system-transforming processes operating, the family organization can change in such a way that the family responds adequately to the situation that it is facing while retaining its sense that it is still the same family.

Some families find these moments when they are required to modify their organizational maps difficult to manage. They respond to the press for organizational change by rigidifying their structure rather than by modifying it (Minuchin, 1974). Frequently, this "freezing" of a family's organization elicits symptoms in one or more family members, symptoms which themselves may serve to reinforce further rigidity in the organizational map. The symptoms may lead the family into the office of a structural family therapist.

Looking through the theoretical lens just described, the structural family therapist will view a family's presence in her office as a sign that the family is already resisting change. Now, here they are, sitting in the presence of someone whose job it is to instigate the very process of change that the family has been resisting thus far. It should, therefore, come as no surprise that the structural therapist expects the therapy she conducts to be a struggle, a contest in which, in order to succeed, she must defeat the forces of stability that are exercising undue influence in the family.

The structural family therapist relies primarily on two tools in her struggle against resistance. The first of these is joining (Minuchin & Fishman, 1981). Joining serves two purposes in the therapist's struggle against resistance. First of all, joining the client family allows the therapist to be experienced by the family as an "insider," as a distant relative, perhaps. This "insider" status will render the therapist's efforts to instigate organizational change somewhat more palatable to the family. Secondly, in the same way that countertransference provides the analytic and symbolic experiential therapist with "in-the-gut" data about a family's workings, the exercise of joining a family provides the structural therapist with experiential knowledge of how the family operates, and, perhaps more importantly, of alternative organizational arrangements that are currently lying latent in the family's repertoire. This latter knowledge will allow the therapist to craft her interventions in such a way that she only asks for organizational changes that are compatible with the family's history, beliefs, values, capacities, and so forth.

Even if the therapist gains "insider" status, and even if she asks for changes that are within the range of the client family, there is no guarantee that the family will quickly change. Client families resist requests for change even from therapists who have joined them well. When resistance remains in the face of good joining, the structural family therapist uses her second tool, intensity (Minuchin & Fishman, 1981). Intensity refers to the process by which the therapist creates "volume" in her requests for change that exceeds the family's ability not to hear. The word *volume* is being used here metaphorically; creating intensity does not necessarily require dramatic emotional displays on the part of the therapist. To be sure, dramatic interventions like confrontation are certainly one way of creating therapeutic intensity, as will be attested by anyone who has seen some of Salvador Minuchin's famous (or infamous) earlier sessions. However, confrontation is by no means the only way to create intensity. Perhaps the best way to produce intensity is via a relentless focus on a particular structural change that one is trying to elicit. The skillful structural therapist can take almost any content that emerges or any event that occurs during a session and "spin" it in such a way that the family's attention is directed toward the therapist's restructuring agenda. Brought back again and again to the therapist's request for change in a particular domain of its functioning, the family will eventually accommodate by beginning to explore alternative organizational arrangements that have been lying dormant in its repertoire.

If a structural family therapist were supervising Tasneem's work with the Aherns, she would probably not ascribe the clinical impasse that Tasneem was experiencing to any lack of joining on her part. Indeed, there is ample evidence that Tasneem is, in fact, overly joined with the family. Tasneem's sense of futility, of having been defeated by the Aherns, bespeaks her induction into the family system, because it is likely that this is exactly what the Aherns experience incessantly in their dealings with each other. It is probably precisely because their therapist has become one of them that the Aherns are perfectly comfortable scheduling a seventh session after a sixth in which Tasneem has done next to nothing. The structural supervisor would likely ascribe the stuckness of the therapy to Tasneem's failure to create intensity within the therapy. While well-intentioned, Tasneem's movement from one therapeutic tack to another during the first few sessions of the therapy has deprived her of any influence over the Aherns. A structural supervisor would push Tasneem to decide which piece of the Aherns' organizational map she would like to change first. She would then challenge Tasneem to construct the next session as one with a single-minded focus on this restructuring agenda.

The Strategic Therapies.   Overcoming resistance constitutes the heart and soul of the strategic therapies. But, whereas the voluntarist therapies that we have examined thus far prefer to make their struggle with resistance overt and direct, the strategic therapies prefer to use indirect and covert tactics. It is this preference that merits these therapies the label *strategic.*

Each of the strategic therapies offers a somewhat different account regarding the source of resistance in client families. In the MRI model, as we have seen, families wind up in therapy because they insist on repeating attempted solutions to their problems that have patently failed to solve the problems. In such families, members maintain allegiance to the cognitive sets that underlie their attempted solutions, even in the face of massive evidence that the attempted solutions are not working. They will also maintain this allegiance in response to therapeutic attempts to get them to try different solutions. While such behavior is utterly incomprehensible to an intellectualist, the originators of the MRI model, rooted as they were in the voluntarist tradition, saw no need to hypothesize further about why people would behave in such a self-defeating way. For them, it was simply par for the course for us human beings.

Although he was as much a voluntarist as were the MRI originators, Jay Haley did offer a somewhat more elaborate account about the origins of resistance. In the view of the Haley-Madanes strategic therapist, people in relationship are involved in constant attempts to control the definition of the relationship, the rules by which the relationship operates. In this view, the subtext of even the most functional of relationships is a power struggle, albeit a low-level one, between the participants. "It is not pathological to attempt to gain control of a relationship, we all do this, but when one attempts to gain that control while denying it, then such a person is exhibiting symptomatic behavior" (Haley, 1963, p. 16). Therapy is a relationship like any other. At its heart lies a struggle for control between the therapist and the client family. Because the family in therapy is by definition a symptomatic one, it will conduct its struggle for control over the therapist covertly. It will engage in all the subtle maneuvers designed to disqualify the therapist that have come to be known under the collective title of "resistance."

The first Milan team offered an explanation for resistance that is almost identical to that offered by Jay Haley. What is distinctive about the Milan team is its use of language that blatantly reveals the team's reliance on the voluntarist philosophical tradition. Note the unabashed use of moral language in the following description. "Our work with the couple in schizophrenic transaction has brought us to the fundamental hypothesis that the mistaken epistemology of such a couple is . . . *hubris*, that is, the hidden presumption which each one holds: that he sooner or later will be able to gain unilateral control of the definition of the relationship" (Palazzoli, Boscolo, Cecchin, & Prata, 1978, p. 30; emphasis added). In the view of the Milan team, members of symptomatic families are devoted at all costs to winning the struggle for relational control that constitutes the very life of these families. So obsessed are these people with winning the game, that their greatest fear is that one or more members will depart the family and so ruin the game. "[T]he game must not end. Everyone hopes that one day he will make it. The essential thing is that the whole team remain on the field" (Palazzoli et al., 1978, p. 29). When such a family enters therapy, it will inevitably attempt to turn its relationship with the therapist into the same kind of power struggle that is at the heart of its own existence. Thus, inevitably, the family will resist any attempts made by the therapist to exercise influence over it.

The strategic therapies share with the other voluntarist models the expectation that the therapist will encounter resistance in the execution of his task. However, the strategic therapies part company with the other voluntarist therapies in the way that they choose to respond to resistance. Where the other voluntarist models tackle resistance head on, the strategic therapist operates on the notion that he can turn the forces of resistance in the client family to his own therapeutic purposes. The strategic therapist does not destroy resistance, he outwits it. Each of the strategic therapies offers its practitioners a way to use resistant maneuvers by a client family so that the maneuvers themselves become mechanisms for change. Thus, the MRI therapist does not challenge the cognitive sets that underlie the problem-maintaining interactional sequences in client families. He accepts the cognitive sets, but then "spins" them in such a way that, in order to maintain their allegiance to these sets, family members find themselves required to act in ways that interrupt the problem-maintaining sequence. A strategist of the Haley-Madanes tradition might use the same tactic. Additionally, he might prescribe the symptom to the family's symptom-bearer. In doing so, he would deprive the symptom-bearer of the power that the symptom gives him, because now when he enacts the symptom he is not defeating the therapist, but rather acting at his behest. The symptom-bearer thus finds himself in a position where he can only defeat the therapist by giving up the symptom. The Milan strategist takes this tactic and extends it to include the entire client family. In the message from the observing team that would typically close a Milan session, the team positively connotes and prescribes the role behavior of each member of the client family, repeatedly observing how each member's behavior is required to maintain family cohesiveness and safety.

Tasneem, you will recall, used some strategic interventions in her work with the Aherns. The interventions did not appear to work. A strategic supervisor, however, might point out to her that no technique, strategic or otherwise, is a magic bullet that will single-handedly turn a troubled family around. The essence of strategic therapy is a mind-set, not a set of techniques. If Tasneem had had a strategic mind-set, she would not have been demoralized when the use of a technique or two failed to produce change in the Aherns. What was required at that point was for Tasneem to congratulate the family for its maintenance of the status quo. In doing so, Tasneem would have achieved what is the ultimate purpose of any strategic intervention, namely, the positioning of herself vis-à-vis the family so that her influence over them is maximized.

The Intellectualist Therapies

Solution-Focused Therapy.   "We had long been puzzled by the notion of 'resistance.' . . . As we watched each other work, we became more and more convinced that clients really do want to change" (de Shazer et al., 1986, p. 209). With this quotation, we leave the world of the voluntarist therapies and enter the world of the intellectualist therapies. As the quotation demonstrates, there is no better place to start our exploration of the intellectualist therapies than with the solution-focused model developed by de Shazer and his colleagues.

In marked contrast to the voluntarist therapies, solution-focused therapy does not assume that clients are wedded to their problems. Neither its original version nor its more recent postmodern variant sees the problems presented by clients as anchored in resistance-producing entities like biological drives or self-protective defenses or fear or inertia or power struggles. Quite the opposite, in fact: the solution-focused therapist assumes that any client system with which he meets already has a sphere of its life that operates outside the influence of the system's presenting problem. It is precisely the task of the solution-focused therapist to direct clients' attention toward that sphere. He is convinced that, if he succeeds in executing this task, clients' presenting problems will wither away from lack of attention. Moreover, he assumes that his clients will be more than willing to allow him to redirect their attention away from their problems and toward the problem-free areas of their lives.

This is not to say that the solution-focused therapist assumes that every one of his interventions will succeed in achieving its goal. Like therapists of any other orientation, solution-focused therapists experience their fair share of interventions that fail. However, the solution-focused model conceptualizes this phenomenon differently than do the voluntarist models. If an intervention fails to achieve its purpose, the solution-focused therapist assumes immediately that *it was an incorrect intervention*. Somehow, it did not fit with this particular client system's worldview, values, or style. While the voluntarist therapies grant that a particular intervention may be ill-conceived, they are also prepared to ascribe the failure of an intervention to client resistance. Apparent failure of an intervention should lead a good voluntarist therapist to examine the aptness of the intervention. However, if the intervention appears to have been vindicated, all of the voluntarist models counsel their practitioners to dig in and to stick with the intervention. It is resistance that is being encountered, and, as we have just seen, resistance is ultimately defeated only by resoluteness on the part of the therapist.

Whereas the voluntarist therapies school their practitioners in endurance and perseverance, the solution-focused model teaches its practitioners how to read feedback from the client system. When clients fail to accommodate to an intervention, they are seen in the solution-focused model as providing the therapist with information as to how he might best help them (de Shazer et al., 1986). The therapist does not "stay the course" in response to such feedback; rather, he modifies his intervention in response to the feedback.

The alert reader will recall that the strategic therapist, especially the practitioner of the MRI model, will also accept without challenge clients' cognitive sets and then use these in the construction of interventions. There is, however, a fundamental difference between the ways in which the MRI therapist and the solution-focused therapist accept and use a client-system's worldview. The MRI therapist does so as a tactic in her battle against resistance. She adopts what looks like a collaborative stance with a client family because she believes that doing so will give her an advantage in the contest that she believes therapy to be. The collaboration here is only apparent; the attitude of the MRI therapist remains that of a contestant locked in a fierce struggle. In distinction, the accommodation of a solution-focused therapist to a client-system's worldview is not a ruse. It emerges out of solution-focused therapy's intellectualist optimism that people will readily accept requests for change that are demonstrably in their best interest. The solution-focused therapist does not feel that he needs to jockey for position in his work with clients. When he accommodates to a client-system's worldview, he is, in his own estimation, doing nothing more than would be expected of someone engaged in a cooperative dialogue with a well-intentioned partner.

A solution-focused supervisor would likely see Tasneem's impasse with the Aherns as resulting from her failure to read the corrective feedback that she was receiving from the family. To be sure, Tasneem had attempted to modify her interventive thrust when her first interventions had failed. But a solution-focused supervisor would notice that Tasneem's choice of subsequent interventions had been driven more by her own predilections than by the feedback that she was being given by the Aherns. In true solution-focused style, the supervisor might try to attune Tasneem to reading the feedback from the family by asking her to notice exceptions, times during the first six sessions when the Aherns, however briefly, had not engaged in their usual pattern of conflictual exchange. The supervisor would go on to ask Tasneem to identify what it was that she was doing during these periods, even if what she was doing did not seem all that complicated or profound. The supervisor would then make the signature solution-focused suggestion that Tasneem "try doing a little more of whatever it is you have been doing that has been working" (Thomas, 1994).

Narrative Therapy. In differing ways, the voluntarist models maintain that client families hold on to their problems, even, perhaps especially, when presented with ways in which they can solve them. Depending on the particular voluntarist model being considered, families may or may not be seen as having caused their problems in the first place. However, once problems emerge, the voluntarist models are united in their expectation that client families will, with greater or lesser degrees of intensity, hold on to them.

Narrative therapy is convinced that client systems do not cause their own problems. It is the "dominant discourse," prevailing sociocultural practices and institutions, that causes clients' problems. The narrative therapist views her clients as truly oppressed, subjugated by powerful, dehumanizing forces that are almost invisible because they are pervasive.

The goal of narrative therapy is to liberate its clients from the debilitating story that they themselves are problematic. Utilizing externalization, the narrative therapist helps her clients see that, far from being problematic, they are, in fact, being oppressed and victimized. Further, the narrative therapist conveys the message to her clients that they have unsuspected, untapped resources to resist and to overcome their oppression. White and Epston (1990) quote approvingly Foucault's use of the word *insurrection* to describe the process by which people overcome dominant sociocultural discourses and replace them with self-authored, preferred stories.

The narrative therapist approaches her clients as a liberator. She brings the good news that they are not the problem and that they are capable of asserting themselves against the forces "out there" that are the problem. Who would resist hearing such good news? In a voluntarist world, perhaps, people might become so identified with their victimization that they would resist the news that there is a way out. But awash as she is in intellectualist optimism, it is inconceivable to the narrative therapist that anyone would resist her news of liberation. Thus, it should come as no surprise to us that resistance is simply not part of the clinical vocabulary of the narrative therapist.

If the Aherns are resisting Tasneem's intervention messages, the likely reason, in the view of a narrative supervisor, is that Tasneem is sending them the wrong messages. All of her messages, in differing ways, are telling them that they are the problem. Who would welcome such messages? The Aherns certainly don't, and, for lack of a better alternative, continue to conduct their business as normal in Tasneem's presence. If Tasneem is to be therapeutic for the Aherns, she must help them to discern how problematic cultural stories are being played out in their day-to-day family life. The narrative supervisor might coach Tasneem on how to use externalization to expose how dominant stories about stepfamilies, or perhaps about child rearing, are victimizing the Aherns. Once the problem is seen to lie "out there," the Aherns will quickly replace their destructive infighting with a mutually supportive effort to self-author preferred stories about their family.

Collaborative Language Systems Therapy.   For the language systems therapist, change in the human world is the rule, not the exception (Anderson & Goolishian, 1988). This axiom is a corollary of the language systems therapist's understanding of the nature of conversation. To be in conversation is, in the language systems therapist's view, the essence of what it means to be human. And conversation, by its very nature, entails the ceaseless questioning and changing of meanings.

This is not to say that the collaborative language systems therapist does not recognize that there is such a thing as a "stuck" conversation. Anderson (1997) refers to these as "conversational breakdowns." "Differing realities develop, continue, and often escalate to *dueling realities. . . .* as members' attentions and energies focus on protecting their views, convincing others of the correctness of those views, and experiencing others' views as unfounded or even crazy. Such competing actions can become divergent and ensconced over time" (p. 124).

Such conversational breakdowns can bring people into therapy. When a language systems therapist meets with new clients, he is not surprised if he encounters a problem-organizing conversation that has broken down in the manner just described. However, the therapist does not assume that clients are either particularly prone or tenaciously committed to such breakdowns. The therapist assumes that, if he himself maintains a dialogical posture in the problem-organizing conversation, one in which any and all viewpoints are simultaneously entertained and explored, then all the other members of the conversation will before long assume the same posture.

A therapist talks with one person at a time. . . . As we talk, others present assume a reflective listening posture in which inner dialogue becomes possible. They listen and hear undefensively because the story being created between a therapist and the person is different, and they have a sense that the therapist also considers what they have to say important, they will also be heard, and they want to add to and expand the story rather than correct or interrupt it (Anderson, 1997, pp. 126–127).

The inevitable result is the reestablishment of fluidity in the problem-organizing conversation. With fluidity reestablished, the conversation eventually will evolve to the point where the presenting problem is defined out of existence.

Clearly evident in this formulation is the intellectualist optimism of the collaborative language systems model. It is not inconceivable to the language systems therapist that a conversational breakdown will occur in therapy. However, if it does, it is not because the client system is being resistant. Breakdown occurs when the therapist abandons an attitude of not-knowing and begins to privilege one set of meanings over others. The fault here lies with the therapist. The language systems model shares with all the other intellectualist models the assumption that, if the therapist does his job well, clients will do theirs.

A supervisor operating out of a collaborative language systems perspective would likely see Tasneem as not having done her job very well in the therapy with the Aherns. While Tasneem has demonstrated some fluidity in switching from one intervention tack to another, each of the intervention postures that she has assumed has been impositional, a posture that has imposed meaning on what is happening among the Aherns rather than elicited it. Because the Aherns are busy trying to impose meaning on each other, Tasneem's interventions thus far have done nothing but reinforce the conversational breakdown that has occurred in the family. In his dialogue with Tasneem about the case, the language systems supervisor would assume a curious, not-knowing posture, fully expecting that Tasneem herself would before long assume the same posture. Established in a not-knowing posture, Tasneem would then be in a position to manage her participation in the Aherns' problem-organizing conversation in such a way that she could be truly therapeutic for the family.

Bowen Family Systems Therapy.   Among the intellectualist-inspired therapies, Bowen family systems therapy is the intellectualist model par excellence. Murray Bowen enthusiastically endorsed the intellectualist position that a well-functioning human being is one whose actions flow out of and are governed by his thinking. The undifferentiated person, in the Bowenian view, is precisely one whose cognitive operations are flooded during times of stress by overwhelming feelings, resulting in behavior that is impulsive and reactive. Bowenian therapy counts itself successful if it produces clients whose actions almost invariably proceed from a calm base of rational deliberation.

The Bowenian therapist recognizes that, if the therapy room becomes charged with intense emotionality, client families are likely to behave toward the therapist in a reactive, resistant manner. Nonetheless, struggling against resistance has never been a preoccupation for Bowenian therapy the way it is for the voluntarist thera-pies. This is so because the Bowen family systems therapist shares with the other intellectualist therapies the assumption that if she does her job well, then her cli-ents will do their part in producing a successful therapy.

Although the models differ in many ways, collaborative language systems therapy and Bowen family systems therapy share similar visions of what it is the therapist does when she is doing her job well. Like the language systems thera-pist, the Bowenian talks with one member of the client system at a time. The intent of both therapists in behaving this way is to discourage the kind of emotion-laden exchanges that can easily occur when client-system members talk directly with each other. Both the Bowenian and the language systems therapist use their ques-tions to promote calm reflection, both in the person to whom their questions are directed, and in the other members of the client system who are eavesdropping on the conversation. Practitioners of both models assume that, if the therapist herself is able to maintain a posture of reflective calm, then clients will be able to assume and to maintain the same posture. Intellectualists both, the Bowenian and the lan-guage systems therapist are certain that people's cognitive functioning will never fail to soothe the savage beasts of emotion and will.

Within the atmosphere of tranquility that each creates in therapy, the Bowenian and the language systems therapist lead their respective clients in very different directions. The collaborative language systems therapist will lead his cli-ents in a process of continual questioning of the meanings that they have gener-ated around the problem that they have defined into existence. The Bowenian, on the other hand, will lead her clients into a consideration of the family-of-origin situations that are, in Bowen's view, the ultimate cause of the clients' current diffi-culties. Where the Bowenian and the language systems therapist find common ground is in their unshakable faith that clients will cooperate in the therapeutic process provided that the therapist creates the requisite therapeutic atmosphere of tranquil reflection.

Watching videotapes of the emotional mayhem that Tasneem has allowed to prevail during her six sessions with the Aherns, a Bowenian supervisor would not be surprised in the least that the therapy with the Aherns has ground to a frustrat-ing halt. How could anything productive emerge out of such a mass of free-floating anxiety and anger? The supervisor would likely counsel Tasneem that, if the therapy is to be salvaged, she needs to regain control of the process so that she can establish a more productive atmosphere. To begin, she needs to centralize her-self in the therapy, so that all communication by any member of the Ahern family is directed to her. She needs to ask questions and make statements that promote thinking and discourage feeling. If any of the Aherns find it difficult to accommo-date to the new therapeutic regimen, she can excuse them from the therapy, at least for now. Even if only a few of the Aherns remain behind in therapy, the therapy can still be successful, provided it teaches the remaining clients to base their actions on a calm, dispassionate understanding of how relational systems operate across generations.

Personal Reflection

Obviously, resistance is entirely in the eye of the beholder. What the voluntarist therapist experiences as resistance, the intellectualist therapist may experience as corrective feedback from the client system. Where the voluntarist therapist sees resistance, the intellectualist therapist may see the unfortunate fruits of the therapist's own failure to maintain an appropriately therapeutic posture.

How Tasneem makes sense out of her situation with the Aherns will depend entirely on whether she views therapy as a contest or a collaboration. In deciding which of these views to accept, it is crucial that Tasneem make a choice that fits well with her view on the larger question of human evil. If she accepts the intellectualist position on this question, Tasneem should choose one of the intellectualist-informed, collaborative models to guide her practice. If she accepts the voluntarist view, then her therapy should be informed by one of the voluntarist-inspired models.

Discerning whether one is an intellectualist or a voluntarist on the question of human evil is somewhat simpler than the task of deciphering whether one is an individualist or a collectivist, a eudaimonist or a deontologist. Because the encounter with human evil is an unfortunately common experience in almost everyone's life, most of us have by adulthood crystallized an interpretive framework by which we cope with the experience of evil, and of which we are more or less consciously aware. If we have been raised within the confines of Western culture, that interpretive framework will almost invariably reflect either the intellectualist or the voluntarist approach to good and evil.

In order to throw into relief your own interpretive framework, think now, if you will, about the first thought that occurs to you when you hear about some egregiously evil action performed by one of your fellow human beings, a school shooting, perhaps, or the murder of her newborn infant by a young mother, or an execution-style slaying that was the culmination of a robbery gone bad. Is your first thought when you hear of deeds like these that there simply *must* be an explanation for why people would behave in such a way? Maybe, you tell yourself, the school shooter had been so desensitized to violence by the media that he did not grasp the reality and the finality of what he was doing to his fellow students. Perhaps the young mother held her own life in such little esteem that it was impossible for her to value the life of her little child. Maybe the thieves-turned-murderers had grown up in a dog-eat-dog environment that rendered their killing a rather unremarkable event in their own eyes.

If your first response when you encounter an evil act is the thought that there must be some explanation that will make sense of the act, then yours is an intellectualist approach to the issue of good and evil. Informing your response is the fundamental intellectualist assumption that, however evil their acts may appear to an outside observer, people always have some rationale for their behavior that makes that behavior justifiable and correct in their own eyes.

If, on the other hand, it is easily conceivable to you that the school shooters, or the young mother, or the execution-style murderers committed their acts with full awareness of and utter indifference to the fact that they were evil, then you subscribe to the voluntarist position on the matter of human evil.

An examination of your spiritual life should provide some confirmation of your appraisal of whether you are an intellectualist or a voluntarist on this question of good and evil. If you are a voluntarist, it is highly likely that dealing with your personal sinfulness, your own evildoing, is an important theme in your spiritual life. Such is not the case in an intellectualist-informed spirituality. A spiritual journey guided by an intellectualist worldview is one characterized simply by ever-increasing awareness or consciousness. It is a linear journey from light into light. Voluntarist spirituality, on the other hand, is characterized in its earliest stages by an encounter with darkness, with our own capacity for evildoing. Expiation and the search for forgiveness are dominant concerns. Light dawns when forgiveness is found, but it is a light discovered only by immersion in darkness. Moreover, it is a light that does not necessarily dispel all future darkness, for the clarity that it brings may well reveal deeper, more radical tendencies toward evildoing. The voluntarist spiritual journey is thus a cyclic rather than a linear one. Light is discovered in this journey by ever deeper plunges into the darkness that is the human capacity for evil.

Reflect now on your spiritual life. If you find that your spirituality provides you with unmitigated consolation, with a steady, peace-filled growth in consciousness, then it is likely that you are an intellectualist. You may, however, find instead that your spirituality is characterized by periods of turmoil. Instinct, or the teachings of your religious tradition, tell you that spiritual peace is to be discovered only by gazing resolutely with anxiety and dread at evil that you have committed and evil of which you still remain capable. If such is the case, it is likely that you are a voluntarist in the matter of good and evil.

Reprise: Tasneem and the Aherns

If Tasneem discerns herself to be a voluntarist, then being therapeutic for the Aherns—and indeed, for most of the client families that she will encounter in the course of her career—means winning the battle against resistance that in the view of the voluntarist-inspired contest models constitutes the essence of therapy. Each of the voluntarist models of therapy has signature techniques for winning this battle. However, when Tasneem chooses to commit herself to one of the voluntarist models, it will ultimately not be the techniques described by that model that will give her the advantage that she needs in order to win the battle against resistance. Ultimately, it is the anchor, the shelter, that the model itself provides that will allow Tasneem successfully to survive most of her encounters with resistance.

But perhaps Tasneem is not a voluntarist. Perhaps the reflection suggested in the previous section will reveal to her that she is an intellectualist on the matter of human evil. Then she will turn to one of the intellectualist-informed collaborative models of therapy to guide her work with the Aherns and with all of her client families. Viewed through the lens of one of these models, therapy will look like a collaborative trek rather than a struggle. If Tasneem chooses to practice within the narrative or the Bowen family systems model, her role in the collaboration will be to teach her client families. As a Bowenian, her teaching will be direct, and she will teach about intergenerational family processes. As a narrative therapist, her teaching will be indirect, and it will be about the ways in which clients are being oppressed by dominant cultural narratives. If Tasneem chooses the solution-focused or collaborative language systems model, her job will not be to teach but simply to influence the flow of the therapeutic conversation. As a solution-focused therapist, Tasneem will direct that conversation toward the problem-free areas of clients' lives. As a language systems therapist, she will direct it always in the direction of the not-yet-said, the not-yet-considered. No matter which intellectualist model she chooses, that model will lead Tasneem to expect that, if she executes her role well, then the Aherns and all of her client families will do their part in constructing a successful therapy.

We have seen in this chapter that how a therapist positions herself vis-à-vis her clients is mightily influenced by whether she sees therapy as a contest or a collaboration. However, there are still more issues at work that equally influence the therapist's intervention posture. As we will now see, how a therapist intervenes with her clients is also determined by where she stands on the perennial philosophical issue of the relationship between mind and body.

4

Mind and Body

Dean had been looking forward to this moment for several weeks.

He had been working with Susie and her four children on and off for about a year now. When Susie first contacted Dean's clinic a year ago, she had presented her older son Juan as the identified patient, reporting that he had been caught twice at his school involved in some minor thefts. Dean had four sessions with Susie, her two adolescent daughters, her ten-year-old son, Juan, and his eight-year-old brother, Carlos. During these sessions, various family members had from time to time made some passing references to Hector, the father. Dean had gleaned from these references that Hector had persistent problems with drugs and alcohol. He also saw clearly that Hector was an object of universal derision in the household. Even in the midst of a heated exchange between Susie and one of her children, the tension could immediately be relieved by mention of one of Hector's recent foibles. The time that he locked himself out of the house. The time that he could not find his way home. How he broke into tears while watching a TV commercial. His latest butchering of the English language. (Hector apparently spoke only broken English; Spanish was his native tongue.) The mere mention of any of these incidents caused Susie and her children to dissolve in unbridled laughter. In the camaraderie of their shared derision of Hector, whatever differences there had been between Susie and the children disappeared. Whatever offense Susie had been chiding one of the children for was forgotten, as was the punishment that she had been threatening. All was swept away in a flood of laughter over pitiful, drunken Hector.

During the four sessions with the family, Dean had made some requests that Hector be included in the therapy, but he had abandoned the requests when he saw the cool reception with which the family greeted them. And so Dean worked with the portion of the family that he had before him and did what, in his estimation, was good work. Juan's misbehavior at school ceased, and at the close of the fourth and final session, Susie informed Dean that she was very satisfied with the service that he had provided.

She must have been satisfied, indeed, because it was barely six weeks later that she contacted Dean again, requesting family therapy this time for Carlos, who had recently gotten into several fairly serious fistfights. Again, Susie politely but firmly denied Dean's request that Hector participate in the therapy. This time, Dean did six sessions of what he thought was good work with Susie and the four children. Again, the family left treatment highly satisfied.

During the course of the ensuing year, Dean saw Susie and the children for a total of four discrete episodes of family therapy, each consisting of from four to seven sessions. Dean thought that each of the episodes, considered in isolation, was a piece of good therapeutic work on his part. But when Susie contacted him for the fifth time, he was forced to admit to himself that his therapy with this family had to be somehow flawed.

Dean did not need a conversation with his new supervisor to figure out that the flaw lie in Hector's non-present presence in the therapy. The good news was that Hector was interested in attending the next session, and Susie was willing to permit him.

Dean realized that the next session was crucial. Hector's ongoing involvement in therapy needed to be cemented. After careful consideration, Dean decided to invite his new supervisor to run the next session as a consultant. The new supervisor was pretty much an unknown quantity to Dean. He and Dean had met together for supervision only twice. But given the fact that the supervisor had twelve years of experience and Dean only one, he figured that it was a decent bet that the supervisor might have a better chance than he of convincing the family that Hector's participation in the therapy was crucial.

It had taken several weeks before the family's schedule could be coordinated with Dean's and the supervisor's. As the plans for the consultation session crystallized, Dean began to look forward to the session with growing anticipation and excitement. He fully expected the session to be a high point in his young clinical career. He was sure that sitting in the session, watching his supervisor work with Hector, Susie, and the children, would be a tremendously educational experience for him.

Ten minutes into the session, Dean's excitement began to wane. By the twenty-minute mark, he was certain that arranging the consultation was the worst clinical blunder that he had ever made.

Without giving it any explicit thought, Dean had assumed that his supervisor did therapy in much the same way that he and his fellow interns did, only more skillfully. Dean's therapy was a highly verbal affair. He asked questions. He made statements. He invited his clients to talk, and his interventions focused on what they said. It never even occurred to Dean that therapy could be otherwise. After all, isn't psychotherapy called "the talking cure"?

Apparently, no one had ever bothered to inform Dean's new supervisor that therapy was about talk. Sure, he was talking in the session; but he was also doing much more than that. The session was not five minutes old before he had changed the family's seating arrangement in the therapy room, moving Hector from an isolated position in the corner of the room into a chair next to that of his wife. Five minutes later, the supervisor was playing choreographer again, this time moving Hector and Susie into chairs that were separated from the children and facing them. Nor did the movement stop there. A few minutes later, the supervisor had Susie and her older daughter standing next to each other to see which of them was taller. Midway through the session, the supervisor picked up a hand puppet that was lying on a shelf in the therapy room and proceeded to wear the puppet on his hand through the next several minutes of the session. When finally he took it off his hand, it was only to give it to Hector, suggesting that he should put the puppet on his hand. (When Hector did so and then proceeded to keep the puppet on his hand for the next ten minutes, Dean was not sure whether to be amazed or appalled.) Shortly before the close of the session, the supervisor sent the children out of the room. Dean soon realized that this latest bit of stage direction was mere preparation for what would prove to be the supervisor's final flourish. As his last "intervention"—the quotation marks were in Dean's mind—the supervisor got Hector to kneel down in front of his seated wife. Then, to Dean's final embarrassment, the supervisor knelt down next to Hector.

After bidding the family goodbye, Dean's supervisor asked him if he had any questions about the session. With every fiber of his being, Dean longed to reply, "Well, yes, in fact, I do. What the hell was that all about?" *Judging that discretion was the better part of valor, Dean asked instead, "Is that the way you do therapy all the time, or was that for the benefit of this particular family?" A mischievous smile creased the supervisor's face. "No, that's the way I do therapy all of the time."*

Dean was almost as disturbed by the supervisor's answer as he had been by the session that the supervisor had just conducted. He would have found it easier to handle if the supervisor had told him that the session was an aberration, an unusually histrionic affair that the supervisor deemed necessary to address the exigencies of this particular situation. While that answer would not have rendered the session any more aesthetically pleasing to Dean, at least it would have allowed him to write it off as a unique piece of therapeutic posturing that he could let sink into the deep recesses of his memory.

However, the fact that his supervisor claimed that he routinely did therapy in the very physical way that he had just witnessed deprived Dean of the opportunity simply to dismiss the session and to forget about it. As soon as he heard the supervisor's answer to his question, it was clear to him that he and his supervisor inhabited different therapeutic worlds. In Dean's world, a session like the consultation was unimaginable; in the supervisor's world, it apparently was routine. It unsettled Dean immensely to realize that he and his supervisor lived in different therapeutic worlds. And he quickly realized that his discomfort was not simply related to the prospect of a possibly difficult relationship between him and this new supervisor. Dean's disquiet had deeper roots than that. Conscientious therapist that he was, Dean felt that he was under an ethical obligation of sorts to journey into the foreign territory that was his supervisor's therapeutic world. Precisely because its contours were so alien to him, Dean felt that he owed it to himself and to the profession that he was entering to enter into and to explore this strange new world. He felt pretty sure that he would come out of the exploration even more confirmed as a citizen of his own therapeutic world. Still, he could not be certain.

Mind and Body

What distinguishes Dean's and the supervisor's therapeutic worlds is the tools that each puts in the hands of the therapist to use in helping clients to change. In Dean's world, language is the privileged tool that the therapist wields in the quest for change. Dean tries very hard to use language carefully and to listen well to the language that his clients use. The supervisor, too, attends to language, but for him language appears to be not an entity unto itself, but part of a larger, more encompassing reality that very much involves physicality and spatiality. The supervisor does not appear content simply to deliver verbal interventions, as Dean does. He manipulates space, moving people around the consulting room. He uses physical objects, like the hand puppet. He even uses clients' own bodies as a tool for change, as when he had Hector kneel down in front of Susie. For the supervisor, what happens in therapy should have a distinctly physical component to it. For Dean, the therapeutic domain is the domain of words.

The discussions in the previous chapters of this book have sensitized us to the fact that differences like the one that we have just described are neither trivial nor accidental. When therapists go about the business of doing therapy in ways that are as different as Dean's and his supervisor's, it is because they are operating on the basis of very different assumptions about the nature of the human world. In this case, Dean and the supervisor seem to hold different assumptions about the relationship between the physical world, including the human body, and the human person. Dean's emphasis on language in the therapy that he conducts appears to bespeak his assumption that that which is properly and uniquely human resides in the immaterial domain of mind and meaning. The supervisor's reliance on interventions that involve a distinctly physical component suggests that he assumes that the physical is a constitutive component of the human.

The previous chapters have also taught us that these assumptive differences between therapists usually have their roots in philosophical debates that stretch far back in the history of Western thought. Once again, this is the case. Almost as soon as Westerners began philosophizing, they began to wonder about the relationship between the material and human worlds. Thus was born what has come to be known as the mind–body problem, perhaps the most vexing issue that Western philosophy has tackled.

Historical Backdrop

All of the philosophical issues that we have examined thus far have been dealt with in a dichotomous fashion within Western thought. Individualism versus collectivism. Freedom from versus freedom for. Intellectualism versus voluntarism. Having struggled through all of these either/or distinctions, you may be relieved to find out that Western philosophers have shown themselves to be a little more creative in their attempts to deal with the mind–body issue. Over the course of the years, they have developed not two, but four, distinct solutions to this philosophical problem. While this has allowed for more nuanced thinking, it has emphatically not produced any kind of consensus in the philosophical community as to the best way to think about the mind–body issue. Currently, all four approaches to the issue have their vociferous exponents. And, as we shall discover later in the chapter, all four approaches are represented in the practice of psychotherapy.

Materialism

The oldest solution to the problem of the relationship between the physical and the human simply denies the existence of the human (Shaffer, 1967). Leucippus and Democritus were two pre-Socratic Greek thinkers who asserted that the only things that exist in the universe are atoms and empty space. In their view, all phenomena are simply physical phenomena. A phenomenon that might appear to be of a qualitatively different nature, such as human perception or thought, is at root nothing more than atoms in motion, colliding with each other in certain ways (Campbell, 1967). The appearance of qualitative difference is illusory. In the final analysis, those things that we think of as being distinctly human wind up being nothing more than physical processes, identical to the physical processes that we observe in the nonhuman world. The human *is* the physical. There is no mind, only body.

In asserting this doctrine, Leucippus and Democritus gave birth to the intellectual tradition commonly known as materialism. "Materialism is the name given to a family of doctrines concerning the nature of the world which give to matter a primary position and accord to mind (or spirit) a secondary, dependent reality or even none at all" (Campbell, 1967, p. 179). Once articulated by Leucippus and Democritus, materialism remained a viable tradition throughout the development of Western thought, even to the present day. Materialism was adopted and refined by the Greek thinker, Epicurus, and by the Roman, Lucretius. In the seventeenth century, it was given vigorous expression by Thomas Hobbes.

Idealism

When a materialist like Hobbes looks at the physical world, he sees a solidity and reality that he perceives to be utterly lacking in what appears to him to be the insubstantial world of consciousness and thought. Plato saw things in exactly the opposite way. When Plato looked at the physical world, he did not see solidity, but constant flux. True stability, as he saw it, exists only in the realm of ideas. Individual trees come and go. They are subject to birth, growth, and decay. But the *idea* of a tree is eternal and unchanging. From this observation, Plato reached the conclusion that only ideas are really real, possessing the fullness of being. The physical world is merely a dim reflection of the luminous, unchanging world of ideas.

In according primary status to the realm of mind and ideas, Plato gave rise to the philosophical tradition of idealism (Acton, 1967). While according the physical world only derivative status, Plato never denied that it actually exists. However, a later idealist did go so far as to make this assertion. George Berkeley, an eighteenth-century Irish philosopher, taught that the only things that exist in the universe are minds. The so-called physical universe exists only as a percept of the minds that inhabit the universe (Shaffer, 1967; Sprigge, 1998). If there were no minds to perceive it, the physical world would not exist. Berkeley's idealism is the mirror opposite of the materialism of Leucippus and Democritus. For the latter, there is no mind, only body; for Berkeley, there is no body, only mind.

Idealists who came after Berkeley were not as radical as he in denying existence to the nonmental world. Immanuel Kant, for example, admitted that something exists in the universe that is independent of mind. However, the human mind, he declared, can know absolutely nothing about these things-in-themselves. When human beings encounter things-in-themselves, the experience of them is mediated through constructs *that the mind itself creates*. Thus, we can never know things-in-themselves; we can only know what they are like after they have passed through the filters imposed by human consciousness.

Kant was the first idealist to proclaim that the human mind plays a pivotal role in constructing what it knows. After Kant, idealists became less concerned with worrying about exactly what kind of existence the physical world has. Because the human mind can only know what it itself constructs, it is a waste of time worrying about the nonmental world. The only proper object of the human mind is the human mind itself.

Dualism

Materialists assert that everything that we think of as quintessentially human is really nothing more than a physical process, one that, in principle, can be thoroughly explained by the laws of physics. The humanities are irrelevant. Physics rules. Idealists assert that the laws of physics really tell us very little about the physical world. The knowledge that we think we have about the physical world bears the indelible imprint of the human consciousness that constructed it. Physics is subsidiary. The humanities rule.

As you have seen in this book, the Western philosophical tradition has tended to be very accepting of either/or formulations, like the materialism/idealism dichotomy. However, for some reason, in the matter of the mind–body problem, Western philosophers have been motivated to hammer out some kind of both/and alternative to the materialism/idealism dichotomy. Their efforts have produced two more approaches to the mind–body issue.

Rene Descartes (1596–1650) was the chief architect of one of these alternative approaches. Descartes refused to be cornered into asserting that, in the final analysis, only one kind of thing, physical or mental, really exists in the universe. Instead, he proclaimed that there are two kinds of things that exist, which are completely opposite in their nature (Williams, 1967). There is matter, whose behavior, in Descartes' view, is absolutely governed by the laws of physics. The world of matter is a deterministic world, completely devoid of freedom, operating as a big, complex machine. Then there is mind, whose very essence it is to be free and spontaneous.

As Descartes saw it, there is only one place in the universe where matter and mind interact, and that is in the human person, who has both a mind and a body (Shaffer, 1967). (Descartes denied that animals have any kind of mind whatsoever; he considered them to be simply machines [Garber, 1998].) However, when they interact in the human person, matter and mind retain their essential properties. Thus, Descartes looked on the human body as a deterministic machine, completely subject to the laws of physics. At the same time, he adamantly insisted that the human mind is free and spontaneous.

If you think you see a problem in Descartes' dualistic solution to the mind–body problem, you are not alone. While his thought has been highly influential, it has been subjected to considerable criticism by philosophers. His critics have claimed that Descartes wedged himself into an impossible situation when he assumed that the universe is composed of two kinds of things with completely opposite characteristics, and then went on to assert that these two kinds of things come into contact in the human person. How, critics ask, does the free human mind influence a human body whose behavior is seen as being completely governed by the deterministic laws of physics? Is the human person a free spirit imprisoned inside of a deterministic machine? While Descartes' dualism avoids the extremes of both materialism and idealism, it does so, his critics say, at the price of describing the human condition in a way that does not seem to fit many people's experience of themselves.

Aristotelianism

The second alternative to the idealism/materialism dichotomy was developed by Plato's student, Aristotle. In distinction from the materialists, Aristotle did not accept that the apparent qualitative difference between mental processes and physical processes is illusory. Mind is real, Aristotle believed. But in distinction from the idealists, he did not accept that mind is the only thing that is really real. For Aristotle, the physical world is every bit as real as the mental. How then are mind and body related? Mind, Aristotle says, is the body's organization. Mind and body are related to each other in much the same way that dance and dancers are related to each other (Swinburne, 1998). Dance only exists when real live concrete dancers are moving with each other in coordinated, organized ways. The dance only exists when there are dancers. Yet, the dance is not illusory; there is, in fact, an organized pattern to the way the dancers are moving with each other. Thus, both dance and dancers are real. Moreover, they are inextricably interdependent. In the same way, mind and body are both real and are inextricably interdependent (Kerferd, 1967). Mind is the dance that is manifest in the body's organization. No mind, no body; no body, no mind.

Thomas Aquinas was the great medieval Christianizer of Aristotle's thought. However, Aquinas found himself in a bit of a quandary when he attempted to Christianize the Aristotelian solution to the mind–body problem. Christianity maintains that the human soul—which for all intents and purposes is equivalent to the philosophical concept of mind—survives the death of the human body. Aristotelian that he was, Aquinas was inclined to view the soul as the body's organization. Yet, as we have just observed, this approach to the mind–body problem carries with it the corollary that, when the body dies, mind dies too. (After all, what is death but the beginning of the body's disorganization?) No body, no soul. As a devoted Christian, Aquinas could not accept that the soul perishes with the body. Thus, Aquinas taught that the soul is immortal. However, in deference to Aristotle, Aquinas asserted that the disembodied soul exists in an unnatural state after death, longing, as it were, to return to its natural condition as the organizing principle of a physical body. This longing will be fulfilled, Aquinas believed, at the general resurrection that Christianity believes will occur at the end of time, when, as part of a new heaven and a new earth, all human beings will receive resurrected bodies.

Therapeutic Ramifications

Dean remembers having heard something about the mind–body problem in one or two of his undergraduate courses. At the time, he considered the problem to be one of those trumped-up, intellectual issues that give professors something to write about, but which has absolutely no relevance to the way that people live their day-to-day existences. Little did Dean suspect that this supposedly abstract issue would slam him in the face a couple of years later as he was sitting in a family therapy session conducted by his supervisor.

For it was, indeed, the mind–body problem that Dean was encountering as he watched the way in which his supervisor worked with Susie, Hector, and their children. Concerned as they are with humans and how they operate, the various models of psychotherapy have had to take a position on the relationship between the human and physical worlds. As they have done so, they inevitably have turned to the four different solutions to the mind–body problem that are afloat out there in the matrix of Western culture. Thus, there have developed materialist models of therapy, models that understand and attempt to change human behavior using modes of thought that are drawn from and modeled on the physical sciences. There are also idealist therapies, which consider the human domain to be one of mind and meaning, minimally impacted, if at all, by the physical world (Lannamann, 1998). There are dualist models, which see the quintessential human drama as resulting from the tension that exists in the individual between psychological and physical processes that are each constitutive of the person, and yet opposed to each other. And there are Aristotelian models, which view the pathway to therapeutic change as necessarily involving interventions in which meaning and movement, language and physicality, thought and action, are inextricably intertwined.

While materialism has had an impact in the broader mental health field, it has not been influential in the field of family therapy. The two most important materialist models of treatment are behaviorism and biological psychiatry. Each of these, in different ways, treats so-called psychological phenomena as nothing more than physical phenomena. In the radical behaviorism of John B. Watson and B. F. Skinner, "mental" phenomena are analyzed into observable behavioral components. It is assumed that these behaviors are caused by stimuli in the environment, in much the same way that the motion of a ball on a pool table is caused by the impact of other balls. Behavioral therapy seeks to discover and then to manipulate these stimulus–response chains that are seen as utterly determining human behavior. Biological psychiatry also deals in deterministic cause–effect sequences, but at a different level than does behaviorism. This model of treatment understands human behavior to be determined ultimately by genes and brain chemistry. Based on this understanding, it seeks to change behavior by changing chemistry.

While there are no materialist models of family therapy, there are, indeed, dualist, idealist, and Aristotelian models. Grounded as they are in very different visions of the relationship between the physical and human worlds, the various kinds of models view clinical phenomena in very different ways and prescribe very different kinds of behavior for the therapist.

Dualist Therapy

A dualist therapy is one that, following Descartes, sees human beings as residing at the intersection of two worlds that operate according to utterly opposite sets of laws. Classical psychoanalytic family therapy is precisely such a therapy.

As adamantly as Descartes, Sigmund Freud thought of the human body as a machine, completely governed by physical and chemical laws (Whyte, 1967). The sexual and aggressive energies that power this machine do not limit their influence to the bodily sphere. Instead, they surge into the mental sphere as well, where they power the unconscious. Freud also agreed with Descartes in equating consciousness with freedom. Each of these men heartily endorses the biblical premise that awareness of the truth will set you free.

Thus, as a result of his dualist worldview, Freud saw the human psyche as a house divided. One part of this house is driven by instinctual energies that are completely governed by deterministic physical and chemical laws. The other part of the house is filled with the clear light of freedom and self-determination. A person with psychological symptoms is one who experiences at least part of her behavior as being un-free, compulsive, outside of her control. Freud theorized that such symptomatic behavior has its roots in the part of the psychic house that is ruled by the blind, unconscious, physical laws of nature. The cure will come when the person's behavior emerges out of the free, conscious, self-determining part of the psychic house. Therapy thus entails helping the symptomatic person to become consciously aware of the instinctual sexual and aggressive drives that are powering her symptoms. Hector, Susie, and their children will cease cycling into Dean's office when he helps them become conscious of the fact that their patterns of daily interaction with each other are rooted in sexual and aggressive fantasies that each of them has about the others. Awareness of this truth will set them free.

Or will it? We noted above that, in the opinion of many, Descartes' dualism led him into an untenable and unacceptable description of the human condition. How can a mind that is free influence a body whose behavior is believed to be

completely determined by physical law? When Freud built his therapy on this dualist worldview, he inherited the same difficulty. However, because Freud was a
practitioner as much as a theorist, his difficulty was as much practical as it was
theoretical. In his therapy, the difficulty took the following form: is it possible for
consciousness ever really to get the upper hand over the unconscious instinctual
energies in serving as the source of a person's behavior? Will insight and awareness really free Susie, Hector, and the children from being governed by their
sexual and aggressive instincts?

     As Freud matured as a therapist, he became decreasingly confident that the
answer to these questions is "yes" (Whyte, 1967). His growing pessimism was
evident when he titled one of his late essays "Analysis Terminable and Intermi-
nable." In this essay, Freud tried to make sense out of the fact that his insight-
oriented therapy so frequently failed to achieve a positive outcome. Marshall
(1982) summarizes for us the gist of the article: "Freud, in conclusion, returns pes-
simistically to his dualistic energy model, wherein the balance of therapy is metaphorically attributed to the 'bigger battalions' to whom God owes his allegiance"
(p. 26). Following the logic of the dualist position, Freud was unable to assert in
the end that consciousness can consistently govern biology. Thus, utilizing the
"battalion" metaphor, he wound up saying that the outcome of any given therapy
is necessarily a crapshoot, with the therapist unable to say with any certainty why
it succeeds or why it fails.

     Other psychoanalytic approaches to family therapy, like the object relations
approach, have downplayed the role of biological drives in the genesis of human
behavior. In doing so, these approaches have distanced themselves from Freud's
dualism, and, as a result, from his therapeutic pessimism. In place of Freud's focus
on the instinctual drives, these other analytic approaches have explored how a
person's developmental history produces in him intrapsychic constructs or "filters" that wind up determining how he experiences relational partners in his later
life. In their emphasis on how the human mind constructs the world that it experiences, these psychoanalytic approaches resemble the idealist therapies, which we
will now examine.

Idealist Therapies

Collaborative Language Systems Therapy. "[L]anguage does not mirror nature . . . ; language creates the natures we know" (Anderson & Goolishian, 1988,
p. 378). This premise lies at the heart of the collaborative language systems model
of therapy. It is this premise that leads the language systems therapist to understand a problem presented as a focus for therapy as something defined into existence in conversation among members of the problem-organizing system. It is this
premise that motivates the language systems therapist to keep the members of the
problem-organizing system in open and fluid dialogue with each other, so that
they can reach the point where they define the presenting problem out of existence. And it is this premise that makes the collaborative language systems model
an idealist therapy.

The essence of the idealist solution to the mind–body problem is its assumption that mind (and those things that are properly "mental," like ideas and language) has primacy over matter. In its various versions, idealism asserts that mind is more real than matter, or, at the very least, imposes its own structures on matter. When the language systems therapist states that language creates rather than mirrors what we "know" about nature, he places himself squarely within the idealist tradition.

The language system therapist's idealism is evident not only in how he thinks about therapy, but also in how he conducts it. As Dean did in his work with Susie and her children, the language system therapist devotes all his attention in therapy to language. He listens very carefully to what his clients say to him. He asks carefully crafted questions that invite his clients to elaborate further their point of view. Via this repeated oscillation between listening and questioning, the therapist elicits ongoing languaging among members of the client system, a languaging that, in its very fluidity, constantly brings new realities into existence.

To the same degree that he privileges language, the collaborative language systems therapist disregards the physical component of what is happening in the consulting room. Things like seating arrangement, bodily posture, and nonverbal gestures remain "off the scope" for him. In the consultation session with Hector, Susie, and the children, a language systems therapist would not have attended to the way in which Susie seated herself in the midst of her children, while Hector positioned himself alone in the corner of the room. He would have paid no attention to the derisive smiles that passed back and forth between Susie and the children whenever Hector struggled to make himself understood in his broken English. This inattentiveness would not have been the result of a lack of skill. Instead, it would have been the result of a deliberate decision. The language systems therapist does not believe that these physical elements of the therapy session have any objective meaning. The only meaning that they could possibly have would be one that is created on the spot in a conversation between him and the client-system members. And then, as far as the therapist is concerned, it would be the conversation, the languaging about these physical elements, and not the elements themselves, that would be important. And so, the therapist simply does not advert to the physical components of the interview. He restricts his attention to the languaging going on in the room, wherever it might lead.

In the same way that the language systems therapist does not attend to the physical component of the interview, he also will not use physicality in his own intervening. All the manipulation of space and objects that Dean found so appalling in his supervisor's intervening would simply never occur to the collaborative language systems therapist. Such behavior, in his view, would do little to promote the elaboration of meaning that he sees as lying at the heart of therapy. Language, and language alone, is the royal road to the evolution of meaning that is the essence of the therapeutic encounter.

Narrative Therapy.   As vigorously as the language systems therapist, the narrative therapist is committed to the idealist notion that language creates rather than reflects reality. But whereas the language systems therapist restricts his attention predominantly to the languaging occurring in the problem-organizing system, the narrative therapist focuses her attention on the way in which the language of the broader society, the dominant stories told by the broader culture, influences the conversations that occur at a local level. In the view of the narrative therapist, the "realities" brought into existence by this broader language are all too often oppressive, robbing people of their right to language their own worlds into existence. The "truths" described in dominant cultural stories deprive people of their right to author their own truth. The narrative therapist seeks to liberate her clients from the influence of this oppressive language. She would try to make Susie and her children aware of how their view of Hector has been influenced by the stories told in the dominant American culture about Hispanics and immigrants. She would try to help Hector see that the story he tells about himself was largely authored by impersonal forces at work in the broader sociocultural context in which he operates. The narrative therapist would endeavor to empower Hector, Susie, and the children to replace these dominant cultural stories with self-authored stories that they prefer.

Because she aims at liberating her clients from language that is oppressive, the narrative therapist is not content, as the language systems therapist is, merely to facilitate the conversation that is occurring in the problem-organizing system. She fears that such a nondirective approach will leave unexposed the insidious and largely covert influence that the broader societal language is having on the conversation occurring in the client system. Thus, the narrative therapist takes a more directive stance. In crafting her questions, she does not simply invite clients to further elaborate their point of view. Instead, she asks questions designed to expose to clients how the language that they are using and the stories that they are telling are not really their own at all, but have been authored by the dominant culture. She also asks questions designed to sensitize clients to the resources that they possess to overcome the oppressive influence of the broader culture. This use of questions to create an awareness of the sociocultural roots of clients' presenting problems is precisely what the narrative therapist refers to when she talks about externalization.

The narrative therapist may be more agenda-driven than the language systems therapist, but her therapy is every bit as much language-centered. Sharing the idealist tenet that language creates reality, the narrative therapist attends only to language and utilizes only language in crafting her interventions. As she sits in a therapy session, she, too, oscillates between listening and questioning. Like the language systems therapist, the narrative therapist would also choose not to respond to the physical component of the interview. And she, too, would not include a physical component in her own intervening. As much as for the language systems therapist, therapy for the narrative therapist is all about talking.

Aristotelian Therapies

Symbolic Experiential Family Therapy.   Consider the following description of a therapy session:

The children are dressed "in their Sunday best" with ties and flashy jackets, sitting beside each other with their arms crossed, and hostile looks, as if they were defending the family fortress. While the children eye the therapist silently and with increasing hostility, the mother lavishes praise on them to "help them" talk to him about their difficulty in getting along with everybody, especially with her.

Foreseeing a total failure if he tries talking to them or, worse, getting them to talk to him, the therapist leaves the room and soon returns, wearing a more garish jacket and a vividly colored tie. He sits down beside them, arms crossed, in total silence, imitating their hostile looks. The scene is so hilarious and at the same time so uncomfortable that even the mother, unsure of the situation, is obliged to be silent. The silence allows her suffering to leak out behind her mask of words.

The therapist remains in this position for several moments. When he feels he is really wearing the uncomfortable clothes of the children, the therapist moves toward them and catches their expressions which are now more cheerful. He places a hand gently on each of their mouths and tells them he will ask some questions that are a little tough. But they must answer without words, only nodding yes or no with their heads (Andolfi, Angelo, & de Nichilo, 1989, p. 72).

With this description, we have left the idealist therapeutic world inhabited by the collaborative language systems and narrative models. We have entered a world in which language and meaning do not exist in splendid isolation, but are inextricably intertwined with objects and movement. We have entered a therapeutic world where clients' clothes and facial expressions are noticed as much as their words, a world where the therapist's jacket and tie are considered to be as much an intervention as are the words that he says. In this world, mind and body are intimately related to and dependent on each other. We have entered the world of the Aristotelian therapies. The first inhabitant of this world that we will examine is symbolic experiential family therapy.

The symbolic experiential therapist is wary of words. In his view, words, and the elaborate cognitive constructions that they can be used to convey, all too frequently are used by people as a defense against the deep emotional experiencing that the symbolic experientialist most prizes in life. Thus, the experientialist would never join his idealist colleagues in constructing a therapy filled only with talk. His must be a therapy that gets his clients in touch with their feelings, impulses, and drives. And the best means available for producing this effect is play (Andolfi et al., 1989).

Therapy *is* play for the symbolic experiential family therapist. It is imaginative and creative, the way play is. It is spontaneous, the way play is. It is only minimally rule-governed, and, as in play, what rules there are are always subject to being amended on the spot. Most germane to the subject at hand, symbolic experiential therapy, like play, uses space, motion, and physical objects in a symbolic, meaning-laden, "as-if" kind of way.

[W]hile he talks to the parents during a session about their concerns over their seven-year-old daughter, Laura, the therapist tactfully removes a shoe from the little girl and holds it on his knees. By taking something personal from her, the therapist communicates to Laura that he understands her problems and that he wants to help her. The shoe becomes a relational link when the therapist suddenly hands it to the father to see what the father does to it. Annoyed by this sudden intrusion into his personal space, the father grabs the shoe and automatically throws it on the floor in front of his wife's chair, who quickly picks it up and puts it back on the child's foot. Now we have a vivid vignette about the functioning of the family when faced with the problem of Laura's behavior. . . .

The shoe, then, changes shape and meaning in the course of the session. From an inanimate object it becomes alive first as part of Laura, when the therapist takes it from her, then as a relational link, and later as a tool to open up otherwise hidden conflicts and rejections (Andolfi et al., 1989, p. 70).

The symbolic experientialist loves the way in which objects and movement can hold several different meanings at the same time. It is this analogical nature of physical play that makes it the gateway into intense emotional experiencing on the part of the participants. The symbolic experiential therapist plays with motion and objects in his therapy precisely because he wants his therapy to be a place where clients will have profound and even primordial experiences.

The literature of symbolic experiential family therapy is laced with stories of how the masters of this approach have used physicality and physical objects in their therapy. There is the famous story of Carl Whitaker wrestling with one of his clients (Napier & Whitaker, 1978). Maurizio Andolfi's first AAMFT Master Therapist session with the family of a thirteen-year-old girl displaying obsessive-compulsive behaviors focused almost entirely on a water glass that Andolfi happened to spy lying on a table in the room being used for the consultation (Andolfi et al., 1989). But one need not be a master to do therapy in this way. I myself have seen several novice family therapists do very credible renditions of symbolic experiential family therapy.

Structural Family Therapy.   Like the symbolic experiential therapist, the structural family therapist is also wary of words. In her experience, simply labeling for a family its dysfunctional organizational map will not induce family members to change the map. Conversations in the therapy room about more adaptive maps will almost never result in those new maps taking hold. It is not words that restructure client families; it is concrete action on the part of family members, in which they enact the relational arrangements that will become part of the new map.

Like symbolic experiential therapy, structural family therapy aims at providing its clients not primarily with new language and new stories, but with new experiences. Similarly to her experientialist colleague, the structural family therapist prefers to have these new experiences occur in the session. However, the structural therapist and the experientialist differ in the kinds of experiences that they attempt to produce for their clients. The symbolic experiential therapist tries to create experiences that put his clients in touch with feared and repressed impulses and drives. The structural family therapist works to create experiences that enact a new relational organization in the family. Thus, while a symbolic experiential therapist might attempt to get Hector in touch with his repressed rage toward Susie, a structural family therapist would likely be interested in getting Hector and Susie to experience what it is like to parent their children together.

Despite their different intents, structural family therapists and symbolic experiential family therapists both make ready use of movement and objects in creating in-session experiences for their clients. The structural family therapist will use clients' position in the therapy room as a metaphor for interpersonal distance. As Dean's supervisor did, a structural therapist might move Susie and Hector into positions next to each other and separated from the children in order to challenge the coalition between Susie and the children, and to provide the family with a concrete, symbolic experience of an organizational map that has the adults working together in parenting their children. The structural family therapist also feels comfortable using physical objects in pursuit of her structural goals. In order to begin bridging the language gap between Hector and his children, she might arrange an in-session enactment in which eight-year-old Carlos teaches his father how to play a handheld video game that he brought into the session.

Even when she is not manipulating space and utilizing objects, the structural family therapist displays her Aristotelian roots in her reliance on enactments to bring about change in client-families' organizational maps. Therapeutic talk between therapist and clients will not change family relational patterns. In the view of the structural therapist, the therapy session must be used to push clients beyond merely talking about change into a here-and-now experience of relating to each other differently. This emphasis on therapy as *doing* rather than simply as talking bespeaks the interdependence of mind and body that defines the Aristotelian position.

The Strategic Therapies.   In a way, the strategic therapies emphasize doing even more than structural family therapy does. While the structural therapist presses her client families to do something new in the here-and-now of the therapy session, she will also usually explain to them (frequently in metaphorical language) the rationale behind her intervening. A strategic therapist might not do so. "[T]he main goal of therapy is to get people to *behave* differently and so to have different subjective experiences" (Haley, 1976, p. 49; emphasis added). The MRI therapist and the Haley-Madanes strategic therapist will tell clients whatever stories they need to in order to get them to behave differently. The stories told— referred to as *reframes* in both approaches—need not and frequently do not reflect the therapist's understanding of the clients' situation. No matter: reframes are simply pragmatic means; the end sought is behavior change.

What the Haley-Madanes and the MRI strategist are trying to change are problem-maintaining interactional sequences. (Of course, we have already noted that, in the Haley-Madanes model, changing problem-maintaining sequences is seen as also requiring a change in families' organizational maps.) Differently than the structural family therapist, the strategic therapist is not interested in having the targeted behavior change occur in the session. In his view, trying to effect in-session behavior change elicits too much resistance on the part of client families. Therapy can be done much more briefly and efficiently if the doing that is required of clients occurs between sessions rather than in them. Thus, the heart and soul of MRI and Haley-Madanes strategic therapy are directives, tasks given to client families to perform between therapy sessions. Reframes are delivered to client families to increase the chances that they will comply with directives. The reframe "sells" the directive, but it is the directive that brings about therapeutic change.

Strategic therapists have described numerous kinds of directives that they employ. Some directives aim directly at interrupting problem-maintaining interactional sequences. Others seek to achieve this end indirectly, perhaps by exaggerating some component of the interactional sequence until the latter collapses under its own weight. These are the kinds of directives described by Jay Haley in *Ordeal Therapy* (1984). And then there are directives that seek to exploit some client-families' tendency to oppose and defy whatever it is that the therapist might direct them to do. These are the famous (or infamous) paradoxical directives that have come to be indelibly associated with strategic therapy.

The therapy of the first Milan team was an exception to the strategic therapy tradition of playing fast and furious with reframes so as to increase clients' compliance with directives. Like the structural family therapist, the Milan therapist believes that he should be straight with client families in telling them exactly what he sees malfunctioning in them, namely, their organizational maps. However, the Milan therapist does not believe that this information will change anything. A thoroughgoing Aristotelian, the Milan therapist is convinced that change requires doing, not simply talking. As is the case with the other strategic models, Milan therapy aims at having this doing occur between therapy sessions rather than in them. The means that the Milan therapist employs to instigate this doing are reminiscent of the directive techniques utilized by the other strategic models, but are given a distinctive twist in Milan therapy. The therapist relies most heavily on positive connotation, a kind of paradoxical technique, in which the therapist honestly informs the client family of how he sees their presenting problem as being embedded in the family's organizational map, but then goes on to tell the family how necessary it is for its cohesiveness and stability for all the members to continue to behave in such a way as to maintain the map. The therapist intends by this message, of course, to provoke a rebellion by the client family, with family members seeking to defeat the therapist by doing exactly what he has told them not to do—change the organizational map. To heighten the intensity of the positive connotation, the Milan therapist may prescribe a ritual for the client family, which, through exaggeration, throws the dysfunctionality of the family's map into sharp relief.

Whether it is the pragmatic reframes used by the MRI and Madanes-Haley models, or the reality-based positive connotation used by the first Milan model, cognitive-level intervention never stands alone in strategic therapy. It is always wedded to and at the service of interventions like directives or rituals, which aim to produce action on the part of clients. It is this interdependence of the cognitive and the behavioral, of mind and body, that makes the strategic therapies Aristotelian.

Bowen Family Systems Therapy.   Murray Bowen so prizes thinking in his view of the human condition that you may be surprised to find the family therapy model that he constructed listed here among the Aristotelian therapies. Would it not be more aptly included, you might ask, in the ranks of the idealist therapies?

It certainly is the case that Bowen family systems therapy aims at enhancing the cognitive functioning of its clients. In her quest to increase their differentiation, the Bowenian therapist strives to help her clients base their actions on calm, rational deliberation rather than on unexamined affect. The Bowenian even resembles the idealist therapist in constructing therapy sessions as a forum exclusively for talk. Not for the Bowenian are the in-session shenanigans of structural and experientialist therapists.

However, as much as the Bowenian therapist values thinking and talking, she parts company with the idealist therapist in her conviction that talking and thinking are insufficient in and of themselves to effect a successful therapy. She joins ranks with all the other Aristotelian therapies in believing that, ultimately, talking must be coupled with doing in order to effect therapeutic change.

Like the strategic therapies, Bowen family systems therapy has the doing occur between sessions rather than in them. What the doing looks like is dictated by the Bowenian view of what leads to human dysfunction. For the Bowenian, any and all maladaptive behavior is caused by lack of differentiation. While it may be displayed in the nuclear family, lack of differentiation has its roots in the family of origin. Thus, differentiation can only be increased by new behavior enacted in the family-of-origin context. The Bowenian family therapist uses sessions to prepare her clients for this difficult task of behaving differently in their families of origin. She would use sessions with Hector and Susie to explore with them how their current behavior toward each other and toward their children is the product of the positions that they occupied and the roles that they played in the families that they grew up in. Teaching them the concepts of Bowen family systems theory, she would strengthen their cognitive functioning by helping them to view their families of origin through a wide-angle lens that helps them to see their childhood, adolescent, and young adult experiences in the context of the broader interpersonal processes at work in their families.

The Bowenian therapist would not impart this insight for its own sake. By itself, it is considered insufficient to enhance Susie and Hector's level of differentiation. What it does do in the Bowenian's view is to provide Hector and Susie with tools that they can use when finally their therapist sends them out on well-planned and well-rehearsed expeditions to change their behavior in their families of origin. As an intellectualist, the Bowenian believes that Susie and Hector's new way of thinking about their families of origin will be effective in enabling them to withstand the emotional pressure that their families will exert on them to return to their habitual roles. As an Aristotelian, however, she does not believe that Susie and Hector will be fundamentally transformed until they actually experience themselves relating differently to members of their family of origin.

For the Bowen family systems therapist, thinking and talking are simply tools, albeit very powerful ones, that find their completion when they are used to produce action. Quintessentially Aristotelian, Bowenian therapy sees talking and doing as interdependent aspects of an organic unity.

Solution-Focused Therapy

As occurred in Chapter 1, solution-focused therapy's existence in two distinct forms will prevent us here from easily categorizing it. In its original form, this model is unmistakably an Aristotelian approach; in its more recent, language-focused form, it clearly subscribes to the idealist position.

Although in creating the solution-focused model Steve de Shazer stood the MRI approach on its head, the therapy that he created resembled MRI therapy very closely at the level of process. Thus, as in MRI therapy, the talking that occurred between therapist and clients during the session was seen as a setup for directives that were delivered near the end of the session. To be sure, solution-focused directives have a different purpose than MRI directives. The former aim at amplifying problem-free interactional sequences, while the latter aim at interrupting problem-maintaining sequences. Still, in both therapies, talk is seen as a preparation for action. The Aristotelian interdependence of thinking and doing, of mind and body, is clearly discernible in this first rendition of the solution-focused model.

The more recent variant of the approach was produced by an explicit turn on de Shazer's part toward the idealist solution to the mind–body problem. De Shazer and his colleagues joined the idealist ranks when they endorsed the proposition that language creates, rather than reflects, reality (Berg & de Shazer, 1993; Miller & de Shazer, 1998). With this turn made, directives quickly disappeared from the tool kit of the solution-focused therapist. Therapy was no longer seen to be about eliciting between-session client behavior that would amplify problem-free interactional sequences. Instead, therapy was conceptualized as an exercise in amplifying in-session problem-free talk by the client. Language became the sole phenomenon of interest and the sole intervention tool to the solution-focused therapist. In this version of the model, the therapist carefully attends to the client's language and carefully manipulates his own so as to increase problem-free talk by the client. Such an increase in problem-free talk is considered to be the only worthy goal of therapy. The idealist contours of this therapy are unmistakable.

Personal Reflection

Following Dean's lead, we have now journeyed through the therapeutic worlds inhabited by the major models of family therapy, examining as we have passed through the stance that each model takes toward the mind–body problem. Dean did not begin this journey for the sheer enjoyment of it all. To the contrary, because he is not given to philosophical speculation, he found that it sometimes made his head hurt! Dean felt obliged to stretch himself into the new world opened by his supervisor's consultation because he judged that his development as a family therapist required him to compare the mind–body solutions endorsed by the various therapeutic models to his own stance on this issue. Dean's journey thus ended in self-reflection on his own personal experience of the relationship between body and mind, with an eye toward discerning whether he was a materialist, an idealist, a dualist, or an Aristotelian. And so, too, our own journey will end for us.

It is fairly safe to assume that none of you who are reading this book are materialists in this matter of the mind–body problem. The fact that you are studying and/or engaged in the practice of family therapy means that, in all likelihood, you do not endorse the materialist position that human phenomena are in the end nothing more than physical or biochemical phenomena. Thus, we can pass over materialism and safely begin our personal reflection by trying to determine whether you are a dualist on the mind–body issue.

The defining characteristic of the dualist position is that it sees the human condition as fraught with tension, stretched out, as it is, between two domains that follow opposed sets of logic. Thus, to discern whether you are dualist, you need to ask yourself whether your life experience has this kind of tension as its centerpiece. Put in bold terms, do you experience yourself and other people as animals that have to be tamed? Is it your experience and belief that, unless people subject themselves to constant rigorous monitoring and discipline, they tend to behave in ways that can best be described as in-, or sub-, or prehuman? Does behaving humanly and rationally always entail a struggle against forces operating deep inside of you that, left to their own devices, will lead you to act otherwise?

As is true on so many other issues, the nature of your spirituality can provide you with an important clue in this matter. For some people, the essence of their spiritual life is that it is a battle. In order that their higher, spiritual nature be freed in order to relate to God, or the Ultimate, it needs to war against and to overcome a lower, physical nature that knows only indulgence and the satisfaction of appetites. For such people, ascetic practices like fasting, sleep reduction, and other means of gaining mastery over the body are central in their spiritual quest.

One person's asceticism is another person's workout regimen. And so, your attitudes and approach to physical exercise may help you to ascertain whether you are a dualist. What is your attitude toward physical exercise? Do you see it as a means, sometimes pleasant, sometimes odious, by which you pursue some desirable higher end, like enhanced health, or a sense of well-being, or proficiency in some sport? Or do you instead look on physical exercise as an end in itself? Is what attracts you to exercise the struggle of it all, the effort to impose your will on a resistant body? If the latter is the case, then it is likely that you never find any given level of fitness or strength sufficient and satisfying for very long. You are soon in the gym again, struggling to push yourself to yet higher levels of attainment. If such is your experience, your relationship with your body has all the essential characteristics of the dualist position.

If your lived experience does not have the flavor of a struggle of mind to prevail over matter, then in all likelihood your personal solution to the mind–

body problem is not the dualist solution. It remains for you, then, to figure out whether you are an idealist or an Aristotelian.

What, for lack of a better term, we can call your interactional "style" can provide you with a strong hint as to whether you are an Aristotelian or an idealist. What is your preferred means for connecting with intimate partners? Is it words? Is the verbal exchange of thoughts and feelings the foundation on which your connections to others is constructed? Or do you find that words are secondary for you, insufficient in establishing connections to another unless they are accompanied by some kind of physical expression, such as touch, proximity, or bodily posture? If words are the *lingua franca* of your relational world, you may be an idealist. If gesture and movement convey relational connection to you as loudly as do words, you may be an Aristotelian.

A look at your recreational life can provide further clues. Do you instinctively rejuvenate by means of some physical activity, such as painting, taking a walk, gardening, or engaging in some sport? Or is your preferred recreational activity more cerebral, such as reading or listening to classical music? As we noted earlier in the book, your leisure time is probably populated with a variety of different types of activities. However, you will likely recognize one of these types as having a special status in your life. If that type is one involving physical activity, your experience of the mind–body relationship may well be the Aristotelian one. If, on the other hand, a more cerebral kind of recreation has a privileged status in your life, you may be an idealist.

Are you very sensitive to your physical environment? Some people are not. The quality of light in a room, the amount of noise, the color scheme, the temperature and humidity are hardly noticed by them. These environmental factors impact their ability to work or to relax minimally, if at all. Such people appear to float above or outside of their physical environment. If you are such a person, you are likely an idealist. You may, however, belong to that group of people who are extremely sensitive to light, color, sound, temperature, and texture. These people are "in" their physical environments in a way that the others are not. If you are such a person, you are probably an Aristotelian.

For a final clue in this matter, examine your spiritual life. To what degree do your spiritual practices involve a physical dimension? Catholic spirituality, for example, makes copious use of physicality as a means of encountering God. Ritualized movement, vestments, sacred objects and places, are all interwoven into the Catholic experience of God. Contrast this approach with the sparse physical minimalism of some Protestant churches. In this spirituality, all the physical trappings of Catholicism have been eliminated so as to produce a single-minded focus on the word of God. If you experience objects and movement as an instrument for contact with God, or the Ultimate, it is likely that you are an Aristotelian. If you experience the physical world as nothing more than a distraction from what is central in your spiritual life, then your experience of the world is likely an idealist one.

Reprise: Dean, Susie, and Hector

You will recall that Dean suspected that his exploration of his supervisor's therapeutic world would only wind up confirming his citizenship in his own therapeutic world. Such, in fact, turned out to be the case. Although he was not aware of it, Dean was an idealist before he had the harrowing experience of sitting through his supervisor's consultation. When the consultation propelled him into learning about the mind–body problem, he became consciously aware of and explicitly committed to the idealism that up to that point had been implicit for him.

Dean's exploration also made him aware that his supervisor was definitely not an idealist. He was, instead, a thoroughgoing Aristotelian. The supervisor's consultation session with Hector, Susie, and their children bore the unmistakably Aristotelian marks of the structural family therapy that he routinely practiced, along with the symbolic experiential flourishes that he occasionally threw in for good measure. (The supervisor explained to Dean that his use of the hand puppet during the session and his kneeling down with Hector in front of Susie had been inspired by the work of symbolic experiential therapists like Whitaker and Andolfi.)

Dean came to appreciate how his supervisor's practice of structural family therapy fit well with his Aristotelian approach to the mind–body issue. Dean also came out of his exploration of the mind–body problem realizing that he had chosen well when he had decided to mold his therapeutic practice on the narrative therapy model. The idealism of that model, he saw, fit well with his own idealist experience of the relationship between body and mind.

However, Dean was not all that consoled by this insight. In the consultation, he had seen Susie and Hector's family respond well to his supervisor's Aristotelian interventions. He wanted to be helpful to the family; he knew, however, that he could not duplicate the Aristotelian session that he had witnessed.

Dean voiced his misgivings to his supervisor, who quickly tried to allay his fears. "The family responded to me in the session because the session was an expression of who I am. If you construct a session that expresses who you are, they will respond to you just as fully. Their response will look different, because they will be responding to something different. But their response will be just as complete."

Dean was a little surprised that he was being urged by his Aristotelian supervisor to construct an idealist therapy. But he was glad for the encouragement that it gave him. He returned to his narrative work with Susie, Hector, and the children. (Following the consultation, Hector agreed to participate in the therapy on an ongoing basis.) The work that he did was much the same as before the consultation, and yet it was also somehow different. It was infused with Dean's newfound enthusiasm for the narrative model, an enthusiasm born of his awareness of the way in which the model expressed something essential about him and his experience of the world. His supervisor's prediction turned out to be correct. The family responded enthusiastically to Dean's narrative work. The therapy ended well. And, this time, there were no return visits.

To Be or To Become?

That Is the Question

"Why did I say that?"

Jamie had just begun her third session with Karyn and Maurice. She had found this case fascinating from the very start. It was Maurice who had contacted the clinic requesting couple therapy for him and his wife. Jamie had noted that fact with interest. Although she was only six months into her internship, she had already grown accustomed to women being the ones to make the initial contact for therapy. The fact that Maurice had been the one to call in this case piqued her interest. She wondered if she was about to meet with people who had managed somehow to free themselves from the pervasive influence of gender-role stereotyping.

Karyn and Maurice did, in fact, prove to be different from the five other couples that Jamie had treated up to this point in her nascent clinical career. The role structure of their marriage was the converse of the arrangement dictated by typical gender-role expectations. Maurice was the more expressive member of the dyad. He was the main customer of the therapy, complaining that Karyn was rarely, if ever, there for him emotionally. He complained that her stressful job as managing partner of a large, successful law firm kept her in her office until very late most evenings and even wound up interfering with a fair number of their weekends. "Even when she's home, she's not home, if you know what I mean. Her head is always preoccupied with this case or that problem employee. I feel that I'm all but invisible to her." Because his job as a high school counselor allowed him to get home most days much earlier than his wife, Maurice also felt that the lion's share of the housekeeping responsibilities fell on his shoulders. "I think that I would be able to accept that without a problem if I felt that I mattered to her."

In the face of Maurice's emotion-laden narrative of complaint, Karyn responded with an air of calm, perhaps even aloof, rationality. She patiently and painstakingly explained to her husband how the current situation of her firm left her absolutely no choice but to put in the long hours that she had been working. In her logical presentation of fact after ineluctable fact, one could easily sense the skills of analysis and persuasion that had allowed her to rise quickly in her profession to the height that she now occupied. A tinge of frustration was evident in her voice. She had clearly made this case before, and one could tell that she fully expected that she would have to make it again.

However, behind the display of analytic pyrotechnics and just beneath the tone of frustration, Jamie could also see unmistakable signs that Karyn truly cared for Maurice and was committed to the marriage.

Jamie fully expected to conduct this case as she had all of her previous cases, utilizing the model of solution-focused therapy. Jamie, in fact, already thought of herself as a solution-focused therapist. In her coursework, she had been drawn to the model's collaborative ethos. She was also attracted to the model's organized and planful approach to therapy, especially as it had been described in some of de Shazer's earlier books (e.g., de Shazer, 1988). She felt that the model's logical manner of proceeding would buffer her from some of the anxiety that she was sure that she would feel in her first few cases. All in all, she thought that the model was a perfect fit for her.

The model had, indeed, served her well in her first few cases. All had apparently had good outcomes, and they had all been relatively brief, just as the model dictated. However, a strange thing had begun to occur a few weeks ago. As Jamie grew more comfortable operating in the role of therapist, she found herself on occasion saying and doing things in sessions that did not fit the solution-focused model in the least. What was worse, she had done these things spontaneously, on the spur of the moment, with no forethought or planning.

An event like that had occurred just seconds ago as Jamie began her third session with Maurice and Karyn. At the end of the second session, Jamie had given the couple an observational task, asking them to note what it was that each of them was doing on occasions when Maurice felt that he was visible to Karyn. Jamie had begun the third session by asking the couple to report on their execution of the assignment.

Maurice was the first to speak, describing a very satisfying dinner conversation that he and Karyn had had the previous Sunday. Jamie was trying to listen attentively to him, attempting to discern what part Maurice had played in helping to create the problem-free transaction that he was describing. However, as she was listening, she found her mind wandering. Something in Maurice's manner of speaking reminded her of her younger brother Kevin. Try as she did to avoid it, she found herself remembering when they were children and Kevin would talk to her in this particular whiny tone that he sometimes used, and she would feel an overwhelming urge to torture him, an urge to which she almost invariably yielded. She had experienced that tone of voice as a sign of weakness in Kevin, and for reasons that she still did not fully comprehend, the sight of Kevin being weak had infuriated her.

It was bad enough that Jamie had drifted off into this reverie while Maurice was dutifully reporting the execution of his homework assignment. What she did next she found absolutely unbelievable. On impulse, she turned to Karyn and said, "You know, I was just thinking about my brother Kevin. He was a great kid, but every once in a while he would get this whiny quality to his voice that would just drive me nuts. In those moments, no matter what he was asking me for, I wouldn't give it to him. I just wanted to kick him 'til he stopped whining. Have you ever felt that way with Maurice?"

Jamie had not even finished saying this to Karyn when she thought to herself, "Why did I say that?" She was so occupied with berating herself that she almost did not notice that Karyn was taking her question very seriously.

"Thank God," she said, "somebody else knows how I feel. I always feel angry whenever Maurice goes into one of his complaining raps, but I feel guilty about feeling that way. So I try to push the anger aside and deal rationally with whatever issue he's talking about. And then he accuses me of being cold and logical, like Mr. Spock on Star Trek. Meanwhile, I'm seething underneath and battling not to show it. I just can't stand it when he sounds weak and needy."

This had happened every single time that Jamie had made what she had come to refer to as one of her spontaneous "blurts." Appalled as she was that she had acted without forethought, her clients had invariably found her "blurts" useful, as Karyn seemed to right now. However, Jamie was little consoled by this fact. As she reflected on what it was about her "blurts" that bothered her, she realized that it was not primarily the fact that they marked a radical departure from the solution-focused model to which she still felt herself committed. What bothered her most about the "blurts" was their spontaneous, "in-the-moment" nature. Isn't therapy supposed to be an organized, planful enterprise, characterized by a logical development leading toward the achievement of well-defined goals? What place do "blurts" have in such an organized enterprise?

Being and Becoming

Jamie's "blurts" exist in the moment. They do not follow logically on what came before in the therapy, and they are not in service of some intended future goal. They simply "are." And that is precisely what bothers Jamie. She fears that if she gives free rein to her "blurts" it may not be long before she is doing a therapy composed entirely of "blurts." What kind of therapy would that be? she wonders.

Such a therapy would be one that privileges a certain mode of existence, a kind of being-in-the-moment, on the part of the therapist. Jamie is correct in sensing that this mode is very different from that which is privileged in therapies that are planful and organized, such as the solution-focused therapy that she was practicing. In such therapies, the therapist at any given moment is always looking back to the way in which the therapy has developed to that point and ahead to the final state toward which he is trying to lead the therapy. In such therapies, the therapist does not exist in the moment, but rather experiences each moment as part of a broader, coherent process that develops over time.

Jamie might be consoled to know that numerous philosophers have experienced and wrestled with the tension that she feels between the "in-the-moment" mode that characterizes her "blurts" and the "in-process" mode that characterizes the planful approaches to therapy. The experience of this tension has given rise to another one of those issues that have become perennial topics in Western philosophy, the issue of being versus becoming.

Historical Backdrop

Becoming

"All things flow; nothing abides." We possess no written work attributed to the pre-Socratic Greek philosopher, Heraclitus. What we know of his thought is gleaned from fragments, isolated aphorisms of his that were reported by later Greek philosophers. Despite this fact, Heraclitus is one of the most influential figures in the Western philosophical tradition. The saying of his that stands at the head of this paragraph is the source of one of the polarities that constitutes the being versus becoming issue.

When he declared that "all things flow," Heraclitus asserted the primacy of change, of becoming, in the universe. For Heraclitus, the universe is not composed of stuff, like atoms or such, which then happens to undergo change. If that were the case, the stable stuff of the universe would be primary and change secondary. On the contrary, Heraclitus sees change itself as the stuff of which the universe is made. Reality *is* change. Becoming is primary (Capek, 1967).

As we will see shortly, Heraclitus' bold assertion did not long go unchallenged by other Greek philosophers. Nonetheless, his declaration of the primacy of becoming established an intellectual tradition that has endured to the present day. Major modern philosophers like William James and Henri Bergson stand squarely in the tradition to which Heraclitus gave rise.

William James showed his debt to Heraclitus when he analyzed human consciousness as an ever-flowing stream rather than a succession of discrete, stable "states" (Capek, 1967). Bergson expanded this analysis when he noted that the stream of human consciousness is essentially temporal in nature. The present moment of consciousness is experienced as *present* precisely because the past is retained in memory and a future is anticipated (Goudge, 1967). Without a remembered past and an anticipated future, our mode of existence would always be in the moment, in a timeless Now. Bergson describes how our past establishes the parameters for our expectations of the future. He further notes how our expectations for the future filter what we perceive in the present. Present perception is thus constructed out of future expectations that are constrained by past experiences (Lacey, 1998). In this way, past, present, and future coexist in human consciousness and mutually influence each other. Bergson judges that music provides a perfect illustration for this mutual indwelling of past, present, and future in human consciousness. A melody is heard as a melody, he observes, only if past notes that have already been heard are retained in memory and the future development of the piece is anticipated. Thus, in music as in human consciousness, becoming is primary and essential. Reality *is* process.

Bergson did not limit his analysis to human consciousness. In his view, human consciousness represents a microcosm of what transpires in the universe as a whole. Thus, he described the universe as one vast process of becoming, temporally structured in the same way that human consciousness is structured.

Being

While not certain of the fact, most contemporary scholars are of the opinion that the pre-Socratic philosopher Parmenides lived some time after Heraclitus. What is certain is that his view of reality was the opposite of that of Heraclitus.

Heraclitus, we have seen, asserted that "all things flow." In distinction, Parmenides argued that any talk about change is essentially and necessarily self-contradictory. Thus, becoming is illusory. We human beings perceive change because of the limitations of our intelligence. But change does not exist. What is, is. What is not, never was and never will be. In denying the reality of becoming, Parmenides proclaimed the primacy of being.

As counterintuitive as it might be, Parmenides' thought has dominated the Western philosophical tradition in the 2,500 years since it was first articulated. "In most, though not all, philosophical systems Being was given prominence while Becoming was placed in an inferior and subordinate role" (Capek, 1967, p. 76). Not many of Parmenides' disciples have been as radical as he in declaring the absolute nonreality of change. However, those that have ascribed some degree of reality to change have been unequivocal in declaring the domain of becoming to be a subordinate and defective domain. Only the timeless domain of being exists in the fullest sense.

The Roman philosopher Plotinus is typical. Plotinus describes the world of becoming in which we human beings live as having arisen out of a process of degradation, a fall of sorts. Where we fell from is the realm of being, which Plotinus calls the One. The One exists in timeless, unchanging simplicity. The One alone truly exists. We and the world of becoming that we inhabit are mere shadows of the One.

Plotinus' thought contains an element that became standard in the Parmenidean tradition. If we human beings lead a defective and insubstantial existence in the domain of becoming, it is natural that we should try to modify our consciousness so that we can ascend to the domain of being. Indeed, Plotinus teaches that the goal of human existence is to experience the One. "This ecstasy—repeatedly experienced by Plotinus himself—is undoubtedly the climactic moment of [human] life" (Merlan, 1967, p. 355). In this experience, human beings leave the world of time and change, the world of memory and anticipation, and enter a timeless, eternal Now.

St. Augustine gave a characteristically Christian spin to the intellectual tradition begun by Parmenides. Augustine assumes that God, precisely because he is God, exists in the domain of being rather than becoming (Matthews, 1998). God exists outside of time. Time, in fact, is the product of human consciousness. It is the goal of human existence to ascend out of time into union with God, seeing him as he truly is. This state, which can only become constant after death, can be experienced in a transitory way while still alive in mystical experience.

You might think that an unbridgeable chasm separates thinkers like Plotinus and Augustine from modern scientific thinkers. Such, it turns out, is not the case.

Most of modern science, in fact, stands firmly within the intellectual tradition begun by Parmenides. As much as Plotinus and Augustine did, science aspires to ascend out of the world of becoming into the timeless domain of being. The means it seeks to employ in this ascent is not mysticism, however, but mathematics. The holy grail of scientific endeavor is to describe the universe thoroughly in mathematical terms. Were this goal to be achieved, becoming would disappear. All past states of the universe and all future states, as well, could be known in the here-and-now by means of the mathematical descriptions that would have been devised. Thus, escape from the flow of time and existence in a timeless Now would be achieved, not by union with God or the One, but by contemplation of the fundamental equations of nature.

The articulation in 1927 of the Uncertainty Principle by the physicist Werner Heisenberg appeared to throw a colossal monkey wrench into this centuries-old scientific dream. By showing that the coordinates of certain subatomic events could not be known with precision, Heisenberg appeared to introduce indeterminacy into the heart of the universe. If the Uncertainty Principle tells us something fundamental about the universe, then the dream of finding a set of mathematical equations that can precisely predict all future states of the universe is dashed. Immersion in the flow of becoming becomes unavoidable, and Heraclitus triumphs.

The dream, however, has not died easily. Albert Einstein, for instance, refused to admit that the Uncertainty Principle tells us something about the nature of things-in-themselves. What it describes, he maintained, is simply the limitations of our ability to observe. We may not be able to specify the coordinates of some subatomic events, but that does not mean that the coordinates themselves are not determinate. Einstein to his death retained the dream of devising a mathematical description of the universe that could, in principle, yield all past and future states of the universe. Contemporary physicists who are pursuing a unified field theory maintain his dream. By means of mathematics, they seek to ascend out of the flux of the world of our experience into an eternal Now that includes all of reality within itself. As much as Parmenides, these scientists proclaim the primacy of being.

Therapeutic Ramifications

Though she was completely unaware of it, Jamie's "blurts" had ushered her into the centuries-old philosophical debate over whether primacy should be assigned to being or becoming. For Jamie, this was not at all an abstract issue. Her "blurts" had led her to wonder whether it is legitimate to construct a therapy in which the therapist operates primarily in the moment, without reference either to the past development of the therapy or to intended future goals. Although she did not know it, what Jamie was asking is whether it is legitimate to construct a therapy that assigns primacy to being over becoming.

If she had had the opportunity to read the previous chapters of this book, Jamie might have felt pretty confident that such a way of doing therapy is, in fact, legitimate. In those chapters, we have seen repeatedly how important debates in the Western philosophical tradition have left their marks on the field of family therapy. Thus, we might expect that the being versus becoming debate has also made its impact felt. We might expect that some of the models of family therapy have been influenced by the intellectual tradition begun by Parmenides. These would be models that organize their practitioners to hold themselves as much as possible in a "now" mode that looks neither back to what has already transpired in therapy nor ahead toward what might happen. These would be models that might countenance Jamie's "blurts" as legitimate interventions. Such models might (somewhat inelegantly) be called "being" therapies. We might also expect to find models that have emerged out of the Heraclitean tradition. Seeing therapy as a coherent process that develops over time, these models would produce in their practitioners a consciousness that immediately relates any given moment of therapy to what has come before and what is expected to come after. These would be the "becoming" therapies.

Our expectations would not disappoint us. As we are about to see, there are indeed "being" models of family therapy and "becoming" models. But before we begin exploring these two distinct ways of doing therapy, we need a word of caution, lest we wind up caricaturing both kinds of models. We will see shortly that the "being" models do indeed privilege an "in-the-moment" mentality on the part of the therapist. However, because therapy is not mysticism—at least, not all that frequently—it would be foolish to think that practitioners of the "being" models are not at all conscious of the temporal flow of the therapies in which they participate. They certainly are aware of what has come before in the therapy, and, more often than not, they have at least a vague idea of the direction in which they would like the therapy to tend. However, assigning primacy to being as they do, these therapists try very hard to experience each moment of therapy on its own terms, as an entity unto itself, without seeing that moment through a lens that is so heavily theorized as to dictate for all intents and purposes how it will be experienced and interpreted.

It is also the case that the "becoming" models of family therapy privilege a "process" mentality on the part of their practitioners, one that sees a given moment of therapy as having meaning only when it is understood as part of a process that develops over time in an orderly fashion. It would be a mistake, however, to think that any of the "becoming" models are deterministic, presuming to know with precision how any given client system will evolve over the course of therapy. Assigning primacy to becoming as they do, these models certainly offer broad, general descriptions of how successful therapies develop over time, and they expect their practitioners to make use of these descriptions as they go about the business of making decisions in therapy. However, not one of these models conceives of therapy as what Humberto Maturana (1978) calls "instructive interaction," that is, the programming of specific outcomes from client systems. Not one pretends that it can predict how a given client system will respond to a given intervention at a given point in therapy. Rather, the description of the therapy process that each of these models provides is intended to provide therapists with nothing more than the means to make informed guesses as to how to proceed at a given juncture of therapy. The guidance that the models provide does not guarantee that a given intervention will achieve its intended purpose. Thus, the therapist is required to think of each and every intervention that she delivers as an experiment or a probe (Giacomo & Weissmark, 1986). How the therapist proceeds after delivering the intervention will depend entirely on how the client system responds to the intervention. Within the overarching frames that the "becoming" models provide, therapy remains a "dance" of sorts, in which the therapist oscillates between leading and following.

Keeping in mind, then, that "being" therapists are not mystics and that "becoming" therapists do not behave as computer programmers, let us proceed to explore the way in which the being versus becoming issue has made itself felt in the field of family therapy.

"Being" Therapies

Symbolic Experiential Family Therapy.   We are most fully human, symbolic experiential therapy proclaims, when we are in the midst of deep, emotional experiencing. Such experiencing knows no logic. It does not arrange itself in nice, neat sequences. It comes when it comes, goes when it goes, and its content is determined by its own inner logic, not by somebody's idea of what "should" be. If human life is to be lived in the service of this kind of experiencing, it cannot be organized according to plans that are the product of rational deliberation. Instead, we human beings should endeavor as much as possible to keep ourselves "in the moment," as radically open as we can possibly be to whatever the given moment may present to us.

Symbolic experiential therapy proclaims the primacy of being in everyday human existence. It exhorts us to live in the Now. Thus, it should come as no surprise to us that the model prescribes that therapy, too, should take place in the Now. The model itself is constructed in such a way as to help its practitioner cultivate an "in-the-moment" mentality. It contains very few theoretical formulations. All human dysfunction is seen to be rooted in one fundamental cause, the repression and denial of feelings, drives, and impulses. Consequently, the model prescribes only one "cure" for all human dysfunction: people who are malfunctioning need to be led to experience and to give expression to their feelings and impulses. Unsaddled by more elaborate theoretical constructs that she would otherwise need to keep in mind, the symbolic experiential therapist is freed to devote her attention to what really matters, in therapy as in life, namely, the experience of the present moment. It is her "in-the-moment" experiencing, and not theory, that provides the experiential therapist with the matter for her interventions. It is her experiencing, and the way in which she gives expression to this experiencing, that holds promise of pushing her clients past their fears, beyond their rationalistic attempts to control and impart order to life, into new zones of deep, emotional experiencing of self.

Dependent as it is on the therapist's idiosyncratic, "in-the-moment" experiencing, symbolic experiential therapy offers almost no description of the way in which a "typical" successful therapy develops over time. In fact, I have heard it reported that Carl Whitaker was so devoted to conducting therapy from an "in-the-moment" posture that he always assumed that any given session with a client family would be the last time that he would see the family. To be sure, Whitaker was not beyond making some general observations about the process of therapy. He spoke, for instance, about two battles that typically occur between family and therapist, the battle for structure and the battle for initiative (Whitaker & Keith, 1981). The first refers to the struggle for control over who will participate in therapy sessions. Whitaker advises that the therapist must win this battle in order for therapy to succeed. The second battle is over who will provide the energy that drives the therapy. Whitaker asserts that the therapist must lose this battle, so that the family is forced to assume primary responsibility for what happens in therapy. While offering some generic descriptions of the therapy process, these observations provide nothing like a cookbook or a manual for how therapy should be done. Generalizations notwithstanding, symbolic experiential therapy is adamant in assigning primacy to the therapist's "in-the-moment" experiencing. In doing so, it marks itself out as a "being" therapy.

When Jamie took seriously the experiences that gave rise to her "blurts," she was behaving like a symbolic experiential therapist. When she warily contemplated what a therapy composed entirely of "blurts" would look like, she was contemplating symbolic experiential family therapy. In order to encourage her to enter the fold, a symbolic experiential observer might ask Jamie to consider how useful Karyn found her "blurt" about the way in which dealing with Maurice reminded her of the fury she used to feel toward her brother Kevin. The adherent to experiential therapy would assess that it was no fluke that Karyn found Jamie's sharing of her personal experience useful. Deep, emotional experiencing possesses a wisdom that is nonetheless real for the fact that it cannot be quantified, dissected, or analyzed. Jamie's spontaneous expression of an experience that she was having catalyzed a similar kind of expression on Karyn's part. If Jamie is able in her work with Karyn and Maurice to continue to blurt out the experiences that they trigger in her, then the couple may become more expressive of the feelings and drives that they are currently repressing. Jamie need not know what those feelings and drives are. All she need do is to maintain an "in-the-moment" attentiveness to her own feelings and impulses, and then to give some kind of expression to them. The rest is up to Karyn and Maurice.

Collaborative Language Systems Therapy.   In a whole host of ways, symbolic experiential family therapy and collaborative language systems therapy are as different as night and day. Yet, they share one crucial element in common. In their vision of therapy, each proclaims the primacy of being over becoming.

As adamantly as Carl Whitaker, Harlene Anderson and Harry Goolishian reject an approach to therapy that preordains how a successful therapy should develop over time. Like Whitaker, they want the therapist at any given moment of therapy to be more involved with the client than with a model that purports to tell the therapist how the client should be interpreted. Along with Whitaker, Anderson and Goolishian want the therapist to be fully engrossed in his experience of the client. Thus, the language systems therapist, as much as the experiential therapist, is counseled to maintain an "in-the-moment" posture, one that accepts the experience of the given moment on its own terms and avoids seeing it as simply an element in a temporal process whose overall contours are known ahead of time.

The symbolic experiential therapist and the collaborative language systems therapist both participate in therapy from an "in-the-moment" posture. However, what each attends to as he or she resides in the moment is quite different. The difference here is the result of the divergent stands that each of these models takes on the mind–body issue, which we explored in the last chapter. Rooted in her Aristotelian view of the interdependence of mind and body, the experiential therapist attends to emotional experiencing, that "in-the-gut" phenomenon in which the boundaries between mind and body are indiscernible. Operating out of his idealist view of the mind–body issue, it is words and meaning to which the language systems therapist attends as he rests in the moment.

While they attend to quite different things, the way in which the language systems therapist and the experiential therapist respond to what they see and hear is very similar. Neither tries to push clients in a preordained direction, as they would if they were practicing "becoming" therapies. Rather, each tries to behave in a way that will spur clients simply to become more fully the unique, idiosyncratic individuals that they already are. Thus, the experiential therapist gives expression to her "in-the-moment" experiences, not to get her clients to have similar experiences, but to help them deepen their own idiosyncratic self-experiencing. In the same way, the language systems therapist does not try to push his clients' meaning-generating talk in any particular direction. Rather, he asks questions designed to help his clients further elaborate the meanings that they themselves have already cocreated in conversation with the other members of the problem-organizing system. These questions are well crafted if they leave clients a high degree of freedom to elaborate those meanings in any way that they see fit. Anderson (1997) calls such questions "process-oriented questions" and distinguishes them from "content-oriented questions," which endeavor to move clients toward content deemed important by the therapist's model. "I do not want to seek any particular kind of information; rather, I aim to stay close to the understanding of the moment, working within and slowly outside that parameter, and make only small shifts in the conversation" (p. 160).

The collaborative language systems therapist's only goal is to keep the conversation in the problem-organizing system going. She is willing to accept whatever direction the clients choose to move the conversation, because she is confident that an evolving conversation inevitably will define the presenting problem out of existence, no matter in what particular direction it evolves. Thus, the therapist feels no need to lead clients; he need not look ahead to where the therapy "should" wind up. The therapist need only stay "in sync" with the client system, maintaining an "in-the-moment" posture. Anderson (1997) makes an implicit reference to the being versus becoming issue when she calls this way of doing therapy a "way of being" rather than a "system for doing." "The uncertainty that results when a therapist's talk, action, and thought are informed on a moment-by-moment basis, and therefore not known ahead of time, is often unsettling because in the Western world we are accustomed to the certainty of recipelike informed behaviors" (p. 98).

Because the collaborative language system model relies so heavily on its practitioner's "in-the-moment" experiencing, it is impossible to fantasize how a language systems therapist might respond to Maurice and Karyn. All that can be said with certainty is that the therapist would listen for meanings that Karyn and Maurice take to be self-evident. For the language systems therapist, no meaning is self-evident; every meaning is worthy of question and of further elaboration. Thus, the therapist might ask Maurice to explain further what he means when he says that Karyn is not "there" for him. He might ask Karyn to explain further what she means when she says that the current situation of her law firm "requires" her to work long hours. The therapist will not ask these questions thinking that he already knows what the answers will be. Nor will he prefer Maurice and Karyn to give one kind of answer rather than another. He questions just to keep the conversation between Karyn and Maurice going, confident that if it does so the conversation will eventually "dis-solve" the problem.

In collaborative language systems therapy and symbolic experiential therapy, we encounter models that purposely keep their theoretical constructs to a minimum so that their practitioners can devote all their attention to a focal, "in-the-moment" attentiveness to their clients. These models are confident that the moment-to-moment experiencing of the therapist will provide her with all that she needs in order to know how to proceed in therapy.

We will now turn our attention to models of family therapy that have no such confidence in the therapeutic potential of the Now. For these models, any given moment of therapy has significance only when it is seen as part of a larger, encompassing process that develops over time. Therapists can discern the therapeutic opportunities latent in any given moment only if they view that moment against the background of where the therapy has been and where they hope to lead it in the future. These are models that assign primacy to becoming over being. They are the "becoming" models of family therapy.

"Becoming" Therapies

The Strategic Therapies.   The strategic therapies are the quintessential "becoming" therapies. As their name indicates, these models are all about planfulness. "In-the-moment" spontaneity is simply not part of the strategic therapist's repertoire. Every intervention that the strategic therapist delivers is part of an elaborated plan that unfolds over time as the therapy develops.

The strategic therapy model developed by Haley and Madanes is typical in this regard.

> Haley's approach could be called "plan-ahead therapy." He helped therapists consider the importance of developing strategies for the overall course of therapy, as

well as anticipating a family's reaction to events in their lives, and in therapy. He also encouraged the planning of each session and developed a how-to model of a first session with families. . . (Nichols & Schwartz, 1995, p. 414).

Haley and Madanes see several reasons why therapy needs to be such a planful enterprise. To begin, in order for therapy to succeed in eradicating a family's presenting problem, a rather thoroughgoing change, in their view, needs to occur in the family. The family organizational map, which the problem-maintaining sequence serves to preserve, needs to be altered. In Haley's experience, it is nearly impossible to move a family's organization from a dysfunctional arrangement to a functional one in one fell swoop. Organizational maps need to be changed in stages, and such incremental change requires the therapist to plan ahead (Haley, 1976). Moreover, most client families can be expected to resist the therapist's attempts to change their organization. In order to have any chance of overcoming such resistance, the therapist needs to exercise foresight and to carefully plan her interventions. Madanes (1990) has provided some general guidelines regarding which kinds of interventions will likely work with which kinds of families. However, the hallmark of Madanes-Haley strategic therapy remains the development of unique treatment strategies that are suited to the unique characteristics of each client family. Such tailoring of treatment to family once again requires careful planning on the part of the therapist.

In order to give you a sense of the kind of planning in which a Haley-Madanes strategist engages, let us consider how such a therapist might respond to Maurice and Karyn. Based on the model's understanding of how family systems malfunction, the therapist might judge that these two people are experiencing problems in their marriage because a hierarchical arrangement is governing a relationship that should be organized symmetrically. (If the therapist has feminist sensibilities, she might also hypothesize that the arrangement is experienced by the couple to be all the more dissatisfying because the particular hierarchical organization that the couple has places Karyn in the one-up position, a position not generally occupied by women in relationships.) Based on this assessment, the therapist would set as the ultimate goal of the therapy the creation of a more egalitarian structure in the relationship.

The therapist would next turn her attention to planning how to get from here to there. As she does so, she might note the following problem. In order for his status in the relationship to be elevated, Maurice would need to experience himself as someone with influence, as someone who shapes Karyn's behavior as much as he himself is shaped by hers. Unfortunately, Maurice seems content to do little more in the therapy than to engage in an unending litany of complaints about how his wife mistreats him. How, then, empower someone who seems committed to being a perennial victim? The therapist could assign all of her directives to Karyn, but giving her all the work would entail the metamessage that she is the only one who can be counted on to work in the therapy. By sending such a message, the therapist would only solidify Karyn's elevated status in the couple system.

To solve this problem, the therapist might devise a sequence of directives to be delivered to the couple over the course of several sessions. The directives might be "packaged" utilizing the following frame:

> Maurice, you have every right to be attended to more by Karyn. However, Karyn, your work is currently subjecting you to demands on your time that are genuinely outside of your control. So, the therapy can do no more than help the two of you practice in preparation for the time when Karyn will be free to give Maurice more of the attention that he deserves.

To provide them with this "practice," the couple might be directed to set aside a specific amount of time when they will pretend that they are client (Maurice) and attorney (Karyn) rather than husband and wife. Karyn is to think of herself as Maurice's advocate, representing him in a complaint that he is filing against his wife. As the client, it is Maurice's job to detail his complaints in as clear and reasonable a way as possible so that his attorney can understand and represent him well. As his attorney, Karyn can make suggestions to him how best to present his complaints, with an eye to increasing the chances that he will "win" his case. Because she is an expert at what she does, it would be in Maurice's best interests to take her advice seriously. However, it remains the case that, as his attorney, Karyn works for him, and so she needs in the end to represent him in the way that he wants.

The therapist would carefully control the amount of time that the couple is directed to engage in this pretend exercise, gradually increasing the allotted time from session to session. As she tracks their reports of how they are implementing the directives, she will look for signs that the couple's engagement in the pretend exercise is having the desired effect of gradually changing the structure of their relationship. Based on her reading of how the directives are affecting the couple's organization, she will either stick with her plan as she originally developed it or modify it in whatever ways seem better suited to achieving the therapy's ultimate goal.

I have engaged in this extended fantasy of how a Madanes-Haley strategist might operate in the case of Karyn and Maurice in order to convey to you how detailed, elaborate, and particularized are the plans that this model counsels its practitioners to develop. Here, we are at the antipodes of the "in-the-moment" spontaneity advocated by the "being" therapies. Here, every moment of therapy makes sense only when it is seen in the context of the entire temporal span of the therapy process, both past and future. This is the essential characteristic of a "becoming" therapy.

The other strategic models of family therapy are every bit as planful as the Haley-Madanes model. In each of the models, the kind of planning in which the therapist engages is determined by the model's view of what goes wrong in a malfunctioning family, and of what, as a result, needs to be changed in therapy.

We have seen that in the MRI model therapy is narrowly aimed at eradicating the circular interactional sequence in which the presenting problem is seen to be embedded. Thus, MRI treatment planning focuses single-mindedly on achieving this goal. The MRI therapist first elicits from the client family a statement of their presenting problem, being careful to prompt the family to state the problem (or at least its solution) in behavioral terms. Once this is done, the therapist will ask questions designed to reveal the sequence of behaviors that family members are currently using to attempt to solve their presenting problem. In the view of the MRI therapist, it is this very interactional sequence that is serving to maintain the problem in existence. After he has assessed the problem-maintaining sequence, the therapist devises a strategy to interrupt the sequence. The strategy will inevitably involve the use of directives delivered to the family. However, what directives will be used, and what reframes will be employed to "sell" them to the family, will depend entirely on the particular characteristics of the family. Once the therapist begins to act on the individualized plan he has devised, he will, of course, look for evidence regarding whether the plan is producing its intended effect. If the evidence indicates that it is not, the therapist will make appropriate revisions.

Like the Madanes-Haley model, the strategic therapy of the first Milan team sees presenting problems as serving to maintain dysfunctional organizational maps in families. But, whereas the Haley-Madanes strategist is satisfied with some generic ideas about how family maps become dysfunctional (i.e., by the presence of incongruous hierarchies), the Milan strategist relishes highly particularized descriptions of the ways in which a particular client-family's map is malfunctioning. As a result of its interest in the idiosyncrasies of each client-family's organization, the Milan model is less devoted to long-term therapeutic planning than are the other two strategic models. In order to make the most of feedback that is forthcoming on a session-to-session basis from the client family, the Milan therapist limits her strategies to one-session increments. However, it would be a mistake to read this fact as indicating that Milan strategic therapy is a "being" therapy. Nothing could be further from the truth.

The practice of the first Milan team was so highly ritualized and formulaic that it left absolutely no room for "in-the-moment" therapeutic spontaneity. Before any given session, the therapy team would meet together to hypothesize about what they would observe in the upcoming session. During the first part of the session, the therapists in the room with the family would utilize the model's questioning technology either to figure out the client-family's organizational map (if this was the first session of the therapy), or to use the family's response to last session's intervention to refine the therapists' understanding of the family's map. While the first part of the session was taking place, the team behind the one-way mirror would also be engaged in this task of reading, or rereading, the family's organization. During the midsession break, the interviewing therapists would join their colleagues behind the mirror so that the team could construct a consensual hypothesis about the family and how it was responding to the therapy. Based on this hypothesis, the team would devise the session's closing message and prescription, which the interviewing therapists would deliver to the family when they returned to the other side of the mirror. Following the session, the entire team would meet again for a post-session discussion, during which further refinements in the team's understanding of the family's organization would be made and plans crystallized for the next session.

In the Milan model, as much as in the other strategic models, planning based on assessment, and assessment refined by feedback, stand at the heart of the therapeutic enterprise. The Milan therapist may not look as far ahead in therapy as her other strategic colleagues do. She may be more apt than they are to make significant revisions in her understanding of client families more frequently. However, for her as much as for them, therapy that is done in the moment is inconceivable. For the Milan strategist, therapy makes sense only as a coherent process that develops over time.

Structural Family Therapy. Organized development over time is also a hallmark of structural family therapy. It is not that the structural therapist has no "in-the-moment" experiences during therapy. A structural family therapist working with Karyn and Maurice could well be viscerally moved by Maurice's incessant complaining or by Karyn's cold condescension. However, he would not treat these "in-the-moment" experiences as therapeutic entities unto themselves, as would a symbolic experientialist, for instance. Instead, the structural therapist would immediately set these experiences in the context of his theoretical understanding of families and how they malfunction. He would mine the experiences for what that can tell him about the dysfunctional map that is organizing Karyn and Maurice's relational life with each other. He would then use this understanding to plan ways in which he might restructure that map. Thus, almost immediately, the structural family therapist's "in-the-moment" experiencing ceases being in the moment. When experience becomes a source of reflection and planning rather than a stimulus for immediate response, it becomes part of a process that develops over time. The structural therapist responds to his in-session experiences not as a "being" therapist would, but as a "becoming" therapist.

The "becoming" therapy that the structural family therapist conducts evolves through distinct phases as it develops over time. In the first phase, the therapist joins the client family. He endeavors to experience the family from an insider's perspective so that he can develop a feel for the family's current organization and for the more adaptive organizational alternatives that are currently lying dormant in the family's repertoire. By relating to the client family from an "insider" position, the therapist also gains leverage with the family, leverage that he will need when he sets about the task of trying to change the family's organizational map. During this joining phase, the therapist seeks and welcomes the kind of "in-the-moment" experiences just described. He uses these subjective experiences, as well as more "objective" observations that he makes in the joining phase, to construct a structural understanding of the client family.

In the process of joining Karyn and Maurice, a structural family therapist would likely come to assess their presenting complaints as being rooted in the same one-up (Karyn)/one-down (Maurice) complementarity that would be noted by a Madanes-Haley strategist. He would experience firsthand how Maurice's emotional complaining invites the kind of cerebral lecturing in which Karyn engages. He would also experience the anger and impotence that Karyn's unflappable, condescending rationality can easily induce in anyone who is subjected to it for any length of time. As he joins the couple system, the therapist would also develop a feel for how long the spouses are willing to engage in open conflict before they seek to end it, perhaps by Karyn taking flight into her work, or the in-session equivalent, attempting to engage the therapist in irrelevant, work-related conversation.

When the therapist judges that he has constructed an adequate structural understanding of the client family, he turns his efforts to restructuring—changing the family's organizational map. This undertaking will pass through two distinct phases. In the first, the therapist focuses on challenging and destabilizing the status quo, the family's current organization. This, of course, will be a planful affair. Based on his reading of this particular family's idiosyncrasies, the therapist will choose interventions from his repertoire that appear suited to the task of undermining the family's map. The therapist anticipates that his efforts during this phase may meet with resistance on the part of the client family, which could well attempt to maintain its current map. Thus, this phase of therapy frequently has the character of a struggle—a "polemic," I have heard Minuchin call it.

A structural therapist working with Maurice and Karyn might utilize the technique of unbalancing during this phase of therapy (Minuchin & Fishman, 1981). To destabilize the couple's structural status quo, he might align himself for considerable periods of time with Karyn, seeking via the coalition to induce her to replace her controlled, controlling lecturing with a congruent display of the anger that she feels toward Maurice but almost never (directly) expresses. If the tactic succeeds in escalating the level of conflict between the spouses, the therapist might seek to undermine their relational organization further by keeping them engaged with each other past the point where they would normally cut off conflictual exchange.

If the phase described above is successful, it concludes with a therapeutic crisis, marked by the definitive dissolution of the client-family's dysfunctional organization. This crisis is frequently accompanied by an intensification of the presenting problem that brought the family into therapy (cf. Stanton, Todd, & Associates, 1982). If the therapist is not induced by the crisis into behaving in ways that allow the family to return to its original organizational map, the therapy enters into the second restructuring phase. Blocked from returning to its old organization, the family begins to activate organizational alternatives in its repertoire that have not been used for a long time, if ever. The family experiments with these new arrangements as it seeks to stabilize a new map. The therapist during this phase tries to give the family as much space as possible to "try on" these new relational arrangements. Some of these arrangements may not, in his judgment, be all that functional. However, if at all possible, the therapist during this phase does not return to the adversarial stance that characterized his posture during the preceding phase of therapy. In the interest of promoting the family's search for a new structure, the therapist during the current phase is more inclined to see the therapeutic glass as half-full rather than half-empty. He sees his job as a nurturer rather than a challenger. He will selectively look for in-session interactional events that he can congratulate and reinforce. In doing so, he may well pass over without comment any number of events that, were the therapy in its previous phase, he might make the focus of intense challenge.

During this phase of therapy, a structural therapist working with Karyn and Maurice would look to reinforce any in-session behaviors enacted by either of them that could become part of a new, more functional relational organization. Toward this end, the therapist might congratulate efforts spontaneously made by Maurice to engage Karyn in collaborative problem solving regarding how the household tasks should be divided. He might reinforce efforts made by Karyn to display to Maurice more vulnerable aspects of herself that she typically keeps private from him.

Once the client-family's work to stabilize a more functional organization develops a momentum of its own, the structural family therapist negotiates the termination of the therapy. In doing so, he brings to an end an enterprise that has undergone a process of organic development over time. No moment of structural family stands as an entity unto itself. Each moment finds meaning only when it is set into the context of the whole sweep of the therapy. For this reason, structural family therapy stands as a classic "becoming" therapy.

Psychoanalytic Family Therapy.   Like the structural family therapist, the psychoanalytic family therapist has her fair share of "in-the-moment" experiences in the therapies that she conducts. However, she, like her structural colleague, tries her best to lift these experiences out of the moment and to set them against a broader, theory-saturated background. She uses her experiences as a source of data, as a springboard for hypothesizing. She does not, as a "being" therapist would, respond to them in the moment. Thus, the therapy that the psychoanalytic therapist constructs also occupies the ranks of the "becoming" therapies.

As is true in the other "becoming" therapies that we have examined thus far, psychoanalytic family therapy follows a course that moves from assessment through planning to intervention. Of course, what assessment, planning, and intervention look like varies widely among the strategic, structural, and psychoanalytic models as a result of their widely varying understanding of human beings and how they malfunction.

The understanding that psychoanalytic family therapy, in all of its various forms, seeks to construct inevitably focuses on the relationship that it believes exists between its clients' current relational behavior and their developmental histories. Different psychoanalytic approaches describe human development differently; as a result, different approaches might offer different conceptualizations of how a given client came to behave in the way that he or she is currently behaving. Nonetheless, all of the analytic approaches see current relational behavior as being "hardwired" by developmental history that makes its impact felt through current intrapsychic structure. In order to know how to intervene with a given client family, the analytic therapist needs to understand family members' intrapsychic structuring and how it was produced by their childhood experiences.

Like the structural therapist, the psychoanalytic family therapist uses both "objective" and "subjective" data to construct her understanding of client families. Objective data consists of information reported to the therapist by family members regarding their families of origin. This data allows the therapist to begin to form hypotheses regarding the developmental trajectories followed by her clients, and the ways in which childhood experiences are influencing their current relational behavior toward each other. It is, however, the subjective domain, the "in-the-moment" experiences that her clients trigger in her, that provides the analytic therapist with the richest source of data about her clients. We are, of course, speaking here about the therapist's countertransferential reactions to her clients. The thoughts, fantasies, feelings, and impulses that arise spontaneously in the therapist as she sits with her client families provide invaluable clues to the intrapsychic structuring of the family members.

These subjective experiences of the therapist can provide this understanding only if they are reflected on rather than acted on. As does her structural colleague, the analytic family therapist does not allow her "in-the-moment" experiences to remain in the moment. She does with these experiences what the "being" therapist adamantly avoids doing; she processes them through the filter of theory. By applying psychoanalytic understanding to her in-session experiences, the therapist distances herself from them. Thus, the experiences cease being in the moment and become part of a larger whole that develops over time.

An analytic therapist working with Maurice might become aware that she experiences feelings of anger as she interacts with him in the therapeutic setting. As she probes her experiencing more deeply, she might also become aware of a felt need to suppress her anger and to protect Maurice from it. The therapist resists the impulse simply to act on these feelings. Instead, combining her in-session experience with what she has been told by Maurice about his emotionally withholding mother and his histrionic, alcoholic father, the therapist uses psychoanalytic theory to begin to construct an understanding of Maurice's intrapsychic structure. She begins to see the anger that she experiences when she interacts with Maurice as really his own anger, which he has induced her to experience through the process of projective identification. In trying to make sense of her felt need to protect Maurice from the anger that she feels, the therapist recalls Maurice's recollection, reported in an earlier session, that the few times that he "lost it" and expressed anger to his mother, she had given him the silent treatment for weeks. The therapist thus begins to see Maurice's current relational behavior toward both herself and Karyn as being driven by a rage whose original object was Maurice's mother, a rage that Maurice denies and covers up with his impotent whining.

As in structural and strategic therapy, assessment leads to treatment planning in psychoanalytic family therapy. However, because analytic therapists do not practice the kind of therapeutic activism that their strategic and structural colleagues do, the kind of planning that they engage in looks very different from the planning that strategic and structural therapists do. The key intervention in psychoanalytic family therapy is interpretation. In this intervention, the analytic therapist helps her clients see how their current relational behavior is rooted in past unresolved conflicts. The insight elicited by interpretation frees clients to cease repeating self-defeating behaviors. It empowers them to resume their developmental trajectories, which got stuck at some point in the past. It allows them to see their current relational partners realistically, as persons in their own right, rather than simply as foils on whom their internal conflicts can be projected.

In order for it to achieve this curative effect, interpretation must be well timed. "[I]nterpretations, to be effective, should be limited to preconscious material—that which the patient is almost aware of; interpretations of unconscious material arouse anxiety, which means they will be rejected" (Nichols & Schwartz, 1995, p. 267). If the therapist interprets too much too soon, clients will either reject the interpretation or accept it in a merely cognitive, superficial manner. Hence, the planning that the analytic therapist does is not so much a planning for action as it is a planning for waiting. The therapist uses the understanding that she has constructed of her clients' intrapsychic functioning as a means to restrain herself from intervening prematurely. Her psychoanalytic assessment of her clients certainly provides her with the material for her interpretations. But, just as importantly, her assessment helps her to know when to interpret and when simply to wait.

> The discipline involved in learning to interfere minimally and to scrutinize one's responses to eliminate unessential or leading interventions is a critical part of psychoanalytic technique, with individuals or with families. . . . Two or three [interpretations] per session is typical. Most of the rest of the analytic therapist's activity is devoted to eliciting material without becoming overly directive (Nichols & Schwartz, 1995, pp. 275–276).

The planning engaged in by the strategic and structural therapist expresses itself in action. The planning engaged in by the psychoanalytic family therapist expresses itself mostly in waiting. However, this should not obscure the fact that analytic therapy is every bit as planful as the strategic and structural therapies. For it, as much as for them, every moment of therapy makes sense only when it is seen as part of a larger process that develops coherently over time. It, as much as they, is a "becoming" therapy.

Bowen Family Systems Therapy. While they do not allow them to remain in the moment, structural and psychoanalytic family therapists do accept that "in-the-moment" experiences can have some utility. Bowen family systems therapists are not willing to grant the same. Murray Bowen was very wary of any kind of "in-the-moment" experience. "In-the-moment" spontaneity looked and felt to him like the kind of nonreflective, impulsive reactivity that he saw as characterizing persons who are undifferentiated. The goal of the family therapy model that he constructed is to lead clients to a state of differentiation in which behavior almost invariably proceeds from a base of calm, rational deliberation. Thus, it should come as no surprise to us that the model counsels its practitioners to anchor their behavior in therapy in the same base of calm, rational thought. "In-the-moment" experiencing has little place in such a therapy.

As befits a model that privileges deliberative thought, Bowenian therapy is a planful enterprise. It is the genogram that serves as the basis for the Bowenian therapist's planning. The genogram helps the therapist to understand the transgenerational processes that have produced the lack of differentiation in the client family that the Bowenian sees as underlying all symptomatic behavior. Thus, the genogram also provides the blueprint for the work that family members will have to do to increase their levels of differentiation. It indicates triangles in their families of origin from which the adult members of the client family will need to extricate themselves. It also highlights cutoffs from the families of origin that the clients will need to repair.

The Bowenian therapist begins therapy by producing enough alleviation of the client-family's presenting problem to attenuate whatever sense of crisis the family may have entered therapy in. For the Bowenian, nothing of therapeutic importance can be accomplished in the swirl of emotionality that characterizes a family crisis. In this initial symptom-focused phase of therapy, the therapist may well make use of techniques borrowed from other models of therapy.

Once the rampant affect in the client family has abated, the Bowenian therapist begins to teach the client family the key concepts of Bowen Family Systems Theory. He helps the family to understand that the presenting problem that brought them into therapy is simply the end-product of relational processes that extend back one or more generations into the adult members' families of origin. At this point, the therapist is likely to excuse any children in the client family from further participation in the therapy. The focus now is on constructing with the adult family members plans to help them behave differently in their respective families of origin. The presence of children in the session would constitute little more than a distraction from this work.

The genogram becomes a key element in sessions at this point. In an atmosphere of reflective calm, the therapist collaborates with his clients in developing a nuanced understanding of the transgenerational relational processes at work in the adults' families of origin. He helps them to identify triangles from which they need to extricate themselves, cutoff relationships that need to be reopened. We saw in the last chapter that the Bowenian does not believe that simple understanding of family processes is sufficient to increase his clients' level of differentiation. Understanding is simply a preparation, albeit an essential one, for action taken by clients to change their usual role behaviors in their families of origin. Thus, after the transgenerational processes in clients' families of origins have been delineated, the Bowenian therapist begins to prepare his clients to engage in "expeditions" back into their families of origin, "expeditions" in which the clients, armed with their new understanding of how their families operate, will attempt to change their usual behavior. In this phase of therapy, known as "coaching," the therapist may engage in role play with his clients, helping them to rehearse their new relational postures so that they will be better prepared to withstand any pressure that may be exerted on them to return to their usual roles.

Clients return from their family-of-origin "expeditions" to report back to the therapist how their attempts to change their behavior went. Successes are congratulated; failures provoke further reflection leading to more refined understanding of the relational processes that the clients encountered. New plans are hatched, and clients are sent out on new "expeditions." As clients gradually succeed in stabilizing new role behaviors in their families of origin, their intrapsychic differentiation increases. They begin habitually to base their behavior in all contexts on calm, rational thought rather than on emotional impulses. As they do so, the risk that they will participate in generating symptoms in some member of their nuclear family decreases.

A Bowenian family therapist working with Karyn and Maurice might note from his genogram that Maurice participates in a triangle with his mother and father. The therapist helps Maurice to see that his behavior in the triangle stabilizes the relationship between his parents. When the emotional intensity between his parents surpasses their threshold of comfort, Maurice's father seeks him out as an ally. He invites Maurice to serve as an audience for his alcohol-enhanced, whining diatribes against his wife's cold insensitivity. Maurice welcomes the camaraderie that these interludes provide. He joins his father, and together they whine about mother's atrocities. Invariably, however, Maurice pays a price for the coalition with his father. As soon as she becomes aware of the coalition, his mother signals to his father that she is willing to accept him back into her good graces, provided that he makes sufficient show of contrition. Father inevitably welcomes mother's invitation. He enters into one of his "dry" phases and a brief honeymoon ensues between him and his wife. Maurice is abandoned, at least for the moment. He blames the abandonment not on his father, but on his mother.

The therapist observes that this cycle that began between Maurice and his parents when he was young has continued unabated since he and Karyn married. The therapist points out that the cycle between Maurice and his parents is the engine that helps to drive the conflictual cycle between him and Karyn. It is during the periods when Maurice and his father are in open coalition that things deteriorate between Maurice and Karyn. Exploration of Karyn's genogram reveals that a cutoff between her and her widowed, dependent father provides the context for her patterned behavior toward Maurice. The therapist works with each spouse to develop plans for how they might change their behavior toward their parents. He assures them that changing their roles in their families of origin will enable them to relate to each other in a more rewarding way.

From the perspective of Bowenian therapy, family processes evolve gradually over the course of several generations. To understand a person's behavior, that behavior needs to be viewed as part of a larger relational process that unfolds over time. So, too, the Bowenian model views therapy as a process that develops over time. No moment in Bowenian therapy stands alone as an entity unto itself. Each moment finds its meaning only as part of a larger whole that evolves in an orderly way.

Solution-Focused Therapy.   "It is clear from watching expert therapists at work . . . that they seem to follow rules, or at least that their decisions can be modeled using rules" (Gingerich & de Shazer, 1991, p. 241). The authors of this sentence were talking about therapists in general, but they certainly believed their observation to be true about therapists who practice solution-focused therapy, the model that they both helped to develop. So convinced were Gingerich and de Shazer that the practice of solution-focused therapy is rule-driven that they attempted to develop computer programs that could predict what an expert solution-focused therapist would do in a given therapeutic situation. When tested, the programs that they developed were successful most of the time in predicting what interventions solution-focused therapists actually delivered at the end of their first sessions with clients (Gingerich & de Shazer, 1991).

If the practice of solution-focused therapy is so predictable, it is clear that this model must be a "becoming" model of therapy, one in which each moment of therapy is linked causally to the ones that came before and to the ones that will come after. The kind of "in-the-moment" spontaneity that characterizes the "being" therapies is just not subject to the prediction and computer modeling to which Gingerich and de Shazer successfully subjected solution-focused therapy.

What makes the practice of solution-focused therapy so predictable is the elegant simplicity of its underlying theory. Because it is solution-focused, the model has no explanation for problem development. Because it has no theory of problem development, the model also has no theory of solution development. Rather, the model is based on the simple premise that every client system that presents itself for therapy is already enacting solutions, already doing things that produce problem-free interludes in its life. Therapy, therefore, need only amplify these already occurring exceptions to the presenting problem.

This goal poses a relatively straightforward agenda for the solution-focused therapist. She needs first to question clients in such a way as to elicit information from them about exceptions to the presenting problem. She then needs to craft and deliver behavioral assignments that are designed to amplify these exceptions.

How the therapist questions and what assignments she gives depends on the quality of the information that she receives from the client system. Consider, for instance, a situation in which a client reports an exception to his presenting problem but claims not to know what he does to bring about the exception. The client may be complaining of depression and report that he has "up days" and "down days," but that he cannot discern what he does differently to create the two different kinds of days.

> In this situation, it seems best to give a message that includes a prediction task. The actual task . . . was:
>
> > "Each night before you go to bed, predict whether the next day will be an 'up day' and then, in the middle of the next day, figure out whether your prediction was right or wrong and then account for how come it was right or wrong" (Gingerich & de Shazer, 1991, p. 248).

Some clients, by contrast, are able to report exceptions and to describe exactly what they do to create the exceptions. In such cases, the therapist need only give a simple assignment that directs the clients to increase the exception-producing behaviors. If, on the other hand, a client system is unable to identify any exceptions to its presenting problem, the therapist will likely ask the miracle question, asking members of the client system to describe in detail how they would know if a miracle occurred that caused their presenting problem to disappear.

In each of these scenarios, the solution-focused therapist utilizes whatever her clients give her and then moves from there toward the amplification of solution behaviors. Her therapeutic behavior in these and in all possible scenarios is predictable because her goal is so simple, straightforward, and unvarying: get the client system to do more of whatever it is already doing that is problem-free.

We have thus far been talking about the earlier, behavior-oriented version of the solution-focused model. However, the more recent, language-oriented version of the model leads to behavior on the part of its practitioners that is just as predictable. In the more recent rendition of the model, the goal of therapy has shifted from amplifying problem-free behavior on the part of the client system to amplifying problem-free talk. But this latter goal is itself so simple and straightforward that, once again, the pursuit of it leads to fairly predictable behavior by the therapist. As the therapist and clients engage in conversation, the therapist will selectively attend to statements made by the clients that are not focused on their presenting problems. The therapist will ask questions designed to amplify this kind of talk. She may ask for elaboration and/or clarification. The questions that she asks, in fact, will likely be quite similar to the ones that a behaviorally oriented solution-focused therapist might ask. Like the behaviorally oriented therapist, she will respond to clients who seem not to produce any problem-free talk by asking them the miracle question. Differently than her behaviorally oriented colleague, however, she will not close her sessions with a behavioral directive.

In both of its forms, the solution-focused model elicits behavior from its practitioners that flows in a logical manner from what clients present to a simply defined, resolutely pursued goal. At every moment, the therapist is aware of where the therapy has been and where she is trying to lead it. It is just such temporal awareness on the part of its practitioners that make the solution-focused model a "becoming" therapy.

Narrative Therapy.   No one, to the best of my knowledge, has attempted to subject the practice of narrative therapy to computer modeling. However, this therapeutic model is similar to solution-focused therapy in its pursuit of a simple, straightforward goal. The narrative therapist seeks to liberate and empower his clients by leading them away from seeing their presenting problems as residing inside themselves to seeing them as being external, located "out there" in the dominant cultural discourses that inform the society in which they live. Like the solution-focused practitioner, the narrative therapist starts with what his clients give him and then moves planfully from there toward his goal. The therapy that he conducts evolves in a coherent way from a beginning, through a middle, to a foreseeable end. It is a quintessential "becoming" therapy.

While duly acknowledging the care that the narrative therapist takes to accommodate the uniqueness of every given client system, it is fairly easy to sketch the broad outlines that narrative therapy follows in most cases. Early in the therapy, the therapist begins the process of externalization by personifying the presenting problem. He gives the presenting problem a clever name and speaks of it as if it were a conscious, malevolent entity, bent on oppressing and dominating the members of the client system. A narrative therapist working with Karyn and Maurice might refer to their presenting problem as The Marriage Destroyer. By asking Karyn and Maurice to describe the pain and frustration that The Marriage Destroyer has caused them, the therapist moves the spouses away from thinking of each other as the problem and instead gets them used to thinking of the problem as an external entity that has oppressed them both and that can be defeated by united action on their part.

People will only take action against an external enemy if they believe that they are strong enough to defeat it. Thus, the narrative therapist turns next to helping his clients become aware of the resources that they have to defeat the problem. The therapist asks his clients about "unique outcomes," times that they have managed, albeit temporarily, to overcome their presenting problem or at least to lessen its effect on their lives. He uses a variety of questions to "thicken" the newly emerging story that depicts his clients as resourceful warriors in their battle against the externalized presenting problem. Included among these questions are "landscape-of-action" questions, "landscape-of-consciousness" questions, and "experience-of-experience" questions (Minuchin, Lee, & Simon, 1996). From the perspective of a narrative therapist, it was a unique outcome that Maurice was reporting when he was telling Jamie about a satisfying dinner conversation that he had had with Karyn a few days ago. Jamie interrupted Maurice's narrative with one of her "blurts." A narrative therapist would have responded to Maurice's story by asking questions designed to explore what resources Maurice and Karyn brought to bear that enabled them to triumph, at least for a brief time, over their enemy, The Marriage Destroyer.

The narrative therapist does not simply want to free his clients from the oppression of their presenting problem. He wants them to join the ranks of those who are dedicated to struggling against the colonizing stories told by the dominant culture, which are the ultimate source of clients' presenting problems. Thus, whenever possible, the narrative therapist takes the process of externalization a step further. He asks his clients questions designed to increase their awareness of the sociocultural forces that have created and sustained their presenting problem. A narrative therapist working with Karyn and Maurice might ask them what culturally sanctioned stories about gender and marriage "feed" The Marriage Destroyer and make him such a formidable enemy. He might ask if the spouses know any alternative stories about marriage and gender that might strengthen them in their struggles against The Marriage Destroyer. If Karyn and Maurice are able to identify such alternative stories, the therapist would be very interested in asking them from whom they have heard these stories. He would also ask them to identify people in their lives who would constitute an appreciative audience to whom they could tell these alternative stories about gender and marriage. In this way, the therapist would seek to link Karyn and Maurice to a community of people who share an interest in overcoming the dominant culture's disempowering stories about sex roles and marriage.

The therapeutic practice propounded by the narrative model is clearly much more politicized than the practice envisioned by the solution-focused model. However, both of these therapies have the same simple goal of empowering their clients to do more of what they identify to be problem-free in their lives. In moving from what clients present at the outset of therapy toward this goal, these therapies develop over time in a coherent fashion. This organized development over time places these therapies squarely in the ranks of the "becoming" therapies.

Personal Reflection

Although she did not know the term, Jamie was attracted to solution-focused therapy because it is a "becoming" therapy. She correctly sensed this therapy's organized, logical manner of proceeding, and thought that its planfulness would provide a buffer against the anxiety that she was sure she would feel in her first several cases.

The occurrence of her "blurts," however, raises the distinct possibility that, in her life outside the therapy room, Jamie assigns priority to being over becoming. If this is, in fact, the case, the solution-focused model provides a poor fit with Jamie's broader worldview. To be sure, Jamie's concern over finding a way to manage in-session anxiety early in her clinical career is valid. However, it would be a mistake for her to attempt to calm her jitters by trying to practice a model of family therapy whose worldview and values differ significantly from her own. There are numerous means available to deal with early career nervousness. Anxiety should not distract Jamie from the crucial early career task of finding a model of family therapy that, in the long run and in the big picture, provides a good fit with her values and worldview.

To decide whether she should practice a "being" therapy or a "becoming" therapy, Jamie needs to assess whether her "blurts" are an aberration, a "hiccup" of sorts, produced by her involvement in the novel activity of doing therapy, or whether they indicate a deeply held view about the nature of reality. In order to make this assessment, she needs to look beyond her practice of therapy to her broader life. There, she needs to look for signs as to whether she assigns priority to being or becoming.

In the Introduction, I objected to the notion that a person's "style" should be consulted in the attempt to figure out which model of therapy provides the best fit for her or him. Fit, I maintained, needs to be sought in the domain of values and worldview, not in the ephemeral domain of "style." However, we are about to encounter an exception. In this matter of being versus becoming, a person's "style" can provide a reliable indication of that person's worldview.

Thus, to begin the process of discerning her position on the being versus becoming issue, it would be worthwhile for Jamie to examine her "style." Specifically, she needs to explore whether spontaneity or planfulness constitutes her usual manner of operating in her day-to-day living. As I have said several times in this book, the lives of most well-functioning people contain a mixture of such disparate elements as planfulness and spontaneity. Nonetheless, for most people, one or the other of these ways of operating comes more naturally and occurs more frequently. Some people feel constrained when they have to operate in a planful way. They feel most themselves when they are able to exercise "in-the-moment" spontaneity. They have constructed their family lives, their work lives, and their recreational lives in a way that allows them a considerable degree of spontaneity. These are people who likely assign primacy to being over becoming in their lives. Others, by contrast, experience "in-the-moment" existence as impoverished. Life feels full to them only when it is oriented toward a fairly well-defined and antici- pated future. Even these people's recreation tends to be a planful affair. These are people who probably privilege becoming over being.

It will also be useful for Jamie to examine her attitude toward history. Is history—her own personal history, the history of her family, of her country, of some other reference group—as vitally real to her as is her experience of the present? Does the present, in fact, only make sense to her when she is able to see its continu- ity with the past? Is the maintenance and honoring of tradition, be it personal, familial, religious, or otherwise, a key value in her life? If so, it is likely that Jamie privileges becoming. It may be, however, that Jamie looks on history, whether her own or that of some group to which she belongs, as an abstraction, an ossified irrelevancy. Not only does the past add nothing to the present, it actually impover- ishes it by forcing it into prefabricated molds. Tradition does not impart meaning; it shackles and deadens. Life is best lived with little reference to what has come before. If history is recalled, it is only so that it can be overturned. If such is Jamie's attitude toward history, then it is likely that she accords primacy to being.

Jamie's politics may provide her with an additional clue regarding where she stands on the being versus becoming issue. Conservative political ideologies treat the past with great reverence. When such ideologies contemplate evolution in a society's institutions and laws, they are willing to grant legitimacy only to developments whose continuity with what has gone before can be rigorously demonstrated. The political process countenanced by such ideologies is one that unfolds gradually and coherently over time. It is easy to recognize in such ideolo- gies the privileging of becoming over being. If Jamie is a staunch political conser- vative, it is likely that she, too, accords primacy to becoming.

Progressive political philosophies, on the other hand, feel far less con- strained to maintain continuity with previous political forms. The legitimacy of any institution or law is to be determined not by its degree of fit with the past but by its efficacy in responding to current needs. If it will serve the needs of the body politic, dramatic, even revolutionary, change will be considered by such progres- sive ideologies. In their privileging of the present moment, these political ap- proaches accord primacy to being over becoming. If Jamie is a committed political progressive, then she probably joins in assigning priority to being.

Finally, Jamie can consult her spirituality to help her assess whether in her world it is being or becoming that is primary. For some people, the search for God, or the Ultimate, entails a flight from the ebb and flow of the world of becoming. God, for these people, exists in a timeless, eternal Now, and so experience of and/ or union with God necessarily must take place in the domain of being rather than becoming. Some of these "being" spiritualities teach that human beings can ascend out of the inferior world of becoming into the divine domain of being by their own effort. Such spiritualities provide their adherents with means by which this ascent can be accomplished. Methods and techniques for meditation abound, all designed to help the seeker turn away from the world of becoming revealed by the senses and ascend into the immaterial domain of the eternal Now. Other "being" spiritualities (e.g., those that are Christian in inspiration) hold that, while human beings can purify and prepare themselves to be transported into an experience of pure "being," such an experience can only occur as a result of God's direct action, something over which human beings can exercise no control. These spiritualities also prescribe means for meditation and focused, prayerful reading. However, in this case, these practices are designed not to produce the experience of "being," but rather to make the seeker ready to receive it should God decide to grant it. Once again, these practices tend to move the seeker from a preoccupation with the material world of the senses toward a sensitivity to the immaterial world of the spirit. If Jamie's spirituality is built on such meditative practices designed to prepare for or to effect an experience of a timeless Now, then she has very strong evidence that hers is a world in which being has primacy over becoming.

There are spiritualities that privilege becoming over being. These spiritualities either identify God, or the Ultimate, with the vast process of cosmic evolution, or they see God as having chosen to reveal himself in the ebb and flow of cosmic and human history. The practices prescribed by these spiritualities to effect or to prepare for union with God have a distinctly "this-worldly" flavor when compared with the practices taught by the "being" spiritualities. They treat the material world revealed by the senses as a sacrament, a means by which God may be directly experienced, rather than as a distraction from which the seeker must resolutely turn his or her attention. The goal of these spiritual practices is to purify the seeker's stance toward the material world of becoming, changing it from an irreverent, grasping, utilitarian stance into a reverent, contemplative stance. If Jamie finds God, or the Ultimate, in nature and human history, then hers is a "becoming" spirituality. In her world, it is likely that becoming has priority over being.

Reprise: Jamie, Karyn, and Maurice

Jamie's self-reflection may reveal that, throughout her life-structure, being is privileged over becoming. If such is the case, her "blurts" were not an anomaly. They are merely the reflection in her work as a therapist of her preference for an existence that is lived as much as possible in the moment.

If Jamie's world is one that accords primacy to being over becoming, then her work with Maurice and Karyn, and with all her clients, needs to be congruent with that position. That does not necessarily mean, however, that hers needs to be a therapy of "blurts." We have seen above that Jamie's "blurts" are typical of the kind of "in-the-moment" spontaneity practiced in symbolic experiential family therapy. However, experiential therapy is not the only "being" model of therapy.

Collaborative language systems therapy is also a "being" model. A collaborative language systems therapist would be appalled by Jamie's "blurts," which resemble not at all the kind of careful questioning to which the language systems therapist restricts himself. While sharing a "being" worldview, these therapies are very different. Thus, simply identifying herself as a "being" therapist, while crucially important to her development as a family therapist, leaves Jamie with work yet to do. In order to discern which of the two "being" therapies best fits her worldview and values, Jamie needs to take into account her positions on the individual versus the group, good and evil, and mind and body, all of which are issues that experiential therapy and language systems therapy take differing stands on.

Of course, Jamie's reflection on her broader life-structure may reveal that hers is a world that assigns primacy to becoming over being. If such is the case, her "blurts" are, in fact, aberrations, possibly the result of lack of therapeutic discipline on her part. If Jamie's world privileges becoming, then she needs to commit herself to one of the "becoming" models of therapy. But to which one? Again, Jamie has more work to do. In order to distinguish which of the "becoming" therapies best fits her, she needs to consult her positions on the other philosophical issues that we have examined in this book and then determine which of the "becoming" therapies takes those same positions.

The task Jamie is facing is one of synthesis. Having discerned her personal position on each of the philosophical issues we have examined in this book, she needs now to assess which of the therapeutic models holds the same configuration of positions that she does. The next chapter is designed to help both Jamie and you with this synthesizing task.

CHAPTER

6

The Underlying Story

Josephine, a forty-two-year-old Italian American woman, contacted the clinic, requesting family therapy for herself and her two children, ten-year-old Mike and seven-year-old Tara. When asked why she was seeking therapy, Josephine reported that Mike's school counselor had strongly urged her to "get Mike some help." Josephine said that the counselor was worried that Mike was not handling well Josephine's recent separation from the children's father. When queried for more specific information regarding the counselor's concerns, Josephine replied that "the counselor says that Mike is holding all of his feelings inside." Asked about the constituency of her household, Josephine reported that following her marital separation, she and the children had moved in with her widowed seventy-two-year-old father.

Those of you who have worked in a clinic setting will recognize in the paragraph above the kind of preliminary case description that you would probably be given when assigned to intake a family into the clinic. While it contains a fair amount of factual data, the description is strikingly flat and lifeless. It is utterly lacking in what, for lack of a better term, might best be called "humanity." There is no third dimension to the characters described. We are told nothing of whatever anger or sadness or confusion or ambivalence they might be feeling. We have no inkling regarding what the facts detailed in the description might mean to them. We have no clue as to their motivations, their hopes, their fears.

The third dimension that is missing in the perfunctory case description just given will be added when Josephine's family meets with the therapist that has been assigned to them. Depth will emerge out of the interaction of therapist and family. However, we must note a remarkable thing about this "humanizing" of Josephine's family that will occur as the result of their meeting with their therapist. The humanity that the family will be seen to have is not a universal humanity. Its contours will depend entirely on the particular therapist that the family sees. With Joe, the family's third dimension will take one form, with Eartha, another, and, with Elona, yet a third form.

Sluzki (1992) has described well this protean phenomenon of client families assuming different forms when interacting with different therapists. It is this phenomenon that is alluded to in the well-known aphorism that a client will have Freudian dreams when analyzed by a Freudian analyst and Jungian ones when he switches to a Jungian therapist. I myself had the opportunity to witness this phenomenon firsthand when I was pursuing my graduate training. At that time—in the era before VCRs were used in the classroom—students in counseling programs were commonly treated to what was known as "the Gloria film" (Shostrum, 1964). Some brave soul named Gloria consented to meet with Fritz Perls (of Gestalt Therapy fame), Albert Ellis (of Rational Emotive Therapy fame), and Carl Rogers (of Client-Centered Therapy fame) in three back-to-back therapy sessions. The sessions were filmed, and the unedited presentation of the three sessions constituted "the Gloria film."

I recall that the professor who showed the film attempted to orient us students to watch the three well-known therapists' different ways of intervening with Gloria. However, as I viewed the film, I was more struck by Gloria than by the therapists. Specifically, I was amazed by the different Gloria I saw in each of the three sessions. With each therapist, Gloria became the kind of person countenanced by that therapist's model. With Ellis, she became a thinker, a person whose behavior was driven by ideas, adaptive or otherwise. With Rogers, she became an experience-er, someone whose behavior emerged organically out of her moment-to-moment experiencing of a benign, growth-oriented self. With Perls, she became an experience-er of a different kind, one contorted by efforts to deny and repress her moment-to-moment self-experiencing. Throughout the three sessions, the "facts" of Gloria's case remained the same. However, Gloria herself was different in each of the sessions. Each of the three therapists elicited from her different aspects of her humanity.

We have reached a point in this book where we can account for this power we therapists have actually to construct to a significant degree the clients who sit across from us in the therapy room. We have seen in this book that the therapeutic models that we use to guide our practice do not simply tell stories about human behavior and the business of changing it. We have come to see that informing and underlying these surface stories are deeper ones. These underlying stories provide encompassing accounts of the human condition, accounts that are far broader in scope than the simple business of doing therapy. These stories are about nothing less than what it means to be human. When we apply our therapeutic models, these underlying stories exert their influence in the therapy room, constructing the view of the human condition that will inform and guide the therapy. It is these underlying stories that provide for us the depth, the humanity, of the clients who sit across from us in the therapy room.

It may be difficult at this point for you to believe that these stories that underlie the models of family therapy have such incredible power. If such is the case, it is probably largely the result of the fragmented manner in which we have examined the stories. In each of the previous five chapters, we have explored one of the perennial philosophical themes addressed by the underlying stories. Hopefully, you have emerged from each of these discussions understanding the philosophical issue in question, appreciating the solutions to the issue that have been devised by the Western philosophical tradition, seeing how the various models of family therapy have aligned themselves with one or the other of these solutions, and discerning which solution you personally endorse. While this kind of issue by issue treatment was necessary, it could easily have created in you the impression that the various philosophical issues are unrelated. Such, of course, is not the case. All of the issues discussed in the previous chapters are related to each other. The stances that one takes in response to these issues hang together and form a single, coherent, powerful story about what it means to be human.

It is time, therefore, for us to synthesize the reflections that we have made in the previous chapters. We need to look at each of the therapeutic models that we have discussed and articulate as a whole its underlying story about the human condition. Table 6.1 will help us begin this synthesizing process. It summarizes for us the stance taken by each of the models of family therapy on each of the philosophical issues that we have examined.

While Table 6.1 is useful in pulling together the various concepts presented in the previous chapters, it, too, is flat and lifeless. The awesome power possessed by the models' underlying stories only really becomes evident when we see how the stories operate to "humanize" a particular client family. Therefore, our discussion of each of the therapeutic models will proceed by focusing on Josephine's family. We will examine how each model's underlying story creates expectations in its practitioner regarding what she will encounter when she meets Josephine, Mike, and Tara.

As you watch Josephine's family assume different forms as it falls under the influence of the various therapeutic models, you will begin to appreciate the power possessed by the models' underlying stories. However, this exercise will hopefully result in an even more important outcome. As you read through the following "versions" of Josephine's family, one will likely strike you as more "real," more lifelike than the rest. This will be the "version" of Josephine's family constructed by the therapeutic model whose underlying story provides the best fit with your own values and worldview. Right now, you should be able to predict with a fair amount of accuracy which of the models it will be that produces this "realistic version" of the family. If you have made the personal reflections suggested at the end of the previous chapters, you should know what positions you take on the philosophical issues discussed in those chapters. You should know whether you are a collectivist or an individualist, whether yours is a deontological or a eudaimonistic approach to ethical decision making, whether you are an intellectualist or a voluntarist, a dualist, an idealist, or an Aristotelian, whether in your world being or becoming has primacy. A glance at Table 6.1 should reveal to you which of the models of family therapy is based on a configuration of positions that most closely matches your own. The fit between you and that model should be confirmed when you see below how that model "humanizes" Josephine's family. As you see the depth that that model imparts to the family, you should feel a visceral flash of recognition. "Yes. That's how I experience my client families to be

TABLE 6.1 Summary of Models' Positions on the Philosophical Issues

	Individual/Group	Freedom from/Freedom for	Good/Evil	Mind/Body	Being/Becoming
Structural Family Therapy	Collectivist	Deontological	Voluntarist	Aristotelian	Becoming
Strategic Therapies	Collectivist	Deontological	Voluntarist	Aristotelian	Becoming
Collaborative Language Systems Therapy	Collectivist	Eudaimonistic	Intellectualist	Idealist	Being
Solution-Focused Therapy	Collectivist* Individualist**	Eudaimonistic	Intellectualist	Aristotelian* Idealist**	Becoming
Narrative Therapy	Individualist	Eudaimonistic	Intellectualist	Idealist	Becoming
Bowen Family Systems Therapy	Individualist	Eudaimonistic	Intellectualist	Aristotelian	Becoming
Symbolic Experiential Family Therapy	Individualist	Eudaimonistic	Voluntarist	Aristotelian	Being
Psychoanalytic Family Therapy	Individualist	Eudaimonistic	Voluntarist	Dualist	Becoming

*Applies to behavior-oriented version of the model.
**Applies to language-oriented version of the model.

when I encounter them in therapy." By the end of this chapter, you will have found the model of family therapy that best fits your worldview. You will have found your therapeutic voice.

Structural Family Therapy

There really is no such thing as a human individual in the eyes of a structural family therapist. A dyed-in-the-wool *collectivist,* the structural therapist sees individual family members as being so interconnected as literally to constitute a single, multibodied organism (Minuchin & Fishman, 1981). The skeleton that holds this family organism together and gives it shape is the family structure, the informal and largely unarticulated rules, rituals, and routines that govern day-to-day living in the family. This family organizational map directs how each family member is to behave in every family situation. The map coordinates each member's behavior with the behavior of all the other members, creating the single organism that is the family.

Carrying this collectivist vision into his first meeting with Josephine, Mike, and Tara, the structural family therapist will not see three individuals named Josephine, Mike, and Tara. Instead, he will see the three as interconnected and mutually dependent components of a larger family organism, of which they constitute parts. Seeing them in this way will dictate the manner in which the therapist seeks to get to know them. He will elicit enactments, activating them to interact with each other. As he experiences how they relate with each other, the structural therapist joins Josephine, Mike, and Tara as he assumes them to be, namely interdependent parts of the larger family organism.

The structural family therapist does not simply listen to the enactments that he elicits. Endorsing the *Aristotelian* approach to the mind–body issue, the structural therapist cannot conceive of relating to his client families merely through the medium of language. Mind and body, language and movement, words and affect, form an indissoluble unity in his view. Thus, the structural family therapist does not just listen to his clients. He also watches, feels, and senses. In his attempts to join Josephine, Mike, and Tara, and to assess their family structure, the structural family therapist would not simply listen to the words that they say to each other and to him. He would also note posture and tone. He would attend to assertiveness or coyness on Josephine's part. He would watch for glances and gestures that might indicate vigilance on the part of the children for any sign of emotional discomfort in their mother. He would look for subtle bodily shifts that might indicate when some interactional threshold had been approached or breached.

The structural family therapist observes the opening enactments of therapy in order to get to know his clients. However, he assumes that he already knows one thing about them before ever he meets them. He assumes that his client families have developed the kinds of problems that have landed them in therapy because they have resisted changing their organizational maps in the face of developmental and/or environmental demands that they do so. The structural therapist does not believe that this resistance is occurring because his client families lack the ability to change. To the contrary, he takes it as an article of therapeutic faith that every single family with whom he meets possesses unutilized or underutilized resources that render them fully capable of meeting the demands that they are facing (Simon, 1995). Moreover, the resistance is not thought to be the result of inadequate or defective knowledge. It is also not the product of any story that the family is telling itself. *Voluntarist* that he is, the structural family therapist assumes that the resistance is ultimately the result of a choice. Families generate symptoms because they rigidly choose stability over change.

As the structural family therapist watches early therapy enactments among Josephine, Mike, and Tara, he assumes that he will see in those enactments the family's stubborn attempts to hold on to an organizational arrangement that is developmentally or environmentally inappropriate. Perhaps he will see Josephine and Mike relating as if they are peers, with Mike exercising parental functions toward his sister, who is only three years younger than he. Then again, he may see Josephine so preoccupied with reconciling with her estranged husband that she is more or less inattentive to her children's needs, who are left, for all intents and purposes, parentless. The structural therapist does not know ahead of time what specific inappropriate organization he may find in a given client family. However, he enters therapy assuming that, before long, one will become evident.

Individual family members become habituated to the roles assigned them by their family's organization, no matter how maladaptive that organization may be. They become so familiar with their roles that they frequently incorporate them into their sense of identity. The behavior entailed by the role comes to be seen as making sense, as being the only viable way to proceed. The structural family therapist considers it his job to change the family's structure. Only if the family's organizational map is modified into a more adaptive, more developmentally appropriate arrangement, will the problem that brought the family into therapy be resolved. The therapist can appreciate that individual family members desire to continue playing the roles dictated for them by the current organizational map. He understands that the members experience their roles as familiar, and even self-defining. However, he will not be dissuaded from his agenda of structural change. As a *deontologist*, the structural therapist is perfectly comfortable asking people to sacrifice their apparent self-interest in behalf of a greater good. He is more than willing to put individual family members through the disorientation and discomfort that are almost always produced when a family's organizational map changes.

Once he has assessed the particulars of the maladaptive organization that is governing the life of their family, the structural family therapist will begin to press Josephine, Mike, and Tara to change that organization. Talking about the change that is needed will not satisfy him. The therapist's Aristotelian view of the mind–body relationship dictates that he push Josephine, Mike, and Tara not simply to talk about change but to enact it. His preference is that the enactment of change occur within the therapy sessions. Utilizing movement and props where appropriate, the therapist will create in-session interactions among Josephine, Mike, and Tara that enact a new, more adaptive organizational map.

The therapist will explain to Josephine, Mike, and Tara the good reasons that he has for asking them to change the way that they relate to each other. The therapist's voluntarism, however, leads him to expect that his explanation will do little, if anything, to reduce his clients' early therapy resistance to change. The therapist may revise his strategies in the face of this resistance, but he will not revise his goals.

The structural family therapist strategizes in therapy because his is a *becoming* therapy. He does not construct his therapy on a moment-to-moment basis. As he walks into his first meeting with Josephine, Mike, and Tara, he has a global idea of how the therapy he conducts with them will evolve. He knows that he will first join the family in ways that reveal to him the family's organization. He will then work to interrupt and to destabilize the family's current organizational map. This phase of therapy will have the tone of a contest. Josephine, Mike, and Tara will resist the undermining of the relational organization with which they are familiar. The therapist will respond to their resistance by continuing to press for change. Finally, the family's current structure will come undone. Josephine, Mike, and Tara will tentatively begin to experiment with new ways of relating to each other, activating in the process aspects of themselves that had not been tapped by the previous organizational map. The therapist will nurture and support these attempts to crystallize a new structure. The therapy will then end.

The structural family therapist "humanizes" Josephine's family in a manner that is dictated by his model's underlying story about what it means to be human. He constructs Josephine, Mike, and Tara not as autonomous individuals, but as interdependent parts of an encompassing family organism. He sees this organism as embodied, and so he experiences Josephine, Mike, and Tara as communicating with gesture and movement as much as with words. He constructs Josephine, Mike, and Tara to be resourceful but resistant. He will ask them to sacrifice self-interest in behalf of improved functioning on the part of the family organism of which they are a part. He assumes that initially they will resist, but that ultimately they will be both willing and able to make the sacrifice. He believes that his therapeutic work with the complex, multibodied, resourceful-yet-resistant organism that is Josephine's family requires him to be planful and process-oriented.

The Strategic Therapies

The strategic therapies share structural family therapy's *collectivist* vision of the human condition. A strategic therapist of any stripe would approach her first meeting with Josephine, Mike, and Tara assuming that they are parts of a larger social entity. An MRI therapist would see them as likely participants (perhaps along with Mike's school counselor) in the circular interactional sequence of attempted problem-solving behaviors that, in her view, is actually functioning to keep Mike's problem in existence. A Madanes-Haley strategist would see them as parts of a family system given shape by a family organizational map. Because the family has identified Mike as the symptom-bearer, the Madanes-Haley strategist would assume that this map creates a hierarchical reversal between Mike and Josephine, with the former occupying a position superior to the latter. A therapist schooled in the strategic therapy of the first Milan team would also see Josephine, Mike, and Tara as parts of a larger family organism governed by an organizational map. Like the Haley-Madanes therapist, the Milan strategist would also assume that power politics dominates the family's organization. However, the Milan therapist would not have a preformed idea of what form the power games take in Josephine's family. Rather, she would attempt to ferret out the details of the game based on the idiosyncratic details of the case. The presence of Mike's school counselor and Josephine's father as possible players in the family's game would likely attract the hypothesizing interest of the Milan therapist.

The strategic therapist assumes that Josephine, Mike, and Tara have little, if any, idea that they are functioning as parts of a larger social entity. Each of them, it is assumed, can see only as far as her or his own motivations and intentions. If, indeed, Josephine and Tara are repeatedly trying to solve the problem of Mike's behavior in ways that are only serving to reinforce and amplify it, the MRI therapist assumes that they have blinded themselves to the failure of their attempted solutions. It is more important that their view of the problem be preserved than that the problem actually be solved. If Josephine is inviting Mike into a role in the family that is more powerful than hers, the Haley-Madanes or Milan therapist assumes that she is choosing to do so because it somehow serves her in negotiating the power politics of her family. Her apparent weakness with Mike may actually strengthen her position in her struggle against someone else (her father? her estranged husband?). She has blinded herself to the negative impact that her behavior is having on her son because she is preoccupied with gaining the upper hand over someone else in the system.

In the *voluntarist* world of the strategic therapist, human behavior is not driven by anything so lucid as stories or rational thought. Blind, fierce self-preservation is the name of the game. Whether it is their view of a problem situation that they are struggling to preserve (MRI therapy), or their position in their family's power game (Madanes-Haley and Milan therapy), clients, in the view of the strategic therapies, enter therapy locked in a single-minded pursuit of self-interest. The irony of the therapeutic situation, as the strategic therapist sees it, is that, in clinical families, the members' blind pursuit of self-interest has become organized into an overall interactional pattern that guarantees that none of them will ever get what they are looking for.

In response to this situation, the strategic therapies take the *deontological* position that individual members of client families need to sacrifice their pursuit of self-interest in order for the families' presenting problems to be resolved. Only if Josephine and Tara stop trying to solve Mike's problem in ways that make sense to them will the problem-maintaining sequence that keeps Mike's problem in existence be dissolved. Only if the power politics in the family is negotiated differently will the organizational map of Josephine's family assume a form that will allow Mike's problem to disappear. Therapy cannot consist simply of talk about these changes. Thoroughgoing *Aristotelians*, strategic therapists believe that therapy must focus on getting the required changes performed rather than talked about.

Indeed, at least in the view of the MRI and Madanes-Haley strategic approaches, talk about the changes that need to occur often proves to be a very dangerous thing in therapy. Clients naturally extend their dogged pursuit of self-preservation into therapy. Leveling with clients about the changes they need to make will frequently serve as a stimulus for nothing more than a simple redoubling of their efforts to do things the way they want to. Remember, it is a voluntarist, not an intellectualist, world, that is inhabited by the strategic therapies. Thus, these models see the need for their practitioners to be, well, strategic. Josephine, Mike, and Tara need to be induced to change in spite of themselves. In order to get them to carry out directives that will dissolve their problem-maintaining sequence (MRI) or change their dysfunctional organizational map (Haley-Madanes), Josephine and her children may need to be sold reframes, stories about their situation that might bear very little resemblance to the way in which their therapist actually sees the situation. Even the Milan approach, which prefers to "tell it as it is" to clients, feels the need to utilize artifice to overcome expected resistance. After "telling it as it is," the Milan therapist tells a client family to keep doing it that way, intending thereby to provoke the family to do it differently.

Struggling against resistance is the heart and soul of the strategic therapies. These therapies are so convinced of the intractability of clients' blind pursuit of self-interest that they feel the need for therapy to be organized in such a way as to stack the cards in the therapist's favor. This is the primary reason that the strategic therapies are *becoming* therapies. So powerful is clients' resistance to change that therapeutic work that remains in the moment is likely, in their view, to fail. Only a therapy process that is planful has any chance of prevailing against Josephine, Mike, and Tara's insistence on maintenance of the status quo.

The strategic therapies "humanize" Josephine's family in a manner that, though similar to the way in which structural family therapy "humanizes" them, has its own distinct emphases. Like structural therapy, the strategic therapies see Josephine, Mike, and Tara not as autonomous individuals, but as parts of larger social entities. In fact, in the view of the strategic therapies, what has landed Josephine, Mike, and Tara in therapy is the fact that, though they are parts of an encompassing social entity, they are trying to behave as if they were autonomous individuals, resolutely pursuing self-interest without reference to the functioning of the group. The strategic therapies will attempt to maneuver Josephine, Mike, and Tara into behaving in ways that sacrifice self-interest in behalf of improved functioning on the part of the social entity to which they belong. The strategic therapies are far more pessimistic than is structural family therapy that Josephine, Mike, and Tara can eventually be directly persuaded to make these changes. See-ing resistance as a much more powerful force than does structural therapy, the strategic therapies assume that, more likely than not, Josephine, Mike, and Tara will have to be maneuvered, rather than persuaded, into changing. As a result, therapeutic work with them will have to be exceedingly planful, with the therapist carefully devising a sequence of interventions designed to counter the idiosyncratic ways that Josephine, Mike, and Tara will attempt to resist the therapeutic changes required of them.

Collaborative Language Systems Therapy

Like the structural and strategic therapist, the collaborative language systems therapist is led by her *collectivism* to see Josephine, Mike, and Tara as parts of a larger social entity. However, the social system of interest to the language systems therapist is not any ready-made, predefined group like "the family." The therapeutically relevant entity to which Josephine and the children belong, in the language systems therapist's view, is the problem-organizing system, that collection of people who in conversation together have defined Mike's problem into existence. Membership in this group belongs to anyone who has an interest in and opinion about Mike's "problem." The intake information strongly suggests that Mike's school counselor is a member of the problem-organizing system. Josephine's father may or may not be a member of this system. There certainly may be other people not mentioned in the intake information who currently are members of the system. The language systems therapist will be interested in including as many of these people as possible in the therapy.

How the therapist relates to these people when she meets with them will be determined by her *idealist* stance on the mind–body issue. Assigning absolute primacy to language in the human domain, the therapist will relate to Josephine, Mike, Tara, and whomever else belongs to the problem-organizing system exclusively through the medium of language. She will not try to read interactional sequences or organizational maps. She will not attend to gesture and movement. Instead, she will simply listen carefully to the content of what these people say to her, to the words that they use. She will listen so that she can ask questions that invite further elaboration of the meanings that these people are creating around the topic of Mike's "problem." The language systems therapist wants to keep the conversation about this topic flowing, because she is convinced that if the conversation evolves it will eventually define Mike's "problem" out of existence.

The language systems therapist is willing to grant that, as she joins the conversation about Mike's "problem," that conversation may be stuck. Josephine, Mike, Tara, and the other members of the problem-organizing system may have drifted into a conversational space where each of them has become focally intent on asserting and defending her or his own views about the "problem." Interested as she is in keeping the conversation flowing and evolving, the therapist obviously wants to get the problem-organizing system past this state of conversational breakdown. As a result of her *intellectualist* stance on the issue of good and evil, she does not expect that she will have to engage in any kind of contest or struggle to get this to happen. In her intellectualist view of the world, clients are not by nature resistant. Conversational breakdowns may occur, but people are neither prone to them nor committed to them when they occur. If the therapist behaves in a manner that signals her interest in and respect for any and all views about Mike's "problem," then Josephine and the other members of the problem-organizing system will quickly and effortlessly move from monologic to dialogic stances. The flow of the conversation will resume.

The collaborative language systems therapist participates in the therapeutic conversation as a *eudaimonist*. She is not an advocate of self-sacrifice. She is not interested in getting Josephine, Mike, Tara, and the other members of the system to sacrifice their individual perspectives in order to create some kind of compromise or consensus. In the language systems therapist's world, a well-functioning conversation is one that not only allows, but invites, each participant to explore and to elaborate his or her particular view. Diversity, not unanimity, is the ideal. Thus, the therapist will behave in therapy in a manner that communicates her view that any and all perspectives on the presenting problem, even ones that are apparently opposed, are plausible and valid. Her intellectualist-inspired optimism leads her to believe that her clients will quickly assume the same posture. The therapeutic conversation will, thus, become a place that operationalizes the language systems therapist's ultimate ideal, the self-authoring by individuals of preferred meanings.

Because the collaborative language systems therapist does not feel the need to lead the therapeutic conversation in a predetermined direction, she constructs her therapy as a *being* therapy. As she sits in therapy, she does not anticipate either the short- or long-term responses of Josephine and the other members of the problem-organizing system to the therapy. Thus, she does not behave with either short- or long-term goals in view. Instead, she remains in the moment, engrossed with the meaning-making being engaged in by whichever member of the problem-organizing system she is currently talking with. She will ask questions suggested by whatever that person has just said, hoping that her questions will invite that person to continue to engage in the process of meaning-making.

As they are "humanized" by the collaborative language systems therapist, Josephine, Mike, and Tara, together and separately, live their lives as parts of temporary social entities, ad hoc groups of people who coalesce around their shared interest in something that, together, they actually language into existence. As far as therapy is concerned, the group that is relevant is the one consisting of those who, in conversation together, have defined Mike's problem into being. Membership in this group is not constant; it will ebb and flow as people enter and leave the conversation about the "problem." If everyone in the group is able to maintain a stance that assigns validity to all perspectives about the problem and that encourages each member continually to elaborate her or his own perspective—and the language systems therapist is optimistic that everyone will be able to do so—then the group will eventually dissolve altogether as the conversation among its members evolves to the point where the "problem" is defined out of existence. The therapist will contribute to this evolution by constructing an "in-the-moment" therapy that has as its sole purpose the continuous self-authoring of preferred meanings by the members of the group.

Solution-Focused Therapy

We have seen in the previous chapters that solution-focused therapy exists in two different forms, an earlier, behavior-oriented version, and a more recent language-oriented version. While clearly related, the stories about the human condition that underlie these two versions of the model have some significant differences. Therefore, we will consider each of the versions separately here.

Behavior-Oriented Version

The behavior-oriented solution-focused therapist is a *collectivist*. Like the other collectivist therapists that have been discussed thus far, he sees Josephine, Mike, and Tara as parts of larger social entities. He agrees with his MRI colleague, for instance, that Josephine and the children are likely participants in a circular interactional sequence that is functioning to keep Mike's problem in existence. But he is not therapeutically interested in this particular social entity. Rather, his interest is drawn to other interactional sequences that he is sure Josephine, Mike, and Tara are part of, sequences that are not organized around Mike's problem. He would like to help Josephine and the children increase the amount of time that they spend engaged in these problem-free sequences. The more time that they spend involved in interactions that have nothing to do with the problem, the less time there will be to engage in the interactions that keep the problem alive. Eventually, Mike's problem will die from loneliness.

The solution-focused therapist does not believe that he will have to engage in a contest with Josephine, Mike, and Tara in order to get them to amplify their problem-free interactional sequences. He shares in the language systems therapist's *intellectualist* optimism that Josephine and the children are not stubbornly attached to their problems. They very much want to change. If the therapist intervenes correctly with them, they will quickly accommodate to his efforts to amplify their problem-free behaviors. It is the therapist's responsibility—one that he readily accepts—to find a manner of intervening with Josephine, Mike, and Tara that activates and reinforces their natural willingness and ability to change.

In order to execute his responsibility of finding the correct way to intervene with clients, the solution-focused therapist deems it necessary to conduct a *becoming* therapy with them. If he is to make use of the feedback that Josephine and the children provide to him, the therapist's mind-set must be process-oriented. His behavior at any given moment in therapy must be responsive to what has come before in the therapy—the way in which Josephine, Mike, and Tara have responded to his previous interventions—and it must take into account the changes that he hopes to be able to produce.

For the behavior-oriented solution-focused therapist, these changes are precisely *behavioral* changes. Subscribing to the *Aristotelian* solution to the mind–body problem, the therapist looks on talk as intimately related to action. Thus, the talk that occurs in therapy sessions is useful in his view only if it produces between-session action by clients that serves to amplify problem-free interactional sequences.

Amplification is precisely the kind of change that the solution-focused thera-pist tries to produce. He is a *eudaimonist*. His therapy will not focus on getting Josephine, Mike, and Tara to stop doing things. He will not ask them to sacrifice self-interest or surrender their points of view. He will simply ask them to do more of whatever it is that they are already doing that they have self-defined to be good and problem-free. His therapy will be an invitation to Josephine and the children to live the good life as they define it.

Language-Oriented Version

One crucial difference distinguishes the behavior-oriented solution-focused thera-pist and the language-oriented practitioner of the model. Whereas the former sub-scribes to the Aristotelian approach to the mind–body problem, the latter takes the *idealist* position. For the language-oriented solution-focused therapist, language is the beginning, middle, and end of the human condition. Any aspect of human life, including behavior, is meaningful only if it is described in language. Language gives shape and form to everything that we consider human. Therapy, therefore, must be entirely about language.

When Josephine, Mike, and Tara first meet with a language-oriented solution-focused therapist, they use language that is problem-dominated. They tell her stories about Mike's problem. The therapist assumes that the three of them also tell other stories that they find more pleasant, stories about things that they describe as good and problem-free. She wants to conduct a *eudaimonistic* therapy that will invite Josephine and the children to spend more time telling these prob-lem-free stories that they prefer. Operating out of the *intellectualist* position on the issue of good and evil, the therapist assumes that Josephine, Mike, and Tara will willingly jump at any opportunity provided them to engage in this kind of problem-free talk. In order to provide them with such an opportunity, the solution-focused therapist will conduct a *becoming* therapy, one whose process orientation will allow her to learn from the three of them on an ongoing basis how best to talk with them so as to invite and reinforce their problem-free talk.

Eliciting problem-free talk from Josephine, Mike, and Tara will be the solution-focused therapist's single-minded focus in her work with them. The therapist will talk now with one of them, now with another, paying careful attention to the way in which each of them responds to her use of language. On the basis of this feed-back, the therapist will continuously refine the way that she talks with each of them, endeavoring thereby to create a linguistic climate that will increase Josephine, Mike, and Tara's use of problem-free language. So intent is the therapist on moni-toring the talk that occurs between her and each member of Josephine's family that connections among the three family members, linguistic or otherwise, disappear from her view. The result is that the therapist winds up constructing an *individual-ist* therapy, one that treats Josephine, Mike, and Tara as if they were autonomous, self-sufficient units.

Not surprisingly, the two versions of solution-focused therapy "humanize" Josephine, Mike, and Tara in similar ways. Both versions see the three clients as being ready, even eager, to change. Both versions operate out of the belief that the only change that the three should be asked to make in therapy is simply to do more of what they already identify to be good and problem-free. Both versions use a planful therapy process to bring about this change.

However, whereas the earlier version of the model sees Josephine, Mike, and Tara as mind–body composites, creatures for whom talk and action are but two inseparable sides of the same human coin, the later version sees their humanity as lying exclusively in their ability to talk. As a result of its dual focus on language and behavior, the earlier version of the model sees Josephine, Mike, and Tara as interacting parts of not one, but several larger social entities. Focusing only on language and, even more radically, only on the languaging that occurs between each of the clients and the therapist, the later version of the model deals with Josephine, Mike, and Tara as if they were self-sufficient, autonomous individuals.

Narrative Therapy

Like the structural and strategic therapist—perhaps even more so—the narrative therapist is keenly aware of the influence of larger social entities on Josephine, Mike, and Tara's lives. His structural and strategic colleagues take a rather benign view of the fact that Josephine and her children live their entire lives embedded in larger social systems that organize and direct their behavior. As collectivists, these therapists see it as quintessentially human to be parts of such systems. Structural and strategic therapists will devote their entire therapeutic effort to getting Josephine, Mike, and Tara to sacrifice self-interest and to behave in ways that enhance the functioning of at least some of the social systems to which they belong.

The narrative therapist sees things very differently. Perceiving their situation through an *individualist* and a *eudaimonistic* lens, he is far less sanguine about the humanizing effect of Josephine, Mike, and Tara's membership in larger social systems. In the *idealist* world that he inhabits, language creates reality. The language that circulates through social systems is an anonymous language. The larger the system is, the more impossible it is to pinpoint who authored any given story. "You know what *they* say. . . ." Who, precisely, are *they? They* are nameless. And because what *they* say cannot be attributed to anyone in particular, the truths that *they* proclaim take on a certain mystique. If *they* say it, it must be absolutely and universally true. Josephine, Mike, and Tara probably accept what *they* say about their current situation. The three probably accept what *they* say about women who cannot make their marriages work, about children who grow up in single-parent households, about boys who do not have male role models to look up to. These stories that *they* tell cast Josephine and her children in an exceedingly bad light. And, because language creates reality, these stories will bring it about that Josephine, Mike, and Tara see themselves as problematic.

Precisely because the stories that circulate through social systems are anonymous and, thus, difficult to critique, the narrative therapist is wary of such systems. As a *eudaimonist,* he wants to bring it about that Josephine, Mike, and Tara each author their own stories about themselves, rather than subscribe to author-less, ready-made stories that exist "out there" in the sociocultural environment. Thus, the last thing that the narrative therapist wants to do is to make the *collectivist* move of treating Josephine, Mike, and Tara merely as parts of some social system. The three of them are already oppressed by social systems; the narrative therapist wants to give them the therapeutic gift of treating them as individuals.

To help them throw off the oppression of the dominant cultural stories that they have accepted about themselves, the narrative therapist will do a *becoming* therapy with Josephine, Mike, and Tara. He will start with whatever the three clients give him, but he knows ahead of time where he will try to lead them. He will externalize Mike's problem, helping Josephine and the children to see it as "out there" rather than "in here." He will question them in a way that sensitizes them to the resources that each of them has to battle against and to defeat the problem. He will ask other questions that help them become aware of the way in which dominant cultural "truths" have given rise to and sustain Mike's problem. He will end by inviting them to speak alternative, self-authored truths that they find preferable. Throughout this process, as befits his idealism, he will limit his intervening to the domain of language.

The narrative therapist brings Josephine, Mike, and Tara the good news that they are not responsible for the creation of Mike's problem. Culpability lies with the anonymous, oppressive stories that form part of the dominant cultural discourse. Firmly committed to the *intellectualist* solution to the issue of good and evil, the narrative therapist is certain that his three clients will enthusiastically welcome the news that they themselves are not the problem. No need here for any of the strategizing and maneuvering that the voluntarist therapies feel themselves required to engage in. Instead, the narrative therapist is confident that the therapeutic trek with Josephine and the children toward the goal of self-authorship will be an entirely collaborative venture.

You may have noticed that narrative therapy and the language-oriented version of solution-focused therapy take identical positions on all of the philosophical issues that we have examined in this book. Thus, it should not surprise you that the two models "humanize" Josephine, Mike, and Tara in very similar ways. Both models see the clients' essential humanity as lying in their ability to use language to construct their worlds. Both models assume that Josephine and the children will be most fully human when they are telling problem-free stories about themselves that they prefer. Both models are certain that the three of them will jump at any chance offered them to act in this self-affirming way. Both models treat Josephine, Mike, and Tara as autonomous individuals rather than as parts of larger social entities.

Where the two models differ is in their willingness to theorize about what happens to Josephine, Mike, and Tara outside of the therapy room. In the interest of parsimony and therapeutic brevity, the language-oriented version of solution-focused therapy focuses single-mindedly on what happens in the therapy process itself. The model provides no story about how Josephine, Mike, and Tara came to tell problem-focused stories about themselves. It is interested only in detailing what the therapist must do in order to help the three of them tell problem-free stories about themselves in the therapy room. Narrative therapy, on the other hand, entertains a highly theorized and politicized story about how Josephine and the children were inducted into problem-saturated self-stories. This detailed account of what happens outside of the therapy room leads the narrative therapist to set himself more elaborate goals than does his solution-focused colleague. It is not enough that he help Josephine, Mike, and Tara start telling preferred, problem-free stories about themselves. He would also like to place them on their guard against the dehumanization that inevitably occurs when people accept the stories that *they* tell.

Bowen Family Systems Therapy

Perhaps surprisingly, Bowen family systems therapy and narrative therapy construe the human world in fairly similar ways. We have just seen that the narrative therapist is wary of how Josephine, Mike, and Tara can "lose" themselves if they fall under the spell of social systems. The Bowen family systems therapist entirely shares this concern. Her therapy is every bit as *individualist* and *eudaimonistic* as is the therapy conducted by her narrative colleague. Both therapists grant that Josephine and the children will have to spend most of their lives dealing with various social systems, including their family system. However, both therapists want to bring it about that their clients leave therapy armed with whatever it takes to maintain their freedom in the face of the constraints that the therapists see social systems as tending to impose on individuals.

For the Bowenian, it is the ability to operate out of a base of calm, rational deliberation that will provide Josephine and the children with the capacity to resist the pull exerted by their multigenerational family system to become simply a cog in the wheel of the family's dysfunctional processes. Rational thought keeps people from knee-jerk, emotion-ridden responses and allows them to base their behavior on self-generated, cognitively evaluated goals and norms. Differently than the strategic or structural therapist, the Bowenian therapist does not do a therapy designed to enhance the functioning of family systems; hers is a therapy designed to help individuals navigate their way through their families in such a way as to preserve their freedom and autonomy. Whole families may, in fact, change as a result of this therapy, and this is certainly not an unwelcome outcome for the Bowenian. However, her primary goal is to enhance the differentiation of individuals.

Like the narrative therapist, the Bowenian makes the *intellectualist* assumption that her clients will participate in therapy in a collaborative rather than a resistant manner. She is very much aware that, if she allows the affective intensity of sessions to rise, Josephine, Mike, and Tara will likely respond with a reactivity that could very well result in resistance on their part to her interventions. However, if this were to occur, the therapist would blame herself, not them. Understanding, as she does, how undifferentiated individuals respond to environments characterized by intense emotionality, she should have known better than to let the affective temperature of the session rise. If, on the other hand, she succeeds in keeping the therapy room a setting of calm, rational deliberation, the Bowenian is certain that Josephine and the children will participate in the therapeutic process in a reasonable, cooperative way.

It is precisely a therapeutic *process* that the Bowen family systems therapist constructs. Again like the narrative model, the Bowenian model prescribes a *becoming* therapy, which begins with whatever clients present, but which then evolves in a predictable direction.

It is in the form that the therapeutic process takes that the Bowenian model parts company decisively with the narrative model. The departure here is the result of the models' differing positions on the mind–body issue. The narrative model's idealism produces a therapy focused exclusively on talk; Bowenian therapy's *Aristotelian* approach to the mind–body issue results in a therapy that views talk and behavior as equal parts of what it means to be human. The Bowenian therapist does not view Josephine, Mike, and Tara exclusively through the lens of their talk. Valuing rational thought as she does, the therapist certainly takes the clients' talk seriously. But, for her, it is the experience of oneself behaving, not the experience of oneself talking, that is crucial in determining one's level of differentiation. Specifically, the therapist believes that Josephine needs to experience herself behaving in an autonomous manner in relation to her father in order for her to become a truly mature, differentiated person. When she has achieved such differentiation, Josephine will then be in a position to relate to Mike and Tara in ways that promote their differentiation.

Thinking in this *Aristotelian* way, the Bowenian constructs a therapy process that moves inevitably in the direction of coaching clients to make behavioral changes. Talk will be a crucial element in this process. By means of talk, the therapist and Josephine will construct a genogram. The therapist will use talk to educate Josephine about the Bowenian understanding of multigenerational family processes. Talk will be used to prepare Josephine to deal differently with her father. However, talk will never be an end in itself, as it is in the idealist therapies. Talk will always be seen as a preparation for differentiated action.

As they are "humanized" by Bowen family systems therapy, Josephine, Mike, and Tara are individuals who function well when their behavior is driven not by processes operating in their family system, but by their own calm, deliberative thinking. The three of them will become ultimately differentiated in the Bowenian view when their behavior answers to no higher authority than to their own self-generated, rationally evaluated norms and ideas. As they approach this level of differentiation, Josephine, Mike, and Tara will rarely, if ever, act on irrational, affect-laden impulses. Their behavior will almost always be a limpid expression of their thinking, with the result that their thinking and their behavior, their talk and their action, will hang together in an organic unity.

Symbolic Experiential Family Therapy

The symbolic experiential therapist's *voluntarism* dominates his view of the human landscape. As he sees them, Josephine, Mike and Tara are not talkers, as they are, say, for the language systems therapist. Nor are they thinkers, as the Bowenian therapist would like them to be. They are, instead, experience-ers, and, in the view of the experiential therapist, much of what they need to experience in order to be healthy, fully functioning human beings is nonverbal and quite irrational.

As the symbolic experientialist sees it, Josephine, Mike and Tara are in therapy because they are frightened by deep, emotional experiencing. To keep their impulses and drives at bay, they are trying to live a life that assigns primacy to becoming, a life that is planful and process-oriented. To put them in touch with their impulses and drives, the experientialist will do a *being* therapy with them, one that has no discernible temporal organization, but that exists, as Josephine and the children should be existing, in an eternal, experience-focused Now. The therapist does not think that the clients will walk quietly and cooperatively into the Now experience that he will try to create for them. Rather, he anticipates much kicking and screaming on their part. He does not fear their resistance. Indeed, it would not be a stretch to say that he welcomes it. At least if they are kicking and screaming, Josephine, Mike, and Tara will be doing something other than thinking, talking, and planning, three enemies of a fully lived human life.

Josephine and the children will kick and scream at the experientialist's interventions because they are afraid, not because the therapist will ask them to make some kind of self-sacrifice. In fact, self-sacrifice is not in the symbolic experiential therapist's lexicon. His is a thoroughly *eudaimonistic* therapy. In the experientialist's view of the human world, an ethic of self-sacrifice is one of those devices that we cowardly human beings use to keep our irrational drives at arm's length. The experiential therapist does not want Josephine, Mike, and Tara to sacrifice themselves; he wants them to become completely themselves, to become the true, essential selves that are manifest precisely in their feelings, impulses, and drives.

Intent as he is on enhancing their self-experiencing, the symbolic experiential therapist will not be inclined to view Josephine, Mike, and Tara as parts of some larger social entity. Examining how their behavior is organized into some larger interpersonal pattern will simply provide him and them with an excuse to avoid the anxiety of "in-the-moment" experiencing. Instead, the symbolic experientialist will view the three clients through an *individualist* lens, focusing on each of them as a self-sufficient, self-experiencing entity unto him/herself.

Symbolic experiential therapy's privileging of deep, emotional experiencing requires that it take an *Aristotelian* approach to the mind–body issue. Emotional experiencing is a phenomenon in which mind and body participate equally. It is, in fact, a phenomenon in which the distinction between mind and body blurs almost to the point of disappearing. Necessarily, the communication of deep, emotional experiencing almost always requires something more than words, some kind of physicality that gives symbolic expression to what one is experiencing. In his *Aristotelian* therapy, the experientialist will feel free to make playful use of motion and objects to communicate his own experiencing. He is hopeful that his behavior will free Josephine, Mike, and Tara to do the same. (In the therapist's view, Mike and Tara have an advantage in this domain. As children, they instinctively know the value of physical play. That is, of course, unless Josephine has ruined them by teaching them to be "mature.")

In the world of the symbolic experiential family therapist, Josephine, Mike, and Tara are most fully human when each of them is giving unedited expression to her or his deep feelings and drives. Such expression will likely involve a physical, symbolic component. Because their feelings and drives may include content that defies familial and social norms regarding what is polite or moral, it will require courage for the three clients actually to feel what they feel and give expression to it. Because they probably lack that courage, Josephine and the children will probably resist the therapist's creation of a therapeutic climate in which people are free to be who they are, however irrational or "crazy" that turns out to be. The therapist will not be moved by their resistance. Nor, however, will he try to "maneuver" them into being themselves. (It is quite a "crazy" thought to think that one could do so.) Instead, the therapist will restrict himself to keeping up his end of the therapeutic bargain: he will try assiduously to stay in touch with and give expression to his own moment-to-moment experiencing in the therapy. The rest is up to Josephine, Mike, and Tara.

Psychoanalytic Family Therapy

The symbolic experiential family therapist believes that we human beings tend to be afraid of our drives and impulses. He foresees that most of his clients will resist a therapy that tries to get them in touch with their impulse life. However, the experientialist sees nothing in the way that human beings are put together that fates them always to be involved in a struggle against their impulses. Provided we are courageous enough, we can, in the experiential therapist's view, live integrated lives of deep, moment-to-moment self-experiencing.

The psychoanalytic family therapist is not at all that optimistic, especially if her therapy remains close to Freud's foundational ideas. Her *dualist* view of the mind–body issue leads her to see the human person as stretched out between two worlds that operate according to opposed sets of laws. We are bodies, and our bodies obey the deterministic laws of chemistry and physics. We are minds, and our minds are free and self-determining. The underlying story of Josephine, Mike, and Tara's lives is their attempt to live as free, self-determining people in the face of sexual and aggressive drives that have their source in the deterministic, physico-chemical processes at work in their bodies. If the three clients have been parented well, they may be more or less successful in bringing it about that a fair portion of their behavior emerges out of mental processes that are conscious and free. However, the specter of the blind, instinctual energies lurking just below their consciousness will never be completely banished from their lives. Life for the mentally healthiest of us always entails an element of struggle against the determinism that we carry around in our biological makeup.

The fact that Josephine, Mike, and Tara are in therapy makes it entirely likely that they have not experienced a salutary developmental history and that they are not all that mentally healthy. As a result, much of their behavior is currently unfree, driven by biologically based instincts. The analytic family therapist will try via the therapy that she conducts to strengthen the clients' conscious functioning so that increasing amounts of their behavior emerge out of freedom rather than determinism. She expects the process to be a struggle, however, and a happy ending is in no way guaranteed.

Part of the difficulty of the therapeutic process will lie in the fact that Josephine, Mike, and Tara can be counted on to resist the therapist's attempts to liberate them from their enslavement to their instinctual drives. As befits her dualism, the psychoanalytic family therapist is also a thoroughgoing *voluntarist*. She does not believe that Josephine, Mike, and Tara will act in their own best interest, even when she points out their best interest to them by means of interventions like confrontation and interpretation. They will, as likely as not, resist the therapist's interventions, continuing to enact behaviors whose self-defeating nature they are well able, in their more lucid moments, to admit. As much as she values insight and awareness, the analytic therapist's dualism prevents her from believing that awareness can infallibly master the impulses that arise out of our biological nature. The therapist will not be in the least surprised when Josephine, Mike, and Tara spend much of the therapy irrationally doing things that they have come to understand are self-defeating.

Even if she has abandoned Freud's dualism in favor of the more idealist outlook of the object relations approaches, the psychoanalytic therapist remains rather pessimistic when it comes to the matter of clients' resistance to change. The object relations therapist will not see Josephine, Mike, and Tara as driven by blind biological impulses; she will, however, see them as motivated by an equally blind instinct for self-protection from maltreatment at the hands of those with whom they relate. While not necessarily rooted in biology, this instinct is every bit as powerful as the sexual and aggressive instincts that the classical analytic therapist sees at work in human behavior. The instinct for self-protection can lead Josephine and the children to continue to utilize self-defeating interpersonal strategies, even after the therapist has helped them to become aware of their self-defeating nature.

In the face of their resistance, the psychoanalytic family therapist will still struggle to liberate Josephine, Mike, and Tara from their instinct-based, irrational, self-defeating behavior. The therapy that she constructs will be one that assigns primacy to *becoming* over *being*. It will be process-oriented in a couple of ways. First of all, it will develop in a coherent and planful manner from assessment, through intervention, to termination. Whatever "in-the-moment" experiences the therapist may have along the way will be lifted out of the moment and placed in a larger context by the therapist's use of analytic therapy's well-developed and complex theoretical superstructure.

Psychoanalytic family therapy is process-oriented in a second way. The insight that analytic therapy will attempt to impart to Josephine, Mike, and Tara will always be about their history and development. The analytic therapist will try to help Josephine—and the children, in an age-appropriate way—to understand that their current behavior is the product of past developmental history. It is only such a *becoming* kind of consciousness that will give Josephine, Mike, and Tara a fighting chance of gaining mastery over their unconscious instincts.

In seeing Josephine, Mike, and Tara's behavior as rooted in their respective developmental histories, the analytic family therapist gives expression to her *individualist* view of the human condition. Josephine and the children's behavior may interlock in a larger interpersonal pattern, but the relational system thereby created is secondary and derivative in the eyes of the analytic therapist. What is primary and causal is what is happening inside of each of the clients, and what is happening inside of them is the product of what each of them has experienced in his or her respective past.

When she makes freedom, self-mastery, and self-determination the ultimate goal of her therapy, the analytic family therapist gives expression to her *eudaimonistic* view of the human condition. As she sees it, Josephine, Mike, and Tara will leave therapy functioning well if each of them has resumed the process of self-development that got stalled at some point in the past. Human life well lived for the psychoanalytic therapist is a process of self-understanding, resulting in self-mastery, resulting in self-actualization. After a successful therapy, Josephine, Mike, and Tara will, of course, in all likelihood continue to relate to each other, but their relating will be a means, not an end, as far as the therapist is concerned. Their mutual relating will be healthy if it provides each of them with "holding," a supportive, nurturing context within which each of them can pursue what is, in the analytic therapist's view, the ultimate human goal, self-development.

Conflict and struggle is the centerpiece of the way in which psychoanalytic family therapy "humanizes" Josephine, Mike, and Tara. To be sure, Josephine and the children may be involved in conflict and struggle with each other, but that is not the conflict that the analytic therapist is primarily interested in. She is focused on the intrapsychic conflict that she is certain underlies whatever struggle they might be engaged in with each other. This intrapsychic conflict is rooted in each of the clients' respective developmental histories. Even more profoundly, it is rooted in the divided condition that the psychoanalytic therapist sees all of us human beings living in, a condition of inhabiting a material world and a mental world that operate according to opposed and irreconcilable sets of laws. Living stretched out between these two worlds makes Josephine, Mike, and Tara prone to behaving in irrational, self-defeating ways. The analytic therapist would like to see them live lives more or less consistently oriented toward freedom and self-development. She realizes that getting them to this point will be an uphill struggle. To increase her chances of success, she will construct a planful, process-oriented therapy with them, using the profound understanding of the human condition embodied in psychoanalytic theory as the Ariadne's thread that will organize and make secure her therapeutic descent into the labyrinth of Josephine's and the children's minds.

Reprise: Josephine, Mike, Tara, and You

It is my sincere hope that, as you read this, you are experiencing a sense of exhilaration. Hopefully, you recognized in one of the descriptions of Josephine, Mike, and Tara given above, the way in which you instinctively experience yourself, your clients, and all the people who inhabit your world. The model of family therapy that "humanized" Josephine and her children in this way is the model whose worldview and values most closely match your own. That model looks at the human world through the same lens that you use in your day-to-day existence. It speaks to clients in a voice that echoes your own. The exhilaration that you felt when you read this model's "version" of Josephine, Mike, and Tara was really the thrill of self-recognition. As you heard the model speak its view of the human condition, it was your own therapeutic voice that you were hearing.

As you bask in this thrill of self-discovery, you may be aware that your exhilaration is tinged with a certain dis-ease. You may find yourself vaguely uncomfortable with the power that the therapeutic models have to "humanize" Josephine, Mike, and Tara in such disparate ways. Are Josephine and the children so plastic that they can be turned into whatever it is a model of therapy wants them to be? And what about how they "humanize" themselves? Should that not be equally as important, perhaps more so, than the ways in which the models "humanize" them? You may have found your voice; what about theirs?

You are to be commended if you are, in fact, feeling such discomfort. It speaks to your concern to do therapy in a way that places clients' concerns first and foremost. However, your discomfort is ill-founded. Allow me to try to convince you of this fact.

This chapter, in fact this entire book, has made clear that each of the models of family therapy is based on a set of assumptions that predetermine how clients will be viewed, not only in the therapy-relevant aspects of their lives, but in the manner in which their very humanity is construed. That this should be the case is inevitable. We human beings seem to be constructed in such a way that we cannot escape or get around the lenses through which we view the world. There is no "immaculate perception." Our experience is always determined by our assumptions. Even if we were to try to lay aside our assumptions in order to see the world as another sees it, that very effort would itself be based on an assumption that viewing the world in such a de-centered way is somehow more accurate or more ethical or more desirable. Our attempt to bypass our assumptions would itself be based on one of our assumptions.

What is true of us as individual human beings is also true of the therapeutic models. They cannot help but be based on certain assumptions regarding what it means to be human. As we have seen in this book, even the postmodern therapeutic models, which place the highest premium on privileging clients' voices and worldviews, have their own underlying assumptive stories about the human condition. It cannot be otherwise.

Nor need it be otherwise. It may very well be the case that some of the therapeutic models "humanize" Josephine, Mike, and Tara differently than they "humanize" themselves. However, their encounter with this difference can be therapeutic for them. Not that they should simply "convert" to the worldview espoused by the model practiced by their therapist. (Such profound and thorough-going change, even if it were desirable, is the stuff of religious conversion, not therapy.) Rather, encountering a world different from the one that they inhabit in their day-to-day lives can help Josephine, Mike, and Tara to discover corners of their native world that they have previously not explored. Think about times in your own life that a trip to a foreign place has helped you to see your own life in a new light. Chances are you did not renounce your former life to take up residence in the place that you visited. You returned from your visit to your own native world. But your encounter with the foreign helped you to see your native world in a new way and, perhaps, to discover aspects of it of which you were previously unaware.

An encounter with a therapeutic model that sees the human world differently than they do can have the same salutary impact on Josephine, Mike, and Tara. Of course, such an outcome is not guaranteed. Sometimes a foreign place is so foreign that it produces nothing in you except an overwhelming urge to leave it as quickly as possible. If you are Josephine, Mike, and Tara's therapist, it is entirely possible that your worldview will be so foreign to them as to render a working alliance between you and them all but impossible. Josephine may recognize the illness of fit and herself exercise the initiative of ending the contact with you and seeking another therapist. But she may not. For any one of a number of possible reasons, she and the children may continue to meet with you week after excruciating week, neither changing in the ways that your model countenances nor leaving the therapy.

If this were to happen, it would be your responsibility to recognize and resolve the impasse. The odds that you will be able to do so increase if, as this book counsels, your therapy is guided by a model to which you have committed yourself on the basis of the fit that the model provides with your values and worldview. The very process of finding that fit, in which you are currently engaged, cannot help but sensitize you to the contingent nature of all views about the human condition. As you explore the various models' underlying stories about the human world and reflect on your own story, you inevitably become sensitized to the fact that there are, in fact, a plethora of plausible stories circulating out there. You are undoubtedly passionately committed to your own story, and you will, no doubt, become passionately committed to the therapeutic model that you discover provides the best fit with your story. However, you will never lose the awareness, gained through your search, that there are, indeed, other plausible stories and other therapists whose commitment to them is as passionate as yours. Paradoxically, consciously committing yourself to a therapeutic model increases your appreciation of the viability of other models.

Thus, if you and Josephine and the children fail to "click" in therapy, you will be in a position to assess the situation as resulting from an incompatibility between your worldview and theirs. Of course, this will not likely be your first hypothesis as to why the failure to "click" is occurring. If you practice one of the voluntarist therapies, you may judge the failure to "click" as resulting from some kind of resistance on the clients' part. If such is the case, you will stay the course, hoping to overcome their resistance by whatever means your chosen model prescribes. If, on the other hand, you practice one of the intellectualist therapies, you may hypothesize that the failure to "click" is the result of your failure to do your part in the therapy. Perhaps you have failed to read correctly the feedback that you were receiving from the clients and, as a result, have not adequately shaped your interventions to fit Josephine and the children's idiosyncratic way of being in the world. Or perhaps you have failed to maintain a calm, differentiated posture in the therapy or have abandoned a position of "not-knowing." Whatever your diagnosis, you will attempt to adjust your behavior so that you and the clients will, in fact, "click."

However, the impasse may never resolve itself. A therapist who has not engaged in the kind of reflective process advocated in this book could easily fall prey at this point to pathologizing Josephine, Mike, and Tara. "WE are not clicking because THEY are sick or flawed in some way." However, a therapist who has come to her therapeutic model in the manner described in this book has a different explanation available to her. "We are not clicking because whatever difference exists between my worldview and theirs is proving to be a hindrance to the therapy rather than a help." The therapist cannot and should not change her worldview. She can, however, discuss the situation with Josephine and the children and refer them to a therapist whose value commitments might be more in line with theirs.

I hope that these comments have allayed whatever dis-ease may have been contaminating your thrill of self-discovery. I am convinced that finding your therapeutic voice makes you a better therapist, both to clients who find a way to harmonize their voices with yours and to clients who, despite your best efforts and theirs, fail ultimately to do so.

In all likelihood, you have now found your therapeutic voice. That voice will be an instrument of change for your clients. The passion that suffuses your voice will make it so. But the use of any instrument can be refined. Passion, without being suppressed, can be channeled and shaped. Supervision is the means by which you refine your therapeutic voice, enhancing its ability to effect change in your clients. Now that you have found your therapeutic voice, let us explore how you can refine it.

CHAPTER

7

Supervision

Refining Your Therapeutic Voice

It is the fundamental thesis of this book that your therapeutic voice should be the very same voice that you use throughout the rest of your life. The values and worldview that inform and shape your therapy should be those that animate your day-to-day living.

It is reasonable to infer from this thesis that your only task in therapy is to be yourself. "Why," you might ask, "did I spend all of that money on a graduate education if the essence of being a family therapist is simply to be myself? Surely I didn't need to be trained to be myself." Being yourself is, in fact, a large part of what it takes to be an effective therapist. However, you need to be yourself in a very deliberate way. You need to be able to be yourself, to use yourself, in ways that will benefit this particular client system at this particular point in its therapy with you. It is not enough just to be yourself; you need to be yourself *on purpose*.

Thinking about the situation of an operatic singer will help you to understand the point that I am trying to make here. The voice that a singer sings with is simply her voice—the one that she uses to talk with her family, to order a meal at a restaurant, or to discuss a movie with a friend. However, when she sings, the singer uses her voice as an instrument that must be manipulated so as to convey the emotional nuances of the aria that she is singing. The skill of operatic singing is precisely the ability to use one's voice differentially, one way with one piece, a second way with another, perhaps several different ways over the course of a third piece. Achieving the ability to manipulate one's voice in this way requires extensive training. At the end of this training, the singer still has the same voice that she began with, the same voice with which she was naturally endowed. However, her training has imparted to her the ability to use that voice purposefully.

In an exactly analogous way, you as a family therapist need to develop the ability to be yourself in a purposeful way. The kind of training that you received in your graduate program was not designed to help you develop this ability. Graduate education in family therapy achieves its purpose if it provides you with a working knowledge of the models of family therapy, if it exposes the underlying worldviews of the various models, and if it helps you to discern your own values and worldview. If you come out of your graduate program having found the therapeutic model that provides the best fit with your worldview, your education dollars have been well spent. Graduate education in family therapy helps you to find your therapeutic voice. Refining that voice is the task of supervision.

Now, that last sentence may have surprised some of you. Many of you may already be working in agency settings where supervision appears to be about anything but the refinement of your therapeutic voice. It may be about case management. It may be about how well or poorly your supervisor thinks that you are doing the agency's required paperwork. It may be about administrative matters, like the size of your caseload or your use of your time. What it definitely is not about is your therapeutic voice.

If this is what your experience of supervision has been like up to this point in your clinical career, you have my sincere condolences. You have experienced oversight, not supervision. Oversight may well have its place when family therapy is practiced in an institutional setting. Oversight, however, cannot and should not take the place of genuine supervision.

What makes supervision "genuine" is its focus on the self of the therapist. As you participate in supervision, you should be very much aware that it is about you, about the refinement of your therapeutic voice. "But isn't supervision," you might ask, "about the therapies that I am conducting, the clients that I am seeing?" Well, yes and no. The therapies that you are conducting certainly provide the material, the raw matter, for supervision. But in genuine supervision, that material is handled in such a way that what is really being focused on, sometimes explicitly, sometimes implicitly, is you, your presence as a therapist (Lowe, 2000).

"But if supervision is about me, how is it different from therapy? Do I get 'therapized' in supervision?" There is no doubt that genuine supervision bears an unmistakable resemblance to therapy. In the same way that the therapy you conduct aims at producing change in your clients, supervision aims at producing change in you. However, there is a crucial difference. In therapy, you hope to change the way that your clients live their lives. In supervision, your supervisor aims only at changing the way that you do therapy. To be sure, changing the way that you do therapy may produce ripples that ramify into the way that you lead your private life. Refining your therapeutic voice may lead to refinements in the way that you use your voice in other areas of your life. After all, it is the same voice. However, this ripple effect, if it occurs at all, is always a secondary and accidental by-product of supervision. What supervision is about, primarily, is enhancing your ability to use yourself purposefully in the therapeutic context.

In and Out

In each and every one of the models of family therapy, it is the self of the therapist that is viewed as the mechanism of change. It is your therapeutic voice, and not any technique you might use, that will ultimately be the instigator of change in the clients that you work with. However, because each of the models sees the human, and, thus, the therapeutic, terrain differently, each prescribes a different way that the therapist must use herself in order to be a change agent for her clients.

One way to compare and contrast the different use of self dictated by the various models is to examine what they have to say about where the therapist should position herself vis-à-vis the client system. One model, for example, exhorts its practitioners to jump headlong into the midst of the processes swirling inside the client family. A couple of the models advise their practitioners to insert one foot into the client system while keeping the other firmly on the outside. A few models want the therapist to maintain a position that is completely outside of the client systems that they work with. And one would like the therapist to be so far outside as to be, for all intents and purposes, invisible.

Because the models of family therapy envision very different uses of self by the therapist, supervision cannot be generic. You found your therapeutic voice by finding the therapeutic model that views the human condition in much the same way you do. You will refine your therapeutic voice by learning to use yourself therapeutically in the way that that model countenances. In order to achieve its goal of refining your therapeutic voice, your supervision needs to be driven by the model within which you have chosen to practice.

Reading a chapter in a book can never take the place of actually participating in the process of supervision. However, it can provide you with a preview of what you will experience when you enter into the supervisory process prescribed by your chosen model. At this point, therefore, let us embark on one last tour of the models of family therapy, focusing this time on the particular use of the therapist's self dictated by each of the models, and on the way in which supervision in the model is designed to elicit this use of self.

Symbolic Experiential Family Therapy

Symbolic experiential family therapy is the model that wants its practitioner to position himself wholly "in" the client family. Indeed, the experiential therapist wants to be more inside the family than even the family wants to be. Families wind up in therapy, in the view of this voluntarist model, because they have dedicated themselves to repressing and denying their impulses and feelings. Client families have chosen to exist superficially, on the outside of their emotional lives.

Seeing the clinical situation in this way, the symbolic experientialist considers it his mission to help his client families by placing himself in a position to experience the families more deeply than they are currently experiencing themselves. Thus, he conducts a "being" therapy. He deprives himself of the protection that the elaborate conceptual schemes of the "becoming" therapies provide to their practitioners. Exposing his own emotional antennae, he turns himself into a human tuning fork, susceptible to whatever vibrations might emanate from the client family. He opens himself to the very impulse life that the client family is trying hard to repress. He plunges headlong into the affective depths of the family.

You might have found in the previous chapters that symbolic experiential family therapy is the model that provides the closest fit with your own worldview. Its devotion to a "being" mode of consciousness and its idiosyncratic combination of individualism, eudaimonism, voluntarism, and Aristotelianism might produce a view of the human condition that largely coincides with yours. However, it is one thing to endorse this model's worldview; it is quite another thing to use yourself as a therapist on a consistent basis in the way that the model demands. Paradoxically, it requires great discipline, great control of yourself, to let go of yourself in the way that experiential therapy requires. It is not an easy thing to hurl oneself, devoid of protection, into the emotional undercurrents that swirl inside of a client family. It is not an easy thing to give expression to the experiences that the family triggers in you when you have immersed yourself in the climate of fear and repression that characterizes these families.

Supervision in symbolic experiential family therapy is designed to produce a therapist who can immerse himself "in" a client family and give expression to what he experiences. In order to achieve this goal, supervision needs to accomplish with the supervisee what symbolic experiential therapy tries to accomplish with client families. It needs to overcome the supervisee's fear of his own impulses and drives. It needs to overcome his resistance. It needs to increase his faith in his instincts. It needs to broaden his ability to give creative expression to his experiencing.

It is not a fluke that symbolic experiential therapy sees the supervisory agenda as being identical with the therapeutic agenda. Because the model has a particular view of the human condition, and because the supervisee is presumably human, the model views the supervisee in exactly the same way that it views clients. It will try to elicit the same changes in the supervisee that it tries to elicit in clients. And, as we are about to see, it will try to effect these changes in a way that closely resembles the way it tries to effect change in therapy. We will encounter this isomorphism, this similarity of structure, between therapy and supervision in every one of the models of family therapy that we consider in this chapter.

Our discussions in the previous chapters have revealed that the symbolic experiential therapist has a very definite view of what he can and cannot do in therapy. He does not believe that he can maneuver or manipulate clients into experiencing themselves more deeply and expressing themselves more congruently. Thus, the therapist does not try to change his clients directly. He devotes himself in the therapy room to being as true to his own moment-to-moment experiencing as he can possibly be. In doing so, he creates a context in which his clients, if they choose to, can begin to deepen their own self-experiencing. Whether or not they actually choose to do so is entirely up to them; the therapist accepts no responsibility for their ultimate decision. He commits himself only to keeping up his end of the therapeutic bargain. Thus, if clients change in symbolic experiential therapy, they are the ultimate agents of their own change. The therapist acts only to establish the appropriate climate.

Symbolic experiential family therapy approaches the change process that is supervision with exactly the same mind-set. The supervisor disavows any intention to change the supervisee directly. He will restrict himself to creating conditions in which the supervisee can change if he wants to. Creating these conditions requires that the supervisor give unedited expression to his own self-experiencing in the supervisee's presence. The best way for this to occur is for the supervisee to serve as the supervisor's co-therapist on one or more cases. Thus, co-therapy is the privileged means for supervision in symbolic experiential family therapy (Minuchin, Lee, & Simon, 1996). By experiencing firsthand the supervisor's unedited use of himself in the therapeutic context, the supervisee is provided with an opportunity to begin shedding the inhibitions that keep him from experiencing himself deeply when he operates as a therapist.

Carl Whitaker was fond of saying that therapy will not be good for the client family unless it is also good for the therapist. A thoroughgoing eudaimonist, he believed that any human relationship, including the relationship between clients and therapist, is good only if it results in self-growth for all of the parties involved. This holds true, as well, for the relationship between supervisor and supervisee. In the world of symbolic experiential therapy, the former should stand to get as much out of the relationship as does the latter. And, indeed, the co-therapy arrangement by which supervision occurs in symbolic experiential therapy does provide a benefit for the supervisor. As much as the experientialist trusts the fundamental wisdom and sanity of deep emotional experiencing, he does recognize the possibility that the therapist who plunges into the emotional whirlpools of a client family could go under, never to be seen again. When a supervisor does co-therapy with a supervisee, it is presumably the supervisor who will be the one who opens himself more profoundly to experiencing the emotional currents of the client family. Thus, it is the supervisor who will be at greater risk of being sucked into the emotional undertow of the family. The supervisee, in his very repression, provides a safeguard against this possible occurrence. From his position outside of the emotional currents, the supervisee can serve as a lifeguard of sorts for his supervisor, ready to jump in and rescue him should the supervisor show signs of drowning beneath the waves of the client-family's emotionality (Minuchin & Nichols, 1993).

Structural Family Therapy

The symbolic experientialist's view of the therapeutic enterprise provides him with the luxury of positioning himself wholly "in" the client family. The experientialist does not have to worry about changing the client family. Because he trusts deep emotional experiencing, he does not have to worry much about things like countertransference. Moreover, if he happens to be doing therapy with a co-therapist, he has the added security of having a lifeguard sitting nearby.

Seeing the therapeutic terrain differently, the structural family therapist is not inclined to position herself simply "in" the client family. She certainly wants to be "in" enough to experience the client family in a visceral way. She wants to be able to experience the family's organizational map from the inside, feeling the rigid relational demands that it makes on family members. She also wants to be "in" enough to experience firsthand relational possibilities that are lying dormant in the family, untapped by the current dysfunctional organization. However, visceral experiencing is not the be-all and end-all for the structural therapist that it is for the experientialist. Hers is a "becoming" therapy, not a "being" one. The structural therapist wants to experience so that she can use her experiences to strategize and to plan. Thus, she cannot simply remain "in" the client family the way that her symbolic experiential colleague does. Having been "in" enough to experience, she moves "out" to a more disengaged position in order to reflect and plan.

What the structural family therapist plans is how she will use herself to change the client-family's organizational map. Differently than the experientialist, the structural therapist does consider it her job to change the family directly. Her instrument for doing so is herself. The therapist will manipulate the way that she presents herself to the client family with an eye toward using her mode of presence as a mechanism for changing the family's structure. From her "out" position, the therapist therefore once again moves "in." Based on her reading of the client family, she may approach in a posture of nurturance, or of confrontation, or of vulnerable self-disclosure, or of expertise. Ensconced in her chosen posture, the therapist activates family members to interact with each other in ways that mark a departure from their old relational routines. She judges whether she has been successful by once again moving "out" to a more detached position from which she can observe what, if anything, she has instigated in the family. Her observations will provide the data on the basis of which she plans her next foray "in." Thus, the structural family therapist spends the entire therapy oscillating "in and out" of the client system (Becvar & Becvar, 2000; Minuchin, Lee, & Simon, 1996; Simon, 1995; cf. Simon, 1992, 1993).

Supervision in structural family therapy has as one of its purposes the cultivation in the therapist of this ability to move "in and out." It aims at helping the therapist both to experience and to observe, and, even more complexly, to observe her own experiences. Additionally, supervision tries to enhance the therapist's ability to make planful use of a broad array of relational postures in the therapy room. It tries to produce a therapist who, as the situation requires, can be everything from indignant to playful, from expert to bumbling. "In order to respond differentially to the needs of the members of the therapeutic system, the therapist must access different aspects of herself. She must therefore be self-reflective, self-knowing, and comfortable with the manipulation of self on behalf of the family's healing" (Minuchin, Lee, & Simon, 1996, p. 70).

In order to produce a therapist who can move "in and out" of client families, supervision of structural family therapy focuses on the review of videotapes of the supervisee's clinical work. As she watches herself engage with client families, the supervisee learns to recognize the idiosyncratic cues that signal to her at what distance she is operating vis-à-vis client families. She discovers the characteristic ways that she behaves when she is "out" and the ways that she behaves when she is "in." As she develops an awareness of these "distance barometers," the supervisee enhances her ability to oscillate at will between the "in" and "out" positions as she does therapy.

The second major goal of supervision is to enhance the supervisee's ability to make broad use of a variety of relational postures in the therapeutic context. In its pursuit of this goal, supervision of structural therapy becomes isomorphic with structural therapy itself. "Where therapy seeks to activate underutilized resources in the family's transactional repertoire, supervision seeks to bring out underutilized alternatives in the supervisee's relational repertoire" (Minuchin, Lee, & Simon, 1996, p. 82). The structural supervisor uses the same mechanism of change to effect this expansion in the supervisee as the structural therapist uses to effect the expansion of client families. Based on her reading of the supervisee, the supervisor planfully assumes a relational posture toward the supervisee that appears to hold promise of eliciting from the supervisee aspects of herself that she currently uses infrequently, if at all, as she goes about the business of doing therapy. With a supervisee, for example, who shies away from being direct and assertive in therapy, the supervisor may assume a confused and scattered stance, seeking thereby to induce the supervisee to display toward her the assertiveness that she has to that point been uncomfortable displaying in therapy. With another supervisee who privileges a posture of expertise in therapy, failing to assume a more intimate tone when it might serve to advance a given therapy, the supervisor may herself assume a posture of vulnerable self-disclosure. Thus, as she relates to various supervisees, the structural supervisor exercises the same skill that she would like to see the supervisees themselves develop, namely, the ability to make broad and planful use of self in behalf of client expansion.

Collaborative Language Systems Therapy

Perhaps surprisingly, the collaborative language systems therapist shares with the structural family therapist the aspiration to be both "in and out" of the client systems with which he works. However, the language systems therapist realizes this aspiration differently from the way in which the structural therapist does. The latter conducts a "becoming" therapy that develops over time. She oscillates sequentially between being "in" and "out." The language systems therapist, on the other hand, constructs a "being" therapy. He looks neither back nor ahead, striving as much as possible to remain in the present moment of the therapy. Thus, the language systems therapist cannot realize his aspirations to be both "in and out" of the client system sequentially, the way that his structural colleague does. Attempting to hold himself in a Now mode, the language systems therapist endeavors to be both "in and out" of the client system at the same time.

The language systems therapist wants to be "in" the problem-organizing system because he wants to respect and accept on its own terms the conversation that has languaged a therapy's presenting problem into existence. He does not want to impose any ready-made, preexisting theories on this conversation. However, the therapist considers it his job to keep the problem-organizing conversation flowing, so that it will eventually reach the point where it languages the presenting problem out of existence. In order to serve as a catalyst to keep the conversation developing, the language systems therapist must also be "out." Meanings that are being articulated in the conversation that members of the client system consider to be clear he must consider questionable. He must be "slow to understand," questioning every meaning put forward, so that members of the problem-organizing system are given an ongoing opportunity to elaborate their ideas further. Being simultaneously "in and out" of client systems in this way is the language systems therapist's way of being respectful of the idiosyncratic ways that his clients have languaged their worlds into existence, while at the same time inviting his clients to remain in the kind of open dialogue that inevitably brings it about that those worlds undergo change.

The ability to be "in and out" of client systems in the way that collaborative language systems therapy advocates is not a matter of techniques. It is very much a matter of attitude, of values and worldview. Thus, when supervision endeavors to help the language systems therapist cultivate this ability, it does not try to teach him anything concrete. Teaching, in fact, is as avoided in language systems supervision as it is in language systems therapy. "I do not believe that I can teach a person to be a therapist, but I can create space and foster a generative conversational process in which he or she can learn to be. . ." (Anderson, 1997, p. 244). The attitude of "not-knowing," which underlies the language systems therapist's "in and out" posture, can be interiorized by a supervisee if he is given the opportunity to participate in a conversation that is informed by this attitude. And that is precisely what supervision of language systems therapy is: a conversation among supervisor and supervisees that is shaped by the attitude of "not-knowing."

Reflecting the model's collectivist ethos, supervision of collaborative language systems therapy tends to occur in groups. Frequently, a reflecting team is used (Minuchin, Lee, & Simon, 1996). The supervisor invites all members of the team to offer her or his ideas about the case at hand. The supervisor participates in the ensuing conversation precisely in the manner that the language systems therapist participates in the therapeutic conversation.

> [T]he responsibility of . . . a clinical team supervisor is to provide room for and encourage all voices in the process. As in therapy, this responsibility entails the ability to participate simultaneously in multiple, sometimes contradictory expressions of viewpoints. The opportunity for learning—for newness and change—resides in this capacity of all participants continually to tell and retell, write and rewrite their unique narratives (Anderson, 1997, p. 246).

In the supervision of structural family therapy, the supervisee is talked about as much as, if not more than, the case that she is presenting. Such is not the case in the supervision of language systems therapy. The content of the supervisory dialogue tends to remain anchored on the case being considered. However, the learning that occurs takes place not at the level of content, but at the level of process. Beyond what is said about this or that case, the supervisees drink up the values of language systems therapy by participating in a conversation that is informed by those values, by the attitude of "not-knowing." "The dialogic process, not its content, becomes the primary agenda" (Anderson, 1997, p. 246).

Psychoanalytic Family Therapy

The symbolic experiential family therapist strives to immerse himself "in" the client family. The structural family therapist and the collaborative language systems therapist attempt to position themselves both "in and out" of the client systems that they work with. We turn now to the models of family therapy that desire their practitioners to remain unequivocally "out" of their client families.

The psychoanalytic family therapist's desire to remain "out" of the families that he treats manifests itself in numerous ways. To begin, the analytic therapist never leaves himself naked, exposed to his client families the way that the symbolic experientialist does. Rather, he always relates to client families through the thick buffer that the elaborate theoretical structure of psychoanalytic therapy provides to him. This buffer of ideas organizes the therapist to relate to his clients cognitively, at arm's length. This distance is further magnified by his model's preference for interventive minimalism. We saw in Chapter 5 that the strategizing in which the analytic family therapist engages expresses itself mostly in waiting. In an average session, the therapist intervenes little, and this relative paucity of activity on his part further amplifies his distance from the client family. When an intervention is finally delivered, it is usually an interpretation, which, while saying something important about one or more of the clients, optimally says little or nothing about the therapist and what he may be experiencing at the moment. Again, the effect is to produce distance between clients and therapist, to place the therapist "out."

Why is the psychoanalytic family therapist so hell-bent on remaining "out"? Analytic therapy's voluntarism produces one impulse toward an "out" position. Analytic family therapists of all stripes expect their clients to engage in significant resistance against their attempts to liberate them from unconsciously based, self-defeating behaviors. Analytic therapists stay "out" so that they can gain leverage in their contest against client resistance.

The analytic therapies that have remained more or less close to Freud's foundational ideas are subject to a second impulse toward an "out" position for the therapist. Freud's dualism led him to see the human interior as a fairly dangerous place, where the light of consciousness and freedom is always at risk of being swamped by the dark forces arising from our biological instincts. The only way for a therapist to assure that he will not be overwhelmed by the unconscious instinctual drives of his clients is to work with them from a safe distance.

Even when he is protected by his theoretical buffer and by his interventive minimalism, an analytic family therapist can, of course, fall under the spell of his clients' projections and fantasies. What his clients say and do in his presence can interact with his own unconscious life to produce therapy-threatening counter-transferences. Unless responded to appropriately, these countertransferences can easily begin to govern the therapist's behavior. Under their influence, he will sur-render his "out" position and begin to become a player in, rather than a commentator on, client-families' dysfunctional dramas. Therapeutic impasse or worse is then lurking around the corner.

Learning the theoretical superstructure of psychoanalytic family therapy can be done in an academic setting. Developing the crucial ability to remain "out," even in the face of strong countertransferential reactions, is the primary agenda of supervision in analytic therapy. Once again, the means by which this agenda is accomplished is isomorphic with the process of therapy itself. Psychoanalytic therapy prizes insight as the means through which clients can come to achieve mastery over their unconscious drives and impulses, so that their behavior emerges as much as possible out of the conscious zone of their psyches. In an exactly analogous way, it is insight that allows a therapist to withstand counter-transferences and to continue to conduct therapies that are based on analytic theory rather than on the therapist's own unconscious fantasies. "Three skills, in particular, are central to the therapist's successful management and use of affect in the treatment setting: to contain, to name or identify, and to analyze a given emotion in oneself and relate it to the unfolding therapeutic process" (Jacobs, David, & Meyer, 1995, p. 143).

Supervision of psychoanalytic therapy has as its primary goal the enhance-ment of the therapist's ability to contain (rather than act on) the feelings that he experiences in therapy, to identify what exactly those feelings are, and to analyze what it is in his own developmental history that has caused the feelings to arise with such vigor with this particular client family at this particular juncture of the therapy. The supervisor will move toward this goal utilizing the very same means that the analytic therapist uses to move his clients toward insight into the nature and source of their own feelings. The supervisor will offer the supervisee interpre-tations that label the unconscious roots of what the supervisee is experiencing in therapy.

A question naturally arises at this point. Because a therapist's vulnerability to countertransference is absolutely related to his idiosyncratic developmental history and to his intrapsychic structure, how personal does supervision need to get in order to accomplish its purpose? Is supervision of psychoanalytic family therapy for all intents and purposes nothing more than therapy for the therapist? Does the supervisor "therapize" his supervisee?

This is a question that has undergone a long, tortuous debate among psycho-analysts (Jacobs, David, & Meyer, 1995). Analytic theorists are almost unanimous in asserting that the prospective analytic therapist needs to undergo his own therapy before he can enter therapeutic practice. It is after the therapist has begun to treat clients of his own that differences of opinion arise. To what degree, it is asked, should the supervisor delve into the supervisee's unconscious life and developmental history? All agree that some amount of exploration of this material is absolutely necessary, for the reasons that I have just described. However, opinions vary as to where the boundary should be marked in supervision's exploration of the supervisee's personal life.

The Strategic Therapies

The underlying worldviews of psychoanalytic family therapy and the strategic therapies share very few elements in common. What they do share, however, is a robust voluntarism, which leads both approaches to expect client resistance to play a key role in the process of therapy. Both approaches are of one mind regarding how the therapist should respond to the prospect of client resistance: she should stay "out" of the client system.

Like her psychoanalytic colleague, the strategic therapist relies on understanding to keep herself "out" of the families that she works with. Of course, their different worldviews lead the analyst and the strategist to seek to understand different things about client families. The former seeks to understand family members' internal dynamics. Depending on which strategic model she practices, the latter seeks to understand problem-maintaining interactional sequences and/or family organizational maps. Despite the differences in what the analyst and the strategist seek to understand, the Herculean efforts that each devotes to the task of understanding produces the same salutary effect: it helps to keep the therapist from being sucked into the dysfunctional dynamics that each assumes is at work in the client family.

Once he understands, the analyst interprets, and does so sparingly, thereby maintaining his distance from the client family. Once she understands, the strategist directs or prescribes. The hierarchical posturing that being directive entails also has the effect of keeping the strategic therapist in an "out" position.

As in psychoanalytic family therapy, supervision in the strategic models has as its primary goal helping the supervisee to cultivate the ability to stay "out." Supervision in the MRI and Madanes-Haley models emphasizes the supervisee's acquisition of the skills required to be directive as the chief means of keeping the supervisee "out" of the families she works with. Supervision in the approach of the first Milan team emphasizes the supervisee's ability to engage in ever more detailed and nuanced hypothesizing as the means of keeping distance (Boscolo & Cecchin, 1982). In all three approaches, the process of supervision is isomorphic with the process of therapy.

The strategic therapist who practices in the MRI and the Haley-Madanes traditions needs to be a used-car salesman of sorts. She needs to be able to sell clients reframes that they are probably not inclined to buy. She needs to get clients to enact behavioral assignments that at best go against the grain, and at worst appear to them to be downright insane. The therapist acquires the skills to be directive in this way by herself being directed. The favored means of supervision in these approaches is live supervision. As she sits in the therapy room with her client family, the supervisee will receive phone-ins from the supervisor who is observing behind the one-way mirror. The content of most of the phone-ins is likely to be a directive from the supervisor. "She may direct the trainee to ask more questions in a particular area. She may direct the trainee to use a certain reframe. Or she may give the trainee a directive to be delivered verbatim to the client" (Minuchin, Lee, & Simon, 1996, p. 46). The supervisee is expected to comply with these directives, just as her clients are expected to comply with the directives that she gives them. Both clients and therapist undergo the same process of change. They change not by first learning something cognitively and then implementing it in action. They change "by doing something rather than by thinking or talking about it. Learning happens indirectly, largely outside of awareness" (Minuchin, Lee, & Simon, 1996, p. 44).

Supervision in the Milan approach wants to teach the supervisee that any understanding of a client family can always be refined and nuanced, and that the ability to engage in ongoing refinement requires distance from the client family. The supervisee acquires this learning by being given the opportunity to work at three different distances from client families. Over the course of a training experience, the supervisee will at times function as the interviewing therapist in the consulting room with client families. At other times, the supervisee will function as a member of the therapy team, which observes the session from behind the one-way mirror and has the responsibility of devising the prescriptive message with which each Milan session closes. At still other times, the supervisee will function as a member of an observing team that observes the interactions occurring in the consulting room, the interactions occurring in the therapy team, and any interaction there may be between these two sets of interactions. "Needless to say, being at a meta level, the [observing] group is often able to produce better ideas and solutions" (Boscolo & Cecchin, 1982, p. 158). Experiencing this fact drives home to the supervisee the essential learning that distance is crucial when trying to change the lumbering, resistant entities that clinical families are. Supervision in the Milan approach thus produces practitioners who "will be able to make valid and useful hypotheses, always aware that the map is not the territory, and able to make effective interventions without unwittingly becoming part of the problem through their very efforts of trying to solve it" (Boscolo & Cecchin, 1982, p. 164).

Bowen Family Systems Therapy

Bowen family systems therapy does not subscribe to the voluntarism that is so central in the worldviews of psychoanalytic family therapy and the strategic therapies. In the intellectualist world of the Bowenian therapist, client resistance is not expected to play a significant part in the development of therapy. Yet, like his analytic and strategic colleagues, the Bowenian wants to stay "out" of the client families that he treats (Kerr, 1984). Why is this so?

The Bowenian seeks the "out" position in therapy because this position reflects his ideal about how all human relationships should be structured. We saw in Chapter 2 that, in Bowenian therapy's eudaimonistic view, a relationship is good only if it is structured in such a way as to allow the participating individuals freedom to base their behavior on their own self-generated and cognitively evaluated choices. Such freedom is not present in a fused relationship. Affect, rather than thinking, is the motor that runs such relationships, and the participants are "in" the relationship in such a way that their individuality, their differentiation, is compromised.

Bowen family systems therapy has as its goal increasing the differentiation of its clients. It tries to move its clients "out" of the emotional system that operates in their nuclear families and in their families of origin. Bowenian therapy will succeed in achieving this goal only if it is conducted by a therapist who, himself, manages to stay "out" of the families that he treats.

Like his strategic and analytic colleagues, the Bowenian therapist utilizes thinking as a means of keeping appropriate distance from client families. What the Bowenian thinks about during therapy is obviously different from what the analytic therapist and the strategic therapist think about. Where the analyst thinks about internal psychodynamics and the strategist thinks about problem-maintaining sequences or family organizational maps, the Bowenian thinks instead about how clients' involvement in triangles in their families of origin has produced the lack of differentiation that has led them into his office.

The concepts that the Bowenian therapist uses to construct his family-of-origin explanations were likely learned in an academic setting. These concepts are crucial to the construction of a successful Bowenian therapy. As crucial as they are, however, the concepts will never succeed in keeping the therapist consistently "out" of the client families that he works with. The therapist will be able to think his way through his therapies only if he is a relatively well-differentiated individual. If he is not, he is liable to find his thinking being overwhelmed by his feeling time and again in the therapies that he conducts. In the end, it is his personal differentiation and not his knowledge of the conceptual apparatus of Bowenian therapy that makes the Bowenian therapist effective.

Increasing the therapist's level of differentiation is the primary goal of supervision in Bowen family systems therapy. Because this goal is identical with the goal of Bowenian therapy, it can be expected that supervision and therapy will be isomorphic processes. And, once again, they are.

Bowenian therapy moves fairly quickly from a focus on the presenting problem that brought clients into therapy to an examination of the interpersonal patterns in adult clients' families of origin that are assumed to be the ultimate "culprits" behind the presenting problem. So, too, supervision in this model moves fairly quickly away from a focus on the "presenting problem," the particular clinical impasse that a supervisee might bring to his supervisor. The supervisor assumes that the part being played by the supervisee in constructing and maintaining the impasse is part of a pattern of interpersonal behavior on the supervisee's part that has its origins in his family of origin. The supervisee's genogram is examined in order to construct an understanding of this relationship between the clinical impasse and the supervisee's family-of-origin situation (Protinsky & Keller, 1984). Mere understanding of this relationship may not be sufficient to help the supervisee behave differently when he is back in the consulting room with the client family. Just as adult clients need to return to their families of origin in order to behave differently "at the scene of the crime," the supervisee may well need to return to his family of origin in order to do the things required to increase his level of differentiation. If such is the case, his supervisor will serve as his calm, detriangulated coach, helping him to develop and rehearse courses of action that will allow him to detriangulate himself when he makes his foray back into his family of origin (Minuchin, Lee, & Simon, 1996). If the supervisee is successful, he will return to his therapy with the client family a more differentiated individual, better able to keep himself "out" of the knee-jerk emotionality that is tyrannizing the client family.

Narrative Therapy

As is the case with Bowen family systems therapy, narrative therapy's preference for the "out" position on the part of its practitioner has nothing to do with the expectation of the need to enter into a contest with client resistance. Indeed, narrative therapy shares Bowenian therapy's intellectualist assumption that clients will wholeheartedly collaborate with the therapy process. Like the Bowenian, the narrative therapist wants to be "out" because she holds the "out" position as an ideal, for her clients as well as for herself.

In the view of the narrative therapist, we are organized by the sociocultural force field in which we live our lives to be too much "in" our stories about ourselves and the world. Being thoroughly "in" these stories is a problem because it never occurs to us that there may be alternative stories that we would prefer to tell and live by. Moreover, all too frequently, the stories that we are "in" colonize and exploit us, persuading us to accept the blame for problems that really exist at the level of society and culture.

The narrative therapist wants to lift her clients "out" of the stories that they enter therapy telling. Through the use of the technique of externalization, she wants to objectify the familiar so that her clients can see these debilitating stories as something from which they are separate—not at all "in" (White, 1991). Separated from the stories that they used to accept as "given" and unquestionably "true," clients can identify unique outcomes, aspects of their lives that do not fit with the "official" story. Clients are then in a position where they can re-author their lives, constructing stories about themselves and the world that they find preferable.

In order to do such an externalizing therapy, the narrative therapist must ensconce herself in an "out" position vis-à-vis her clients. Unlike the collaborative language systems therapist, the narrative therapist does not want to expand her clients' stories from within, respecting and accepting those stories on their own terms. (It is this desire to expand the stories from the inside that leads the language systems therapist to strive to be simultaneously "in and out" of the client systems with which she works.) The narrative therapist is too wary of the power exerted by dominant sociocultural discourses to trust that such an "inside out" expansion will truly liberate her clients from the ready-made, culturally endorsed stories that oppress them. In the same way that the analytic and the strategic therapist seeks to gain leverage over resistance by means of distance, the narrative therapist arms herself in her struggle against oppressive dominant discourses by assuming an "out" position in her therapy. From her "out" position, the narrative therapist uses an elaborate technology of questioning to help her clients also assume an "out" position relative to the stories that they entered therapy telling.

Supervision of narrative therapy aims partly at helping the supervisee acquire skill in utilizing the technology of questioning that Michael White and other leading practitioners of this model have developed. However, supervision also has a more profound and important goal.

> Perhaps more important than its technical goal is the opportunity supervision provides for the supervisee to experience firsthand the partial nature of any story. Thus, part of supervision involves interviews with the supervisor, who endeavors to elicit the supervisee's story about herself, her history, her professional career, her work. Through a process of questioning identical to that of therapy, the supervisor leads the supervisee to a "re-authoring" of her autobiography in a way that is richer than the original story. Thus, the supervisee is able to participate directly and personally in a process of re-storying (Minuchin, Lee, & Simon, 1996, p. 52).

Having been led to an "out" position relative to her own cherished and valued story about herself and her history, the supervisee is helped to develop the habit of viewing all deeply held stories from the distance that an "out" position provides.

Solution-Focused Therapy

Steve de Shazer was among the first to announce the "death" of resistance. Intellectualist to the core, solution-focused therapy, in both its behavior-oriented and its language-oriented versions, assumes that therapy will be a collaboration between clients and therapist, rather than a contest. Thus, when the solution-focused therapist maneuvers himself to an "out" position in the therapies that he conducts, he does not do so in order to gain an advantage in any struggle against resistance. Nor does the solution-focused therapist see himself engaged in a struggle against insidious sociocultural forces, the way that the narrative therapist does.

If the solution-focused therapist is struggling against anything, it is against superfluity. The ceaseless quest of the solution-focused therapist is to construct a therapy that is as brief, as economical, and as parsimonious as possible. In the pursuit of this goal, he conducts a therapy that not only has no interest in "extraneous" constructs like family of origin, developmental history, family organization, level of differentiation, or intrapsychic structure; it does not even have an interest in the presenting problems that bring clients into therapy. Solution-focused therapy aims at nothing more than amplifying whatever clients identify as already being problem-free in their lives.

The solution-focused therapist keeps himself in the "out" position in his thera-pies because he considers his idiosyncratic personhood to be as "extraneous" to the therapeutic process as the concepts mentioned above. What's more, he sees the intrusion of his personhood into therapy as constituting a potential distraction from and encumbrance on his mandate to do therapy as briefly as possible. Why muddy the therapeutic waters by putting the therapist in any kind of an "in" position, where person-of-the-therapist variables could begin to become a factor in the therapy? Instead, let's keep the therapist so far "out" that his behavior in therapy is reducible, at least in principle, to the workings of a rule-governed computer program.

In his therapy, the solution-focused therapist strives for near invisibility. Sym-bolic experiential family therapy is all about the therapist and his experiencing. At the opposite extreme, solution-focused therapy is all about clients and the prob-lem-free behaviors that they are already enacting or the problem-free language that they are already speaking. Amplify what's already there and problem-free, and then just disappear: this is the aspiration of the solution-focused therapist.

If the solution-focused therapist wants to be invisible in his therapy, it is not at all likely that he is going to be center stage in supervision. "[Supervision of] solution-focused therapy, with its minimalist orientation toward client-defined goals, has tended to restrict its focus to the case story or other client-driven issues" (Lowe, 2000, p. 516). Supervision in this model does not use the clinical problem brought by the supervisee to his supervisor as a point of entry into some broader or deeper agenda. The supervisor does not reframe the supervisee's problem as having something to do with the supervisee's family of origin, or with some un-conscious process that is going on inside of him, or with some limitation in his interpersonal style, or with some oppressive dominant cultural discourse. Nor does the supervisor believe that he needs to teach the supervisee anything in order to help him resolve his clinical problem. Supervision assumes, as does solution-focused therapy, that the supervisee already has solutions to his clinical problem. The supervisor need only access and amplify already existing exceptions to the problem. And so the exchange between a supervisor and supervisee might be no more involved than the following:

CONSULTANT: "When in the session does she experience change?"
THERAPIST: "When I keep her on task and hold her to the topic."
CONSULTANT: "How do you do that?"
THERAPIST: "I interrupt her!"
CONSULTANT: "Could you do more of that?" (Thomas, 1994, p. 14).

Supervision of solution-focused therapy strives to be as brief and as parsi-monious as the therapy itself is. Both processes achieve the brevity that they seek in the same way: by keeping the therapist "out."

Conclusion: Refining Your Therapeutic Voice

I began this chapter by characterizing supervision as a process wherein you are helped to refine your therapeutic voice. The description that you have just read of what supervision is like in the solution-focused model may have caused you to have some doubts about this characterization. With its aspiration of producing a nearly invisible therapist, solution-focused supervision may appear to be about anything but the refinement of the therapist's voice. However, even in solution-focused therapy, with its therapist positioned completely "out" of the client system, it remains the person of the therapist who is the mechanism of therapeutic change. Being "out" is simply the solution-focused therapist's way of using himself to effect the kind of change that he is trying to produce. "Invisibility" is not a lack of presence; it is merely a certain kind of presence. Thus, even the solution-focused therapist has a therapeutic voice that he uses to beckon clients to change. Thus, even supervision of solution-focused therapy is an exercise in the refinement of the therapist's voice.

The process of becoming an effective family therapist is one that encompasses every aspect of who you are. Learning about the models, about their views of therapy, and about the views of the human condition that underlie their therapeutic visions, is a challenging intellectual exercise. Identifying your own values and worldview is an exercise in honest and rigorous self-reflection, issuing ultimately in your commitment of yourself to the model that best reflects your understanding of the human condition. Both of these exercises are appropriate to and usually take place in academic settings. Both exercises are liable to expand radically your views both of yourself and of what it means to be human.

This process of expansion intensifies and becomes even more personal when you enter into supervision. As we have seen in this chapter, supervision challenges you to use yourself purposefully in therapy, in the particular "in," "out," or "in-and-out" mode that your chosen model prescribes. Your effort to learn to use yourself in this way is an exercise that at different points in the supervisory process will likely activate your head, your heart, your gut, and even your soul. It can be quite a daunting task to learn to use yourself as an instrument. Yet, in the final analysis we have no other means available to do our jobs as therapists than ourselves, our voices. That is why, whatever else it may concern itself with, supervision is always ultimately about you. It always has as its ultimate goal the refinement of your therapeutic voice.

CHAPTER

8

The Therapist's Story

*As we encourage family members to investigate the mysteries of their hearts
and souls, so should every therapist articulate the origins of their beliefs about
human relationships and change; every therapist should examine their role as a
stranger invited into an intimate land.*

—Henry, 2001, p. 229

Each of you, if asked, could provide a story of your life. The stories that all of you
would tell would vary almost infinitely in style. Some would be brief, others of
epic proportions. Some would be abstract, others rich in anecdotal detail. Whatever their stylistic differences, however, the stories would have one central element in common: all of your life stories would be about origin and development.
All would seek to explain how you have arrived at the point in your life that you
currently occupy. All would try to answer the timeless question, "How did I get
here?"

It is doubtful whether any of us could manage the business of day-to-day
living if we did not have such stories of self to provide coherence and meaning to
our lives. Certainly, we could not live our lives with any depth without such
stories.

If you have followed the thinking that I have laid out in this book, it should
come as absolutely no surprise to you that I believe that living our lives as family
therapists also requires us to tell stories about ourselves. As I have tried to make
clear throughout this book, I do not believe that family therapy is something you
do. It is not a protocol or set of techniques that you "administer" to client systems.
Rather, being a family therapist is something you are. If, as I advocate, you base
your practice of family therapy on a model that you have chosen for the fit it
provides with your values and worldview, then your practice is nothing less than
an expression of yourself, an exercise in who you are as a person. Just as living a
coherent, meaningful life requires you to be able to tell a story about how you
came to be the person that you are, so, too, being a passionate, effective therapist
requires you to be able to tell a story about how you came to be the family

therapist that you are. The two stories, in fact, should fit together seamlessly. The story of who you are as a therapist should be a chapter in the larger story of who you are as a person.

If you have done more than simply skim through this book, then you have exerted considerable effort to get to this point. You have wrestled to understand philosophical issues to which you may have never given much explicit thought previously. You have struggled to grasp how these issues impact the way in which the various models prescribe that family therapy should be done. You have engaged in searching self-reflection to determine where you stand on these issues.

To bring this effort to completion, I would very much like you now to tell yourself—and anyone else who might be interested—the story of your development as a family therapist. I would like you to tell how, in the course of your life to this point, you developed the view of the human condition that this book has, hopefully, helped you become more aware of. I would like you to tell about the fit between this worldview and the model of family therapy that you have chosen as your own. In short, I would like you to tell the story about your finding of your therapeutic voice.

I would hazard a guess that there are some of you who are not quite comfortable with the idea that your professional life, your life as a therapist, is worthy of such a story. After all, you might think, I'm not a Satir, a Bowen, or a Minuchin. I'm not the originator of a model. In fact, I've never even had a professional publication. I'm not sure that I've ever had a single original thought about the business of doing therapy. Few of you, I would venture to say, would experience difficulty with the idea that your *life* is worthy of a story. But many of you might balk at the idea that your professional life is important enough to merit a story.

You should already be able to anticipate my answer to this misgiving. Precisely because your life as a therapist should be an extension of your *life*, the former is as worthy of a story as the latter. It does not matter that you did not author the model that you have chosen to practice; what will make the model a powerful instrument of change in your hands are the details of your life that led you to adopt the model as your own. If you practice narrative therapy, the story of your life and professional development is more important for your practice than Michael White's story. If you practice structural family therapy, your story is more important than Salvador Minuchin's.

My Story

Still, especially if you remain in frequent contact with teachers, mentors, or supervisors whom you respect and hold in something approaching awe, you may be shy about thinking your professional story worthy of being told. I would like to encourage you to overcome your shyness.

To help you do so, I have decided to share with you the story of my own development as a family therapist. I thought long and hard before deciding to do this. I am aware that telling you my story might only serve to reinforce whatever

prejudice you might have that only people who write books have professional stories worth telling. I was persuaded to tell my story, however, when I thought
about its contents. As you will see in a few minutes, the story of how I came to my
current commitment to structural family therapy does not contain any elements
that set me apart or make me special. The influences that led me to my values and
worldview are the common stuff that makes up life for most people—family, culture, education, religion. My story does contain one distinctive element: I had the
good fortune to be supervised by and then to work with Salvador Minuchin, one
of the leading figures in our field. But my commitment to structural family
therapy had crystallized long before I ever met Dr. Minuchin. And the material
out of which it crystallized was emphatically common and everyday.

So, I will now tell you my story. It is my fervent hope that, as you read it, its
very un-remarkableness will convince you that whatever misgivings you have
about telling your own story are ill-founded.

Family Origins

All of the elements that characterize structural family therapy's view of the human condition were present in my family-of-origin's view of the world. To begin,
we were collectivists. Both of my parents were first-generation Americans, emerging out of families that still had their centers of mass in Old World cultures that
tended to be collectivist in their outlook. My mother's family was from Naples,
Italy, my father's from Damascus, Syria. I remember visits to grandparents, aunts,
and uncles as loud, boisterous affairs. (I found out as a young adult that I was not
related to many of these "aunts and uncles"; the title was honorific.) Conversations never seemed dyadic. The idea that two people would have a one-on-one
conversation seemed never to have occurred to these people. Everyone seemed
always to be talking with everyone else, all at the same time.

Even among my mother, father, sister, and me, one-on-one conversations
were rare in my memory. Conversation was always a group affair. So, too, was
every other major life activity. There was no question but that the group, not the
individual, was the fundamental unit of the human in my family.

Without knowing it, we were also deontologists. Self-sacrifice was raised to
a high art in my family. Any expression of self-interest was discouraged. The pursuit of self-interest by anybody inside or outside the family was labeled with the
most damning adjective there was in my family's moral vocabulary, *selfish*. My
mother's story of her life was a tale of continuous self-sacrifice. Though she was
bright, she left school after eighth grade to care for her newly widowed father and
her younger brother and sister. Her mother, she told us, had been a model of self-
sacrifice, unappreciated, as she herself came to be, by my selfish grandfather. In
my mother's view, my own father was also largely a selfish man. It was clear that
if my sister and I were to turn out well we should imitate her and not him. My
own reputation in the family was that I had dangerous selfish proclivities. To this
day, any intimation by someone that I love that I am being selfish wounds me
deeply.

The world occupied by my family was not an optimistic one. Not for us was the sunny outlook of those who see the world through an intellectualist lens. We were voluntarists. Human behavior was not seen as being driven by anything so limpid as rational thought. As we sat around the dinner table and tried to digest what had occurred at work, in school, or in the world that day, the unspoken assumption underlying our shared musings was that, by and large, people cannot be trusted. It was unquestioned that there is something dark and sinister in human nature, rendering the world a place where one always had to be wary. I can still recall the near panic that would emanate from my mother on those occasions when my father was significantly late arriving home from work. Inevitably, it was snarled traffic that had detained him. Clearly, however, my mother's first assumption was that something tragic had occurred.

This ugly underside of the human condition that was dreaded in my family was all the more frightening for the fact that it could not quite be named or its presence accounted for. What my sister and I breathed in from our family was that it was simply there, and that it required constant vigilance to overcome. My parents themselves exercised this vigilance in what seemed to my sister and me like a never-ending litany of correction, criticism, and warning directed our way.

Words were of secondary value in my family. The consistently enacted rituals of day-to-day living were the bedrock on which my family's life was constructed. Words drew their meaning from the routines that they were embedded in. Playing with words, as if they had some existence of their own, never occurred, in my memory. Thus, we were Aristotelians in our approach to the mind–body issue. Meaning and physical activity were inextricably intertwined. Our daily round of activities was loaded with symbolic value. The fact that we ate our meals together everyday at almost exactly the same time had tremendous, yet unspoken, meaning for us. Tracking dirt onto a kitchen floor still wet from having just been washed by my mother was not a simple childish faux pas. There was a significance there that was no less understood for the fact that it could not quite be put into words.

You may have noted the reference to routines in my description of my family's life. Ours was not a "being" world of "in-the-moment" spontaneity. We were a "becoming" family. Every event found its meaning by occupying its proper place in a temporal sequence that was highly predictable. Weekday or weekend, I rose at the same time. I have already mentioned that we ate at the same time everyday. Needless to say, my sister's and my appointed bedtimes were unvarying. In the vaguely malevolent world in which we lived, security was found by always knowing that what had just occurred foretold what would soon be coming.

It has not required the exercise of significant therapeutic acumen on your part for you to recognize the tone of discontent informing the description of my family that I have just given. Indeed, I found the world inhabited by my family to be a disturbing, disquieting place. Alternative worlds opened to me as I entered adolescence. I was accepted into a high school populated largely by young men who came from cultures different from my own and from families more affluent than mine. In the flush of discovery that there are different ways to understand and to live what it means to be human, I was poised to execute what thirty years later I would term a "reactive distancing" from and rejection of my family. Had I made that reactive move, it might well have been a narrative therapist rather than a structural therapist who is writing this line. I might well have adopted a worldview characterized by the individualism, eudaimonism, intellectualism, and idealism that underlie narrative therapy.

Religious Retrieval

Why didn't I reactively adopt a worldview that was the opposite of that which informed my family's life? I certainly flirted with doing so throughout my high school years. Most of my friends clearly already inhabited such a world. (I don't want to give you the impression here that my friends and I sat around during high school discussing the relative merits of varying views of the human condition. We were much too busy being 1960s teenagers to do that. It was in their behavior, in the way that they related to each other and to me, that my friends opened up to me the vista of a different worldview.)

However, it was not just my friends who opened up alternatives for me in high school. The school that I attended was run by Jesuit priests and seminarians. In these men, I encountered a fresh rendition of the Roman Catholic faith in which I had been raised. These Jesuits reflected deeply on their faith. Moreover, I sensed from my first encounters with them that their faith resided not only in their heads but also in their hearts and in their guts. These were prayerful men whose intellectual ruminations were grounded, ultimately, in deep spiritual experience.

Profoundly influenced by my Jesuit teachers, I began to plumb more deeply the Catholic faith that, even in my preadolescent years, had occupied an important place in my sense of myself. While still flirting with a wholesale rejection of my family's worldview, I began to read Catholic theologians and philosophers. I also began to engage in meditative, contemplative prayer.

The deepening of my faith begun in high school continued through my undergraduate career. As I approached graduation, I decided that I wanted to become a Jesuit. I applied to and was accepted by the New York Province of the Society of Jesus (the formal name of the Jesuit order). During my novitiate—the first two years of Jesuit formation—my attraction to a life devoted solely to contemplative prayer led me to consider seriously asking my superiors for permission to transfer from the Jesuits to the Trappists, an order of cloistered monks within the Catholic Church. Ultimately, I decided to remain in the Jesuits. I pronounced my first vows of poverty, chastity, and obedience, and went on to take a master's degree in philosophy, the first phase of education in preparation for ordination to the priesthood. Philosophy studies were followed by a three-year period during which I taught in a high school run by the Order. During this time, prayerful reflection led me to an awareness that I did not, in fact, have a vocation to the priesthood. At the end of the three years, I petitioned to be released from my vows. The petition was granted, and I left the Jesuits.

It has now been twenty years since I left the Jesuits. During this time, my Catholic faith has grown even more central to my sense of who I am. This faith determines not only how I understand and experience God, but also how I understand and experience the human world. It has been pivotal in shaping my view of the human condition. Because it has been so, I will now devote a few pages to summarizing for those of you who may be relatively unfamiliar with Catholicism how the Catholic faith sees the human situation.

Catholicism views the world of human beings through a thoroughly collectivist lens. "I" has no place in this world. Not even God is an "I." As understood and experienced by the Catholic Church, God is Trinity, a tri-personal community of persons who are so present and devoted to each other in self-emptying love as to constitute a single entity despite the differentiation of persons (Maloney, 1993; O'Collins, 1999). Nor is this radical "we-ness" seen as something that is restricted to the domain of the divine. The very reason that one of the divine persons entered into human history in the person of Jesus Christ was to bring together human beings into a radically communitarian life that reflects and is an extension of God's triune life. "Jesus reveals God to be a communion of persons; he dies in order to bring human beings together into unity" (Rossé, 1998, p. 44).

A worldview that idealizes self-emptying love is not likely to be one that promotes self-actualization as a goal to be pursued by human beings. Indeed, in the view of many, if not most, Catholic theologians, a genuinely Christian ethic must of necessity be deontological in nature. (You will recall from our discussion in Chapter 2 that it was precisely what they saw as the incompatibility between eudaimonism and Christianity that led the Franciscan friars Duns Scotus and William of Ockham to lay the foundation for the deontological ethical tradition.)

For these deontological theologians, it is the interior life of the Trinity that is seen as providing the model for ethical human conduct. Inside the Trinity, there is not a shadow of self-interest. "No person exists by him/herself or is referred to him/herself. . . . Each divine person is irresistibly drawn to the other, taking his/ her existence from the other, containing the other in him/herself, while at the same time pouring self out into the other" (LaCugna, 1991, p. 271). The life of the Trinity is a never-ending circulation, which finds each divine person at every moment simultaneously receiving his entire existence from the others and giving his entire existence back to the others. John's gospel makes reference to this circulation when it relates the following prayer spoken by Jesus to God the Father: "All I have is yours and all you have is mine. . ." (John 17:10). (All biblical quotations in this section are from *The New Jerusalem Bible: Reader's Edition*, H. Wansbrough, editor.)

Jesus' prayer in John's gospel goes on to draw out the implications that God's Trinitarian life holds for human behavior. "May they all be one, just as, Father, you are in me and I am in you, so that they also may be in us. . ." (John 17:21). St. Paul, in his letter to the Christians in the city of Philippi, describes what kind of human conduct is required by this unity: "Nothing is to be done out of jealousy or vanity; instead out of humility of mind everyone should give preference to others, everyone pursuing not selfish interests but those of others" (Philippians 2:3–4). A more succinct statement of a deontological ethical position is difficult to conceive.

Created in the image of God, human beings, in the Catholic view, are fundamentally good. However, they remain free to act in ways that are at odds with their fundamental goodness. Catholicism takes the voluntarist position that human beings possess the capacity knowingly and willfully to rupture the web of relationships, human and divine, in which they are suspended. The first story narrated in the book of Genesis after the account of the creation of the world tells how human beings chose to exercise this capacity not long after they entered on the cosmic scene.

The ripple of evil that Genesis mythologically pictures beginning in the Garden of Eden grew inevitably and inexorably over time, in the Catholic view, into a veritable tsunami that swept human beings away from each other and from God. Left to their own devices, human beings became constitutionally unable to make their way back to intimacy with each other and with God. Thus would things have remained had God not chosen to make his way back to us.

Because God had to come to us, Catholic spirituality tends to favor a "becoming" mode of consciousness over a "being" mode. True it is that in the Catholic view, God's Trinitarian life occurs in a timeless Now. It is also true that humanity's ultimate end is to share in the Trinity's intimate Now. However, the route toward this goal is not an escape from the time-bound, "becoming" mode in which we live our daily lives. Because, as a result of our sinfulness, God had to come to us, he has made our time-bound, "becoming" existence his own. In essence, he has made our history his own. This is how Catholicism understands the grand epic of Israel's history that makes up the Old Testament. God chose Israel as his own people. Freely and out of love, he made their historical situation his own. So close was the bond that God created between Israel and himself that what happened to them happened to him. When Israel went into slavery in Egypt, God went with them and brought them out. As they wandered for forty years through the desert, he wandered with them, his presence concretely manifested in the Ark of the Covenant that the Israelites carried with them wherever they went. When they settled in the Promised Land, God settled, too, his glory filling the Temple built for him in Jerusalem by Solomon.

The people of Israel learned from their experience of God to look for him not so much in transcendent "being" experiences, but predominantly in the events of their history. God was to be sought in the recollection of their past, in the exigencies of their present, and in their hopes for the future. Even when prophets were granted transitory "being" experiences, it was so that they could be provided with the wherewithal to help their fellow countrymen discern the presence of God in the events of their mundane "becoming" world.

As seen through the eyes of the Catholic faith, God's entrance into and identification with our history reached an unexpected fulfillment when one of the Trinitarian divine persons actually became one of us in the person of Jesus Christ. In this event, Catholicism sees God as bringing to fruition his pledge, repeated frequently throughout Israel's history, of a uniquely close relationship with his chosen people. Catholic faith also sees in the life, death, and resurrection of Jesus the opening of a new historical epoch. In this epoch, intimacy between the divine and the human, sundered by sin but restored by Jesus, ripples outward across time and space beyond the confines of Israel, gathering ever more people into union both with God and each other. As he did with Israel in the Old Testament, God continues, now in a supereminent way as a result of the Jesus event, to draw close to us by making our history his own.

As much, then, as their Jewish brethren, Catholics find God predominantly via a "becoming" mode of consciousness. God is primarily encountered by remembering his past deeds in the history of Israel and in the life of Jesus, by searching out his current activity in the world, and by hopeful anticipation of his future action. Moments of "being" encounters with God that Catholics may experience always prove their validity by the degree to which they orient the recipient toward the grand sweep of God's saving activity played out in the "becoming" events of human history.

When God personally entered into human history in the person of Jesus, he assumed, in the Catholic view, a "flesh-ly" existence. "In the beginning was the Word: the Word was with God and the Word was God. . . . The Word became *flesh*, he lived among us. . ." (John 1:1, 14; emphasis added). Catholicism's insistence on the "flesh-ly" existence of Jesus, on his bodily resurrection, and on the fact that all human beings will themselves experience a bodily resurrection at the consummation of human history, bespeaks an approach to the mind–body issue that in this book I have termed *Aristotelian*. Catholic faith sees the spiritual and the material as being radically interdependent aspects of human existence. In opposition to idealist positions on this issue, Catholicism understands human beings' embodiedness as central to their humanity. In opposition to dualist philosophies, it does not see "flesh" as subject to determinism or as inherently evil. On the contrary, Catholic faith sees all of material reality as destined ultimately to share in the intimate communion between God and humanity that will be brought to fruition at the consummation of human history.

This respect for material reality is manifest in Catholic spirituality, which is not at all shy about using objects and movement as a means to foster communion among people and between people and God. Dress, ritual, music, statues, paintings, and icons all claim a rightful place in Catholic spiritual practice. And, while numerous Catholic spiritual masters have warned against making these material realities and the experiences that they create into ends rather than means, none has ever called into question their potential fruitfulness in catalyzing the connection between God and human beings.

To no one's greater surprise than my own, I found myself in my early thirties committed to a view of the human condition that, formally at least, was identical to the worldview which had held sway in my family of origin. My view of the human world was still collectivist, deontological, voluntarist, and Aristotelian. I still accorded primacy to becoming over being. Though my discontent with my family's worldview had left me ripe for a reactive rejection of that worldview, my commitment to the Catholic faith had kept my late-adolescent flirtation with alternative worldviews from turning into full-blown love affairs.

My Catholic faith kept me ensconced in a worldview structured along the same lines that I had become familiar with in my childhood. However, Catholicism painted between those lines with colors that were far brighter and immeasurably more beautiful than the hues that had formed the background of my childhood. My family's collectivism had been a noisy, confusing, chaotic affair. The Church's collectivism is suffused with stillness and peace. My family's deontological ethic was founded on guilt. The Church's version of deontological ethics is founded on love. My family's voluntarism was pessimistic and fatalistic. While fully acknowledging the reality of human evil, the Church's voluntarism is hope-filled, because its awareness of human evil is balanced by its awareness of the definitive action taken by God over the course of human history to rescue us from our own evil. My family's devotion to a "becoming" mode of consciousness had to it a distinctively obsessive quality. Because it sees God as having entered into the flow of history, the Church's experience of becoming is marked by joy. In the Aristotelian world of my family, physical objects and daily rituals were latent with an unspoken meaning that was almost invariably dark and sinister. In the Aristotelian world of the Catholic Church, physical objects and rituals are filled with the ineffable presence of the Trinitarian God whose innermost reality is love.

Therapeutic Choices

I decided to become a family therapist within three years of leaving the Jesuits. There were no graduate programs in family therapy within easy reach, so I enrolled in a counseling program that offered a concentration in marriage and family therapy. I can still remember the excitement that I experienced in my theory courses, as I encountered for the first time the various therapeutic models that were available to family therapists in those days. As many models as there were, they were fewer in number than are available today. Some models that had exercised considerable influence in family therapy's early days were already distinctly on the wane when I entered the field. While they were still being taught, John Elderkin Bell's family group therapy, Virginia Satir's humanistic therapy, and Ross Speck and Carolyn Attneave's family network therapy were already being presented to us students as historical relics of a bygone era. Solution-focused therapy was in its infancy at that point, and we students were told nothing about it. There were as yet no postmodern therapies, although the great "aesthetics versus pragmatics" debate, published in the pages of *Family Process* just around the time that I became a student, was laying the foundation for what later would become narrative therapy and collaborative language systems therapy.

The major theoretical contenders for my allegiance as I entered the field were psychoanalytic family therapy, Bowen family systems therapy, structural family therapy, symbolic experiential family therapy, and the various strategic therapies. While these models were relatively few in number by today's standards, I was struck even then by the very different ways in which they viewed not only the therapeutic enterprise, but, more profoundly, the very nature of the human condition. And so I set off to do then what I hope this book is helping you to do now: I tried to find the model of family therapy that would provide the best fit with my worldview and values.

Predictably, I was drawn from almost the beginning of my graduate studies to structural family therapy and to the strategic therapies. In their collectivism, voluntarism, and Aristotelianism, in their deontological ethics and their assertion of the primacy of becoming over being, these models offered a view of the human condition that immediately felt familiar to me. Early on, I did not find much to distinguish structural therapy and the strategic therapies. During my internship and the first couple of years after graduation, I practiced a structural/strategic blend, which had quite some currency in the literature at that time (see, for example, Stanton, 1981; Stanton, Todd, & Associates, 1982).

With the passage of time, however, I began to experience a growing discomfort with the strategic part of the structural/strategic blend that I was practicing. If you were to ask me at the time about the nature of my discomfort, I probably would have been relatively inarticulate on the matter. In hindsight, however, I have come to recognize that my discomfort had two components, one stylistic, the other ideological.

One of the strengths of strategic therapy, in any of its three variants, is its individualized nature. Part of the joy of reading one of the books written by Jay Haley or Cloe Madanes or the members of the Milan team is to see how carefully, cleverly, and creatively these strategists craft interventions to fit this particular client family, dealing with this particular symptom or problem, at precisely this particular point in therapy. To excel at this way of doing therapy, the therapist must have an exquisite eye for detail. She must be finely attuned to discerning that which is idiosyncratic in this particular family's rendition of a symptom-maintaining sequence whose general characteristics the therapist has encountered in dozens of other families. I do not naturally possess such an eye for detail. It may be all too obvious to you at this point that I dwell more naturally in the abstract than in the particular. Stylistically, I am not a natural for the crafting and delivery of strategic interventions.

Still, style can be modified by supervision. If my stylistic deficiency were the only difficulty I had with strategic therapy, I could still have been helped to improve the strategic end of the structural/strategic mix that I was practicing.

Style, however was not my only difficulty with strategic therapy. It was not very long before I also began to sense an important ideological difference between myself and the strategic therapies. At the core of the strategic therapies lies the assumption that clients' devotion to self-interest is so entrenched that they will almost never willingly sacrifice self-interest in the service of the improved functioning of the social systems to which they belong. Thus, the strategic therapies maneuver clients into changing rather than asking them overtly to make the changes that they need to. Clients of the strategic therapies change in spite of themselves rather than because of themselves.

As a voluntarist, I certainly shared the strategic therapies' view that people are perfectly capable of choosing to behave in ways that are detrimental to self and others. However, in the course of my own life, I had grown to appreciate that different versions of the voluntarist view are possible. The version adopted by the strategic therapies reminded me of the dark, pessimistic voluntarism that had animated my family's life. In this version, people are seen not simply as capable of evil, but almost as inherently evil. Why should a therapist take the time to let clients know what he sees as maladaptive in their lives and ask them to change, when that very request is seen as being fated to elicit nothing more than a redoubling of their insistence that the status quo be maintained? It is far more efficient for the therapist to devote himself from the outset to devising strategies that will cause clients to change outside of their awareness.

While this was the kind of voluntarism I had experienced in my family, it was not the kind that I encountered in the practice of my Catholic faith. As I described above, Catholicism takes very seriously the reality of human evil. However, it does not see evil as so corrupting human beings as to render them incapable of cooperating with their own salvation. As the Catholic Church experiences him, God so prizes our dignity and freedom that he invariably asks our permission to act in our behalf. We could not be rescued from our evil unless he came toward us; however, he will not come toward us until we give him our consent. By consenting to God's saving activity in our behalf, we cooperate, in the Catholic view, in our own salvation.

Coming from this background, I found myself far more comfortable with the version of voluntarism that informed the structural component of the strategic/structural mix that I was practicing at the time. Differently than a Haley-Madanes or an MRI strategist, a structural family therapist does take the time to tell client families what she sees as malfunctioning in the way that they operate. Her voluntarism keeps her from thinking that her telling will work any magic. Most times, clients will resist accepting what the therapist has to tell them about themselves. But the expectation of resistance does not dissuade the therapist from delivering the message. The structural therapist wants her clients to change because of themselves, not in spite of themselves. She wants them to cooperate in the process of change. For that reason, she is overt in declaring what she sees as wrong, and she is overt in letting families know what she sees as requiring change. She is willing to wrestle with the resistance that her overtness is likely to kick up. She expects that in most cases it will subside as the therapy continues. But even if it does not, she values the transparency on her part that being overt entails, and she values giving her clients the right to know what their therapist thinks about their situation.

I am confident that my stylistic deficiency in delivering strategic interventions could have been remedied by good supervision. However, my growing ideological difficulty with strategic therapy left me reluctant to seek the supervision that I needed. Gradually, I found myself delivering fewer and fewer strategic interventions. My therapy, which had begun as a structural/strategic mix, became increasingly a pure form of structural family therapy.

Supervisory Refinements

By the third year after my graduation from my master's degree program, I had stabilized an identity as a structural family therapist. At about this time, I became aware that Salvador Minuchin, who had left the Philadelphia Child Guidance Clinic a few years earlier, was operating a small family therapy institute in New York City, then called Family Studies, Inc., and since renamed The Minuchin Center for the Family. At my wife's urging, I decided to enroll in the institute's extern program.

It is a very humbling thing to look back at oneself from the vantage point of increased maturity and years of experience. It is humbling for me to recall the arrogance that was mine as I entered the extern program at Family Studies. I was certain at the time that I had a thorough understanding both of the theory of structural family therapy and of its underlying worldview and values. In that particular certainty, I may not have been far off the mark. However, I also had another certainty: I was certain that the therapy that I was doing was a faithful rendering of my thinking. I may not have admitted this to anybody, but I was quietly confident as I entered the extern program that the videotaped sessions that I brought for review by my supervisors—Dr. Anne Brooks in the first year and Dr. Minuchin in the second and third—would consistently elicit admiring nods of approval from them.

I should have known better. (I'm pretty sure that my wife knew better. In all likelihood, that's why she urged me to go to the Institute in the first place.) The fact that I did not know better indicates how very much in need of supervision I stood. True it was that the thinking informing my therapy at that time was comprehensive, nuanced, and consistent. What I was blind to—ironic, given my voluntarist assumptions—was the fact that my behavior in many instances was not following my thinking.

That such a schism existed between my therapeutic thinking and my therapeutic behavior is really not all that surprising. Recall my history. I developed a significant portion of my relational repertoire in a family whose manner of operating I frequently experienced as toxic. To survive the toxicity, I developed a style of relating that provided me with an illusory sense of separateness from the family. I countered their concreteness by becoming excessively abstract. In an effort to strike a pose of aloofness, I became very restrained in making physical displays of any kind. In a quest to achieve a kind of invisibility in the family, I developed the habit of never disclosing any kind of feeling that I was experiencing.

Of course, this interpersonal style that I developed never really provided me with anything like genuine differentiation within the family. Indeed, although I was completely unaware of it at the time, my behavior was simply a piece in my family's mosaic, doing more than its part in helping the family to maintain the very manner of operating that I found so toxic.

When I began to function as a therapist, it was almost inevitable that what, at that point, constituted my interpersonal style also became my therapeutic style. The result was the schism between my therapeutic thinking and my therapeutic behavior that I mentioned above. In the matter of the mind–body issue, for example, I was committed in my thinking to doing a therapy that was Aristotelian. However, in my actual practice, my abstract wordiness and my privileging of my clients' words rendered the therapy that I was doing thoroughly idealist. Ideologically, I was a collectivist. Yet, my rigid maintenance of an aloof, distant posture from my clients was blinding me to the circular processes that my model maintains connected me to them and rendered them and me parts of a single social system. In short, I was behaving as if I were an individualist. The model of therapy to which I was intellectually committed values the therapist's ability to relate to clients from a variety of interpersonal postures. Yet, in my self-protective avoidance of self-disclosure, I was foreclosing a whole domain of interventions that might, in some circumstances, prove useful to my client families.

The task fell to my supervisors and to the other members of the extern group to challenge me to expand my therapeutic style, so that my behavior in therapy conformed to my theoretical and ideological commitments. Had I found myself unable to respond to this challenge, some crucially important questions would have been raised for me. I would have found it necessary to reconsider the aptness of my commitment to structural family therapy. Even more profoundly, the fit between me and my professed view of the human condition would have been called into question. As it turns out, however, I was able to respond to my supervisors' interventions. Steadily, the videotaped sessions that I presented to the extern group began to show a different, more complex therapist, one who was able to use silence and movement as much as he was able to use words, one who developed the ability to relate to clients from a position of proximity as well as of distance, one who was able to risk self-disclosing his emotional responses to clients when it appeared that such feedback might prove useful to them.

I left my three years of supervision at Family Studies a more complex, more integrated, more consistent therapist. By committing myself to structural family therapy, I had already found my therapeutic voice before I entered the extern group. What occurred for me in the group was that I discovered a range to that voice that I never suspected existed. Thanks to this newly discovered range, I have found myself during the intervening years able to harmonize my voice with a broader spectrum of client families. As importantly, and quite to my surprise, my enhanced voice is more intimately recognizable to me as my own. In an effortless way, I now feel more like myself as I go about the business of doing therapy.

Your Story

You have now been gracious enough to sit through my telling of the story of how I came to find and to refine my therapeutic voice. My sole purpose in telling you this story was to spur you to tell your own. If you have found any elements of my story familiar in any way, let that fact encourage you to deem your own story as worthy of telling as mine. If you judge my story to be peculiar or out of the ordinary, let the fact that I have ventured to tell such a peculiar story overcome any misgivings that you might have that your story is too unusual to be told.

Begin, then, to tell your story of how you came to hold the view of the human condition of which this book has hopefully made you more aware. What were the key influences in the development of your view? Family of origin? Culture? Socioeconomic class? Religion? Education? Politics? Did your view develop gradually and organically over time, or did it at some point undergo a radical change? If the latter, what experience led you to change your worldview? Is your worldview currently stable, or do you sense that it is still in flux?

Tell about what fit you see existing between your worldview and the way in which you are currently doing therapy. Were you committed to a model of family therapy before you began this book? If so, what led you to that commitment? Now that you have become more sensitized to your own worldview and values and those that underlie the various therapeutic models, what do you think about the fit between yourself and your chosen model? Has reading this book served to confirm you in your commitment to the model, or are you now thinking seriously about committing to another model? If you began this book without being committed to a model, which model do you now think provides the best fit with your view of the human condition?

Tell about how well you think your current interactional style fits with the use of self that your chosen model prescribes for its practitioners. Does your style render you a "natural" for the model that you have chosen, or are you aware of some disjunction between the way that you generally relate to people and the therapeutic behavior countenanced by your model? If the latter, is the matter of changing your therapeutic style a significant focus of your supervision?

Finding Your Voice

In the course of working your way through this book, you found your therapeutic voice. Now you have told your story about the way in which your voice developed. Though they almost certainly were not part of the audience for your narrative, it is your clients, present and future, who will be the ultimate beneficiaries of your storytelling. For I am certain that, as you told the story about the development of your therapeutic voice, you found yourself coming to a new and heightened appreciation of and respect for that voice. Inevitably, that appreciation and respect will lead you to use your voice with greater clarity, confidence, and depth in your work with your clients. For most of them, encountering this clarity in your voice will lead them to a heightened appreciation of theirs. Clarity will beget clarity, voice will summon voice.

And that, regardless of the model that informs its practice, is the one thing that this enterprise called therapy is really all about in the end: people finding their voices.

REFERENCES

Acton, H. B. (1967). Idealism. In P. Edwards (Ed.), *The encyclopedia of philosophy* (vol. 4, pp. 110–118). New York: Macmillan & Free Press.

Anderson, H. (1997). *Conversation, language, and possibilities: A postmodern approach to therapy.* New York: Basic Books.

Anderson, H., & Goolishian, H. A. (1988). Human systems as linguistic systems: Preliminary and evolving ideas about the implications for clinical theory. *Family Process, 27,* 371–394.

Andolfi, M., Angelo, C., & de Nichilo, M. (1989). *The myth of Atlas: Families and the therapeutic story* (V. F. DiNicola, ed. and trans.). New York: Brunner/Mazel.

Becvar, D. S., & Becvar, R. J. (2000). *Family therapy: A systemic integration* (4th ed.). Boston: Allyn & Bacon.

Berg, I. K., & de Shazer, S. (1993). Making numbers talk: Language in therapy. In S. Friedman (Ed.), *The new language of change: Constructive collaboration in psychotherapy* (pp. 5–24). New York: Guilford.

Boscolo, L., & Cecchin, G. (1982). Training in systemic therapy at the Milan Centre. In R. Whiffen & J. Byng-Hall (Eds.), *Family therapy supervision: Recent developments in practice* (pp. 153–165). London: Academic.

Boss, P., Dahl, C., & Kaplan, L. (1996). The use of phenomenology for family therapy research. In D. H. Sprenkle & G. M. Moon (Eds.), *Research methods in family therapy* (pp. 83–106). New York: Guilford.

Breunlin, D. C., Schwartz, R. C., & Mac Kune-Karrer, B. (1992). *Metaframeworks: Transcending the models of family therapy.* San Francisco: Jossey-Bass.

Buchanan, A. (1998). Community and communitarianism. In E. Craig (Ed.), *Routledge encyclopedia of philosophy* (vol. 2, pp. 464–471). London: Routledge.

Campbell, K. (1967). Materialism. In P. Edwards (Ed.), *The encyclopedia of philosophy* (vol. 5, pp. 179–188). New York: Macmillan & Free Press.

Capek, M. (1967). Change. In P. Edwards (Ed.), *The encyclopedia of philosophy* (vol. 2, pp. 73–79). New York: Macmillan & Free Press.

Cranston, M. (1967). Liberalism. In P. Edwards (Ed.), *The encyclopedia of philosophy* (vol. 4, pp. 458–461). New York: Macmillan & Free Press.

de Shazer, S. (1982). Some conceptual distinctions are more useful than others. *Family Process, 21,* 71–84

de Shazer, S. (1985). *Keys to solution in brief therapy.* New York: Norton.

de Shazer, S. (1988). *Clues: Investigating solutions in brief therapy.* New York: Norton.

de Shazer, S., Berg, I. K., Lipchik, E., Nunnally, E., Molnar, A., Gingerich, W., & Wiener-Davis, M. (1986). Brief therapy: Focused solution development. *Family Process, 25,* 207–222.

Dray, W. H. (1967). Holism and individualism in history and social science. In P. Edwards (Ed.), *The encyclopedia of philosophy* (vol. 4, pp. 53–58). New York: Macmillan & Free Press.

Fraenkel, P., & Pinsof, W. M. (2001). Teaching family therapy-centered integration: Assimilation and beyond. *Journal of Psychotherapy Integration, 11,* 59–85.

Garber, D. (1998). Descartes, René (1596–1650). In E. Craig (Ed.), *Routledge encyclopedia of philosophy* (vol. 3, pp. 1–19). London: Routledge.

Giacomo, D., & Weissmark, M. (1986). Systemic practice. *Family Process, 25,* 483–512.

Gingerich, W. J., & de Shazer, S. (1991). The BRIEFER project: Using expert systems as theory construction tools. *Family Process, 30,* 241–250.

Goudge, T. A. (1967). Bergson, Henri. In P. Edwards (Ed.), *The encyclopedia of philosophy* (vol. 3, pp. 459–465). New York: Macmillan & Free Press.

Griffith, J. L., & Griffith, M. E. (1994). *The body speaks: Therapeutic dialogues for mind–body problems.* New York: Basic Books.

Haley, J. (1963). *Strategies of psychotherapy.* New York: Grune & Stratton.

Haley, J. (1976). *Problem-solving therapy: New strategies for effective family therapy.* San Francisco: Jossey-Bass.

Haley, J. (1984). *Ordeal therapy.* San Francisco: Jossey-Bass.

Held, B. S. (1995). *Back to reality: A critique of postmodern theory in psychotherapy.* New York: Norton.

Henry, P. W. (2001). [Review of *Love's hidden symmetry: What makes love work in relationships*]. *The Family Journal: Counseling and Therapy for Couples and Families, 9,* 229.

Jacobs, D., David, P., & Meyer, D. J. (1995). *The supervisory encounter: A guide for teachers of psychodynamic psychotherapy and psychoanalysis.* New Haven, CT: Yale University Press.

Janaway, C. (1998). Schopenhauer, Arthur (1788–1860). In E. Craig (Ed.), *Routledge encyclopedia of philosophy* (vol. 8, pp. 545–554). London: Routledge.

Keith, D. V. (1998). Symbolic-experiential family therapy for chemical imbalance. In F. M. Dattilio (Ed.), *Case studies in couple and family therapy: Systemic and cognitive perspectives* (pp. 179–202). New York: Guilford.

Kekes, J. (1998). Evil. In E. Craig (Ed.), *Routledge encyclopedia of philosophy* (vol. 3, pp. 463–466). London: Routledge.

Kerferd, G. B. (1967). Aristotle. In P. Edwards (Ed.), *The encyclopedia of philosophy* (vol. 1, pp. 151–162). New York: Macmillan & Free Press.

Kerr, M. E. (1984). Theoretical base for differentiation of self in one's family of origin. In C. E. Munson (Ed.), *Family of origin applications in clinical supervision* (pp. 3–36). New York: Haworth.

Korsgaard, C. M. (1998). Theories of the good. In E. Craig (Ed.), *Routledge encyclopedia of philosophy* (vol. 4, pp. 130–135). London: Routledge.

Lacey, A. R. (1998). Bergson, Henri-Louis (1859–1941). In E. Craig (Ed.), *Routledge encyclopedia of philosophy* (vol. 1, pp. 732–737). London: Routledge.

LaCugna, C. M. (1991). *God for us: The Trinity and Christian life.* New York: HarperCollins.

Lannamann, J. W. (1998). Social construction and materiality: The limits of indeterminacy in therapeutic settings. *Family Process, 37,* 393–413.

Larmore, C. (1998). Right and good. In E. Craig (Ed.), *Routledge encyclopedia of philosophy* (vol. 8, pp. 322–325). London: Routledge.

Leftow, B. (1998). Voluntarism. In E. Craig (Ed.), *Routledge encyclopedia of philosophy* (vol. 9, pp. 663–664). London: Routledge.

Lowe, R. (2000). Supervising self-supervision: Constructive inquiry and embedded narratives in case consultation. *Journal of Marital and Family Therapy, 26,* 511–521.

Madanes, C. (1990). *Sex, love, and violence: Strategies for transformation.* New York: Norton.

Maloney, G. (1993). *God's community of love: Living in the indwelling Trinity.* Hyde Park, NY: New City.

Marshall, R. J. (1982). *Resistant interactions: Child, family, and psychotherapist.* New York: Human Sciences.

Mason, A. (1998). Solidarity. In E. Craig (Ed.), *Routledge encyclopedia of philosophy* (vol. 9, pp. 23–25). London: Routledge.

Matthews, G. B. (1998). Augustine (AD 354–430). In E. Craig (Ed.), *Routledge encyclopedia of philosophy* (vol. 1, pp. 541–559). London: Routledge.

Maturana, H. R. (1978). Biology of language: The epistemology of reality. In G. A. Miller & E. Lenneberg (Eds.), *Psychology and biology of language and thought* (pp. 27–64). New York: Academic.

Merlan, P. (1967). Plotinus. In P. Edwards (Ed.), *The encyclopedia of philosophy* (vol. 6, pp. 351–359). New York: Macmillan & Free Press.

Miller, G., & de Shazer, S. (1998). Have you heard the latest rumor about. . . ? Solution-focused therapy as a rumor. *Family Process, 37,* 363–377.

Miller, S. D., Duncan, B. L., & Hubble, M. A. (1997). *Escape from Babel: Toward a unifying language for psychotherapy practice.* New York: Norton.

Minuchin, S. (1974). *Families and family therapy.* Cambridge, MA: Harvard University Press.

Minuchin, S., & Fishman, H. C. (1981). *Family therapy techniques.* Cambridge, MA: Harvard University Press.

Minuchin, S., Lee, W.-Y., & Simon, G. M. (1996). *Mastering family therapy: Journeys of growth and transformation.* New York: Wiley.

Minuchin, S., & Nichols, M. P. (1993). *Family healing: Tales of hope and renewal from family therapy.* New York: Free Press.

Moody, E. A. (1967). William of Ockham. In P. Edwards (Ed.), *The encyclopedia of philosophy* (vol. 8, pp. 306–317). New York: Macmillan & Free Press.

Nahm, M. C. (1964). *Selections from early Greek philosophy* (4th ed.). New York: Appleton-Century-Crofts.

Napier, A. Y., & Whitaker, C. A. (1978). *The family crucible.* New York: Harper & Row.

Nichols, M. P., & Schwartz, R. C. (1995). *Family therapy: Concepts and methods* (3rd ed.). Boston: Allyn & Bacon.

Nussbaum, M. C. (1998). Love. In E. Craig (Ed.), *Routledge encyclopedia of philosophy* (vol. 5, pp. 842–846). London: Routledge.

O'Collins, G. (1999). *The tripersonal God: Understanding and interpreting the Trinity.* New York: Paulist Press.

Palazzoli, M. S., Boscolo, L., Cecchin, G., & Prata, G. (1978). *Paradox and counterparadox: A new model in the therapy of the family in schizophrenic transaction.* New York: Jason Aronson.

Prochaska, J. O., & Norcross, J. C. (1994). *Systems of psychotherapy: A transtheoretical analysis* (3rd ed.). Pacific Grove, CA: Brooks/Cole.

Protinsky, H., & Keller, J. F. (1984). Supervision of marriage and family therapy: A family of origin approach. In C. E. Munson (Ed.), *Family of origin applications in clinical supervision* (pp. 75–80). New York: Haworth.

Raitt, D. (1988). Survey results. *Family Therapy Networker, 12,* 52–56.

Rediger, S. L. (1996). Critical theory research: The emancipatory interest in family therapy. In D. H. Sprenkle & S. M. Moon (Eds.), *Research methods in family therapy* (pp. 127–144). New York: Guilford.

Rossé, G. (1998). *The spirituality of communion: A new approach to the Johannine writings* (M. J. O'Connell, trans.). Hyde Park, NY: New City.

Sander, F. M. (1998). Psychoanalytic couple therapy. In F. M. Dattilio (Ed.), *Case studies in couple and family therapy: Systemic and cognitive perspectives* (pp. 427–449). New York: Guilford.

Scanlan, J. P. (1967). Voluntarism. In P. Edwards (Ed.), *The encyclopedia of philosophy* (vol. 8, pp. 270–273). New York: Macmillan & Free Press.

Scharff, D. E., & Scharff, J. S. (1987). *Object relations family therapy.* Northvale, NJ: Jason Aronson.

Scharff, D. E., & Scharff, J. S. (1991). *Object relations couple therapy.* Northvale, NJ: Jason Aronson.

Shadish, W. R., Montgomery, L. M., Wilson, P., Wilson, M. R., Bright, I., & Okwumabua, T. (1993). The effects of family and marital psychotherapies: A meta-analysis. *Journal of Consulting and Clinical Psychology, 61,* 992–1002.

Shadish, W. R., Ragsdale, K., Glaser, R. R., & Montgomery, L. M. (1995). The efficacy and effectiveness of marital and family therapy: A perspective from meta-analysis. *Journal of Marital and Family Therapy, 21,* 345–360.

Shaffer, J. (1967). Mind–body problem. In P. Edwards (Ed.), *The encyclopedia of philosophy* (vol. 5, pp. 336–346). New York: Macmillan & Free Press.

Shostrum, E. (Producer). (1964). *Three approaches to psychotherapy.* Santa Ana, CA: Psychological Films.

Simon, G. M. (1992). Having a second-order mind while doing first-order therapy. *Journal of Marital and Family Therapy, 18,* 377–387.

Simon, G. M. (1993). Revisiting the notion of hierarchy. *Family Process, 32,* 147–155.

Simon, G. M. (1995). A revisionist rendering of structural family therapy. *Journal of Marital and Family Therapy, 21,* 17–26.

Sluzki, C. E. (1992). Transformations: A blueprint for narrative change in therapy. *Family Process, 31,* 217–230.

Sprigge, T. L. S. (1998). Idealism. In E. Craig (Ed.), *Routledge encyclopedia of philosophy* (vol. 4, pp. 662–669). London: Routledge.

Stanton, M. D. (1981). An integrated structural/strategic approach to family therapy. *Journal of Marital and Family Therapy, 7,* 427–439.

Stanton, M. D., Todd, T. C., & Associates. (1982). *The family therapy of drug abuse and addiction.* New York: Guilford.

Swinburne, R. (1998). Nature and immortality of the soul. In E. Craig (Ed.), *Routledge encyclopedia of philosophy* (vol. 9, pp. 44–48). London: Routledge.

Taylor, C. C. W. (1998). Eudaimonism. In E. Craig (Ed.), *Routledge encyclopedia of philosophy* (vol. 3, pp. 450–452). London: Routledge.

Thibaut, J., & Kelley, H. H. (1959). *The social psychology of groups.* New York: Wiley.

Thomas, F. N. (1994). Solution-oriented supervision: The coaxing of expertise. *The Family Journal: Counseling and Therapy for Couples and Families, 2,* 11–18.

Wansbrough, H. (Ed.). (1990). *The new Jerusalem Bible: Reader's edition.* New York: Doubleday.

Whitaker, C. A., & Bumberry, W. M. (1988). *Dancing with the family: A symbolic–experiential approach.* New York: Brunner/Mazel.

Whitaker, C. A., & Keith, D. V. (1981). Symbolic-experiential family therapy. In A. S. Gurman & D. P. Kniskern (Eds.), *Handbook of family therapy* (pp. 187–225). New York: Brunner/Mazel.

White, M. (1991). Deconstruction and therapy. *Dulwich Centre Newsletter, 3,* 21–40.

White, M., & Epston, D. (1990). *Narrative means to therapeutic ends.* New York: Norton.

Whyte, L. L. (1967). Unconscious. In P. Edwards (Ed.), *The encyclopedia of philosophy* (vol. 8, pp. 185–189). New York: Macmillan & Free Press.

Williams, B. (1967). Descartes, René. In P. Edwards (Ed.), *The encyclopedia of philosophy* (vol. 2, pp. 344–354). New York: Macmillan & Free Press.

INDEX